W9-AOQ-541

GARDENS
OF THE
ARTS & CRAFTS
MOVEMENT

GARDENS
OF THE
ARTS & CRAFTS
MOVEMENT

REVISED EDITION

JUDITH B. TANKARD

TIMBER PRESS • PORTLAND, OREGON

Frontispiece: Folly Farm, Sulhamstead, Berkshire, England
Copyright © 2018 by Judith B. Tankard. All rights reserved.
Photo and illustration credits appear on page 291.

Published in 2018 by Timber Press, Inc.
The Haseltine Building
133 S.W. Second Avenue, Suite 450
Portland, Oregon 97204-3527
timberpress.com

Printed in China

Text and jacket design by Kelley Galbreath

Library of Congress Cataloging-in-Publication Data

Names: Tankard, Judith B., author.
Title: Gardens of the arts and crafts movement / Judith B. Tankard.
Description: Revised edition. | Portland, Oregon : Timber Press, 2018.
    Includes bibliographical references and index.
Identifiers: LCCN 2018014599 (print) | LCCN 2018021820 (ebook)
    ISBN 9781604698947 | ISBN 9781604698206 (jacketed hardcover)
Subjects: LCSH: Arts and crafts gardens—England. | Arts and crafts
    gardens—United States. | Arts and crafts movement—England.
    Arts and crafts movement—United States.
Classification: LCC SB454.3.A76 (ebook) | LCC SB454.3.A76 T36
    2018 (print) | DDC 635.9—dc23
LC record available at https://lccn.loc.gov/2018014599

A catalog record for this book is also available from the British Library.

CONTENTS

PREFACE

IN RECENT YEARS, the Arts and Crafts Movement has been enthusiastically hailed by historians, architects, designers, antique dealers, and a host of entrepreneurs. Its rich legacy of architecture and decorative objects continues to inspire designers and homeowners alike. Museums on both sides of the Atlantic boast collections of the work of the movement's star designers, and surviving houses, furniture, textiles, wallpapers, ceramics, metalwork, and books gloriously portray this short-lived, but enlightened, period of design that was cut short by World War I. A romance continues to be spun about this extraordinary era and its iconic buildings, such as William Morris's Red House in England and the Gamble House in America. The fact that the movement was a philosophical approach to design, rather than an identifiable style, is often overlooked.

Though much has been written about the architecture and decorative arts of the period, informed discussions about garden design lag behind. It is a topic worthy of study that goes beyond descriptions of individual gardens and features. The paucity of serious publications on Arts and Crafts garden design is due in part to the fact that gardens are often viewed as isolated entities, dismissed as the sum of their plantings and decorative features, rather than properly understood for their function in an overall scheme. The Arts and Crafts Movement gave the garden a new definition as a harmonious component of the house. It is, in fact, impossible to appreciate garden design of the Arts and Crafts era without understanding the house, or the house without its garden.

PREVIOUS
C. F. A. Voysey, *Bird and Bramble*, wallpaper, 1901

8

This book takes as its theme the inspiration, characteristics, and development of garden design during the Arts and Crafts era. Not surprisingly, William Morris, who stands at the heart of the Arts and Crafts Movement, provided the fundamental philosophy for these gardens. The Arts and Crafts Movement, which focused on raising the standards of architecture and design, owes its greatest debt to Morris. In his own homes and his writings, he demonstrated how gardens were as integral to the home as its architecture and furnishings. Morris's followers provided individualistic and regional stamps to the basic tenets of Morris's philosophy.

Arts and Crafts gardens were not nearly as complex and self-conscious as iconic modern gardens such as Sissinghurst. Instead, they were conceived on a more intimate scale, with well-crafted detailing and a special approach to planting design. They were never an end in themselves, but were intertwined with the house like ivy growing on a wall, blurring the distinctions between indoors and outdoors. Their simple structuring and romantic, medieval-inspired imagery derived from old English manor house gardens. Nothing about them was ostentatious, contrived, or foreign. Hand-built stone walls, hedged enclosures, colorful flower borders, whimsical topiary trees, small structures, sundials, and other traditional ornament made for memorable storybook gardens.

Here you'll find a highly personal selection of houses and gardens of the Arts and Crafts era, with an emphasis on the diversity of designers who helped forge a special approach to garden design. Arts and Crafts gardens are presented through the eyes of artists and the words of the designers, gardeners, and critics, drawing on the most influential publications of the era: *Country Life* magazine, *The Studio* magazine, Gertrude Jekyll's *Gardens for Small Country Houses*, and Thomas Mawson's *The Art and Craft of Garden Making*, among others. As one might expect, the thread of Gertrude Jekyll runs through most of the chapters of this book because of her collaboration with several important Arts and Crafts architects, her finely honed planting skills, and her incomparable writings.

Although the Arts and Crafts Movement eventually fell out of favor because of changing aesthetics and altered economic conditions, it left a rich legacy throughout Britain, where its influence was felt in the Garden City Movement and later filtered down to ordinary suburban homes. It also left an unmistakable imprint on American architecture and garden design through the 1920s. Amateur American gardeners responded with a homespun Craftsman style, and architects, designers, and reformers tempered the movement's fundamental ideology to the country's diverse regionalism. In recent years, a renewed interest in traditional building crafts and small enclosed gardens returns the movement to the forefront. In some respects, there's scarcely a contemporary garden designer who does not acknowledge the principles of the Arts and Crafts garden, whether in a simple layout or in the choice of building materials, traditional ornament, and sophisticated planting design.

While a graduate student in art history, I was first introduced to the world of Arts and Crafts architects and designers, notably Morris and C. F. A. Voysey, whose wallpaper designs were the subject of my master's thesis. Having grown up in a house permeated with American Victorian furnishings avidly collected by my parents, I found that the Arts and Crafts era offered a breath of fresh air. Living then in Forest Hills Gardens, an ideal garden suburb designed by Frederick Law Olmsted, Jr., and Grosvenor Atterbury, may have sparked my slumbering awareness of landscape architecture and English-inspired domestic architecture. A seminal visit to Philip Webb's Standen in 1965, while it was still owned by the original family, opened my eyes to another world. Helen Beale welcomed us with homemade scones dripping with butter and cream that had gone sour in the dairy and regaled us with her youthful memories of the dashing architect, heavily enveloped in a large cape, arriving on the building site. Years later, my discovery of Edwin Lutyens and Gertrude Jekyll cemented my addiction to the Arts and Crafts Movement and unwittingly thrust me into the relatively new discipline of garden design history.

This book has grown from a desire to present Arts and Crafts gardens in the broad context of art, architecture, interior design, and decorative arts, in which they need to be appreciated. It was fueled by my personal library of period books and magazines devoted to architecture, garden design, and decorative arts as well as a personal collection of paintings, etchings, and decorative objects by artists and designers of the era. This approach definitely has its limitations, and I leave it to others to write the penultimate studies on American Arts and Crafts gardens, the ramifications of the movement on international garden design, and other related topics.

INTRODUCTION

IN THE 1870S, ENGLAND BEGAN TO EMERGE from the heavy shroud of Victorian design sensibilities by embracing a new aesthetic that would have ramifications on the design of houses, interiors, and decorative arts until the First World War. The Aesthetic Movement, which centered on the world of James McNeill Whistler and Oscar Wilde, ushered in a new concept in domestic architecture and interior design known as the "The House Beautiful."[1] The concept of artistic houses characterized by the lightness of their interiors and decorated with beautiful objects was a welcome relief from the heavy furnishings, dark interiors, and somber palette of the Victorian era. This new aesthetic was especially appealing to the growing middle classes with newfound artistic yearnings.

The parallel Queen Anne Movement, with its distinctive style of architecture that harked back to an earlier period in English history, took hold in London's newly fashionable enclaves, such as Chelsea and Bedford Park. The leading architect was Richard Norman Shaw (1831–1912), who, along with Ernest J. May, designed the artists' suburb in Bedford Park. There, red-brick houses featured picturesque turrets and gables, with artistic interiors in soft, pleasing colors. The

12

Queen Anne style was personified in nursery books written and illustrated by Walter Crane, Randolph Caldecott, and, above all, Kate Greenaway, whose books *Under the Window* (1878), *Mother Goose* (1881), *A Day in a Child's Life* (1881), and *Marigold Garden* (1885) depict caricatures of Shaw houses. Her own brick house in Hampstead was designed by Shaw in 1885. In her books, children decked out in sunbonnets play outdoors amid green croquet lawns and gardens filled with colorful flower borders and enormous topiary shrubs and trees. The steep, red-tile roofs of houses peek over the tops of high green hedges and garden walls. Young ladies enjoy a leisurely afternoon tea on the lawn, with flower borders bursting with sunflowers and roses and the Shaw-inspired house on the other side of the wall.

The Queen Anne style, for all its quaintness, was more suited to townhouses, shops, and suburban neighborhoods than to country houses, for which something more traditionally English was called for.[2] It was during this period that former country seats were replaced by smaller houses inspired by old English models of many forms. According to Ernest Newton (1856–1922), one of Shaw's pupils, these pioneer architects "aimed at catching the spirit of the old building rather than at the literal reproduction of any defined style."[3] Newton's genteel houses, such as Fouracre, in Winchfield, Hampshire, of 1901, definitely catch this spirit. The red-brick house, with decorative bands of trim and the front door opening out onto the garden, is simple, genial, and welcoming. As with many of the architects of the era, Newton's career advanced from Queen Anne and Tudor to Georgian revivals.

Shaw was a versatile architect best known for his old English style. His country houses, such as Cragside in Northumberland, are generously sized and include half-timbering and other traditional details. Perched on a steep ledge, Cragside is surrounded by acres of naturalistic woodland gardens (primarily rhododendrons,

heathers, and alpines) and numerous water features. In addition to Shaw, the leading practitioners of the new architecture were George Devey and Philip Webb. Devey (1820–86), a superb watercolor artist known for his picturesque approach to design, was one of the first Victorian architects to create houses based on the local vernacular, an important issue for Arts and Crafts architects.[4] Devey's sympathetic restorations of older buildings were drawn from an extensive knowledge of Elizabethan and Jacobean architecture.

Philip Speakman Webb (1831–1915) undoubtedly had the most far-reaching influence of the trio. His houses evoke the old in detailing but are innovative in planning, reflecting his passion for traditional building and local materials without copying them in a historicist fashion. A master of understatement, Webb profoundly influenced the coming generation of architects. Standen, which he designed in 1891 for London solicitor James Beale, is his masterpiece. The brick-and-stone house, with its distinctive wooden gables and tile-hung façade, takes its cue from the old farm buildings on the site that other architects might have torn down. Webb's unusual sensitivity to vernacular buildings and details had an enormous influence on the design of country houses in England.

Richard Norman Shaw, Cragside, Northumberland

In 1886, at Great Tangley Manor, near Guildford, Surrey, Webb redesigned and extended a half-timbered house with origins in the sixteenth century. He returned in 1894 to add a stone library wing that complemented the old half-timbered front. Webb's garden architecture included a timber-roofed bridge over the moat and a rustic pergola. These improvements drew considerable comment from Gertrude Jekyll, who lived nearby and had known the house in its former, more dilapidated and overgrown state. The ancient enclosure, with its arched doorway and loopholed walls, inspired Edwin Lutyens at Millmead and elsewhere.[5] The flower borders within the enclosure, which were characteristic of the era, were filled with a pleasing mixture of lilies, irises, and larkspur.

Small country houses within easy reach of London for weekend retreats for the upper middle class would become the realm of a new generation of architects, mostly born in the 1860s, who trained in some of the most prestigious offices of the day. In addition to Newton and May, Shaw's office produced William R. Lethaby (a major theorist of the era), Gerald Horsley, Mervyn Macartney (the influential editor of *The Architectural Review*), Edward S. Prior, and Robert Weir Schultz. Ernest George's office trained Herbert Baker, Guy Dawber, and Edwin

Philip Webb, Standen, East Grinstead, West Sussex

Lutyens, while John Sedding's office trained both Ernest Barnsley and Ernest Gimson.[6] Beginning in the 1890s, these architects and a host of others would create some of the signature examples of domestic architecture associated with the Arts and Crafts Movement, bringing England to the forefront of architectural design.

Unquestionably, the stars were Lutyens, whose romantic Surrey houses built from local stone gave new definition to the concept of vernacular; Voysey, whose quirky, whitewashed, roughcast houses and austere furnishings were universally hailed; and Baillie Scott, whose half-timbered suburban cottages had a profound impact on domestic architecture. Despite the various sources of design inspiration, whether Gothic Revival, Byzantine Revival, classicism, or vernacular, these architects were united by their staunch individualism, regionalism, and respect for traditional building arts.

In the early 1900s it took an enlightened foreigner to appreciate the importance of architectural developments in England. Hermann Muthesius (1861–1927), the court-appointed attaché to the German Embassy in London, extolled the new "free" style in his three-volume work, *Das Englische Haus*, the result of his detailed study of English domestic architecture. While living in Hammersmith, Muthesius fell in with the Morris circle and came to admire the recent work of Shaw, Lethaby, Voysey, and Charles Rennie Mackintosh. Muthesius credited the phenomenon of the English country house to the Englishman's desire for "sincerity and unpretentiousness" in his house, as well as the avoidance of any kind of display, rather than deliberately aiming at a specifically modern look. "The fundamental traits of the English house are its reserve, modesty, and charming sincerity."[7] He singled out Jekyll's Munstead Wood as a worthy contrast to the English house of fifty years earlier, a period he considered a low point in domestic architecture.

Sparked by John Ruskin, William Morris, and their followers, who called for design reform based on simplicity and utility, the new movement championed the England of happier, preindustrial days. Picture books and paintings of the latter part of the nineteenth century portrayed a romanticized rural England, its

TOP
Thomas H. Hunn, *Great Tangley Manor*, watercolor, early 1900s

ABOVE
Thomas H. Hunn, *The Lily Border at Great Tangley Manor*, watercolor, early 1900s

ABOVE
Helen Allingham, *Cottage Near Brook, Witley, Surrey*, watercolor, early 1900s

OPPOSITE
George S. Elgood, *The Twelve Apostles, Cleeve Prior* (Elgood and Jekyll, 1904)

landscapes, vernacular architecture, traditional crafts, and leisurely pursuits. The artist Helen Allingham's book *Happy England* (1903) paints an evocative picture of the English countryside filled with quaint cottages, lush flower borders, and beautiful children. Allingham's nostalgic view of country life is one seemingly devoid of hardships and the negative effects of industrialization.[8] Legions of artists, poets, and writers extolled the virtues of country living as opposed to the grim realities of city life. The back-to-the-land movement was sparked by a newfound reverence for the unspoiled English countryside and its rural traditions as an escape from the unhealthful atmosphere of cities, as well as their inherent social strictures. Ruskin's plea for recognition of artists and artisans alike was only one manifestation of the underlying social dissatisfaction of the day.

The Arts and Crafts Movement emerged from deep moral and social concerns. The complexity of the movement's origins, ideals, and manifestations has been the subject of many detailed studies, but its basic tenets were a fundamental disdain for the falseness of High Victorian design, a rediscovery of nature and English traditions, and the idea that manual work could be personally fulfilling.[9] Inspired by Morris, those who embraced the movement sought to bring together architects and craftsmen to work in harmony. In 1884, a group of Shaw's assistants founded the Art Workers' Guild to provide a meeting place for architects and craftsmen to discuss their work, which quickly fused together some of the movement's early objectives.[10] One of the guild's early ventures was the establishment of the Arts and Crafts Exhibition Society, which eventually provided a name to the new movement. Beginning with its first exhibition of members' work in 1888, it served to spread the word about design reform. Founded in 1893, *The Studio* magazine published illustrations of their architectural perspectives, garden designs, metalwork and jewelry, ceramics, textiles, and wallpapers, all of which rubbed shoulders happily with one another.

The Arts and Crafts Movement championed the unity of the arts, in which the house, the furnishing of its interiors, and the surrounding garden were considered a whole, or as Muthesius expressed it, "garden, house, and interior—a unity."[11] The parallel revival of the art of garden design came into play at a time when architects not only saw to every detail of the house and its interiors, but routinely laid out the gardens. These gardens, with their neatly clipped hedges and ordered geometry, harked back to the England of the sixteenth and seventeenth centuries, the pleasure grounds of the Tudors and Stuarts. In contrast to nineteenth-century estate gardens that were vast in scale and stiffly planted with brightly colored annuals and jarring foliage, gardens designed by Arts and Crafts architects and their collaborators were intimate in scale, with soothing colors and textures. They harmonized perfectly with the house and were often distinguished by individualistic architectural components, such as garden houses, dovecotes, and pergolas, all constructed using the local materials of the region.

1

GARDENS
OLD AND NEW

CHANGING ATTITUDES ABOUT GARDEN DESIGN in late-nineteenth-century England reflected the undercurrents of unrest in architecture and design. John Sedding, Reginald Blomfield, H. Inigo Triggs, and other architect-theorists began to reevaluate gardens and their ideal configuration. They rejected both the horticulturally driven gardens of the Victorian era and the idealized nature of the eighteenth-century landscape style.[1] What emerged during this period were theoretical debates representing two opposing viewpoints, pitting the architects against the horticulturists.

Blomfield's influential book, *The Formal Garden in England*, published in 1892 and considered a key work of the period, was the first to adopt the word "formal" to describe the architectural gardens of the Tudor and Renaissance periods that he proposed as models for new gardens. Blomfield had little interest in horticulture. As he wrote, "Horticulture stands to garden design much as building does to architecture; the two are connected, but very far from being identical."[2] Even Hermann Muthesius, who distanced himself somewhat from these debates, remarked that in England it was typical for the design of the

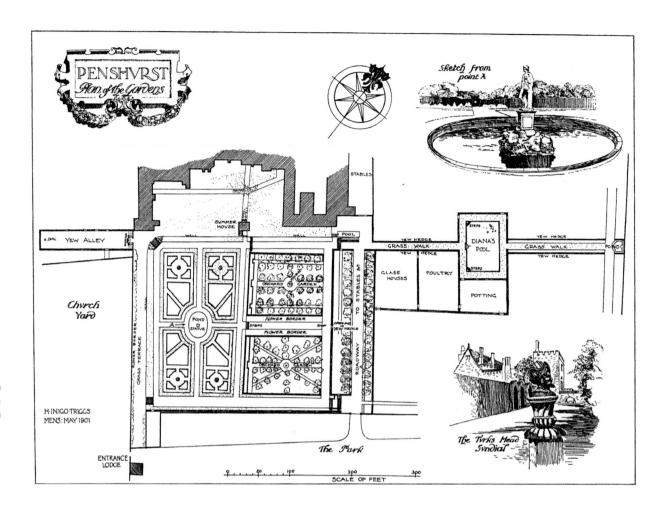

ABOVE
H. Inigo Triggs, *Penshurst:
Plan of the Gardens*, 1901
(Triggs, 1902)

OPPOSITE
Ernest Arthur Rowe, *Penshurst Place*, watercolor, 1891

PREVIOUS
Ernest Albert Chadwick,
Summerhouse at Montacute,
watercolor (Mawson, 1901)

garden to be placed in the hands of the architect, whose role was to conceive it in relationship to the house, while the gardener was left to execute it.[3] According to Ernest Newton, architects who in the past had been forced to delegate the garden layout to "alien hands" rejoiced at the "dethronement of the nursery gardener [who specialized in] the cult of the curly path, of the kidney-shaped bed and clump of pampas grass."[4] This stance, which was shared by other architects of the era, was held in disdain by horticulturists and gardeners alike, who countered that architects knew nothing about garden design.

Blomfield singled out George Devey for his successful efforts in designing a unified house and grounds. In the 1840s, Devey had revitalized the ancient gardens at Penshurst Place in Kent for Lord de L'Isle when he restored the old house with origins dating to the sixteenth century. His sensitive refurbishment of the gardens set the precedent for future generations of architects to draw upon. Some of the individual garden compartments were surrounded by yew hedges or walls within the original asymmetrical configuration. The grander formal gardens, on

axis with the house, include two ornamental orchard gardens and a large parterre. The central pool and fountain set within a patterned framework of low hedges are depicted in Ernest Arthur Rowe's watercolor of 1891. A dense backdrop of ancient trees among the old buildings was the perfect setting for the garden.

The career of Blomfield (1856–1942) owed much to the success of his book on garden design. An early supporter of the Arts and Crafts Movement, Blomfield was a member of the Art Workers' Guild and a partner in Kenton and Company, a short-lived business enterprise specializing in handmade furniture that was a predecessor to some of the regional craft guilds that sprang up later.[5] In the course of his work, which was mostly devoted to the classical style, Blomfield was frequently asked to design gardens evoking the old English style. Godinton House in Kent, with its smooth lawns, terraces, distinctive topiary, and hedges clipped to reflect the gables of the house, serves as a good example of his elementary garden-planning skills. Another commission is the large formal garden at Mellerstain House in the Scottish Borders, an exceptionally fine Georgian house

Reginald Blomfield,
Godinton House,
Ashford, Kent

built by William Adam in 1725, with later additions by his famous son, Robert Adam. Blomfield's garden, laid out in 1909 and consisting of twin parterres, with terraces overlooking the Cheviot Hills, unfortunately obliterated the earlier canal garden that was more appropriate to the period of the house. Although a successful architect, Blomfield's historical interpretation of gardens was often fanciful.

Another early twentieth-century book that extolled the architectural gardens of the sixteenth and seventeenth centuries as models for new gardens is *Formal Gardens in England and Scotland* (1902), a lavish, large-format folio with exquisitely drawn plans and elevations of historic gardens. It was prepared by Harry Inigo Triggs (1876–1923), a young architect who specialized in romantic Elizabethan houses and sunken water gardens. *Gardens Old and New* (1901–07), a three-volume compendium of articles first published in *Country Life* and illustrated with sumptuous photographs, glorified the best of England's old historic gardens as well as new gardens designed along old themes.

H. Inigo Triggs, *Montacute in Somersetshire*, line drawing, 1900 (Triggs, 1902)

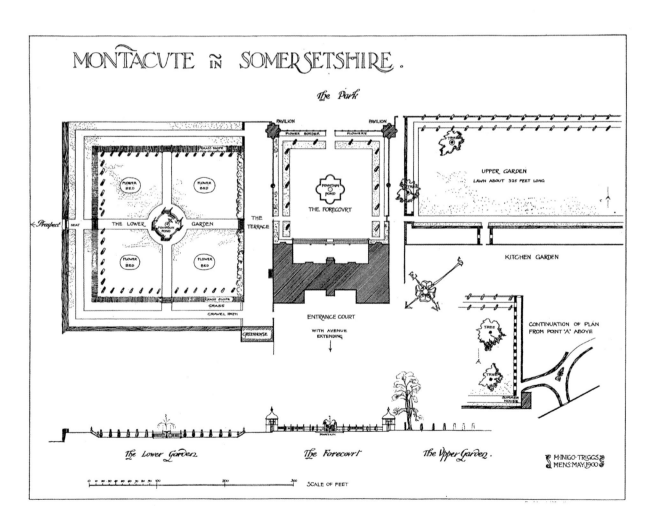

Ironically, by the end of the nineteenth century, little survived of most manor house gardens of the sixteenth and early seventeenth centuries, except possibly the original outlines. Montacute House in Somerset, which was hailed in many period books, including Blomfield's and Triggs's, took most of its identity from a restoration of the early 1890s. Montacute's simple garden layout, as rendered by Triggs, is basically a series of formal garden terraces. The Upper Garden is a simple bowling green or lawn with ancient cedar trees, and the North Garden is divided into four quadrants with a central pool and fountain. The central courtyard, with the distinctive detailing of its walls and its twin garden pavilions, served as an inspiration for architects who were actively engaged in restoring old gardens as well as creating new ones that evoked the old. Gertrude Jekyll wryly noted, however, that the obelisk-shaped finials at Montacute "were borrowed straight from the Italians [but without] their marvelous discernment."[6]

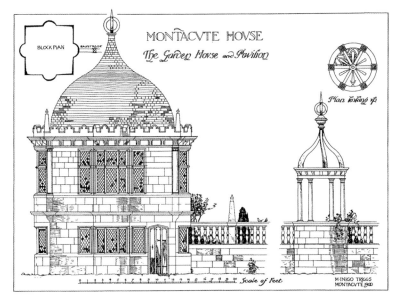

TOP
H. Inigo Triggs, *Montacute House: The Garden House and Pavilion*, line drawing, 1900 (Triggs, 1902

ABOVE
Garden house at Montacute House, Somerset

Francis Inigo Thomas (1866–1950), Blomfield's protégé who prepared the drawings for *The Formal Garden in England*, excelled at restoring and remodeling existing gardens using the vocabulary of older gardens.[7] At Athelhampton, a late-fifteenth-century manor house in Dorset, he rehabilitated the deteriorating old hall and made a new garden in the old manner by creating a series of interrelating enclosures evoking those of the Elizabethan era, with specific quotations from Montacute. The enclosure walls were built from warm-colored Hamstone, acquired not far from Montacute in Somerset.[8] At the center of the garden, Thomas added a circular Coronet (or Corona), with raised stone obelisks on the surrounding wall and a circular pool, and adjacent to this is a large rectangular garden, or Great Court, with two garden houses. This garden is distinguished by dramatic rows of pyramidal yews, with a central basin and fountain. On axis with the house, and on the other side of the Coronet, lies the third enclosure, a companion pool garden. In all, it was the quintessence of an architectural garden. Parnham, also in Dorset, and thought to have been designed by Thomas, also has many echoes of Montacute, including its balustrading, obelisks, and two pavilions.

Gothic Revival architect John Dando Sedding (1838–91), who had an affinity for decorations drawn from nature, wrote another important treatise on garden

design, *Garden-Craft Old and New* (1890), in which he presented a practical, if romanticized, approach to garden design. It laid the foundation for Arts and Crafts gardens in the early 1900s. "The old-fashioned garden," Sedding wrote, "represents one of the pleasures of England, one of the charms of that quiet beautiful life of bygone times." Because these gardens are "beautiful yesterday, beautiful to-day, and beautiful always . . . we do well to turn to them, not to copy their exact lines, nor to limit ourselves to the range of their ornament and effects, but to glean hints for our garden-enterprise to-day, to drink of their spirit, to gain impulsion from them."[9]

CLOCKWISE FROM LEFT
F. Inigo Thomas, the Great Court at Athelhampton, Dorchester, Dorset

John Daddo Sedding, A Garden Enclosed, line drawing (Sedding, 1890)

F. Inigo Thomas, formal gardens at Parnham, Beaminster, Dorset

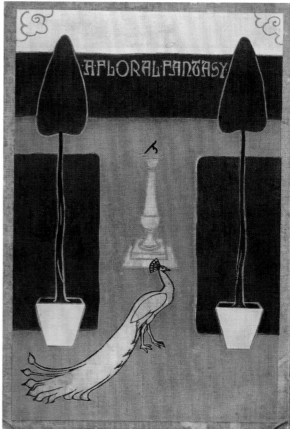

Walter Crane, front and
back covers of *A Floral
Fantasy in an Old English
Garden*, 1899

Sedding championed the "garden enclosed," with high box hedges and ornamented with flower borders and whimsical yew topiaries clipped into birdlike forms that were beloved of the Arts and Crafts architects.

Old-fashioned gardens, with their smooth bowling greens, massive hedges, overflowing flower borders, clipped topiaries, and other characteristic vocabulary, formed the basis for new gardens made by architects during the Arts and Crafts era. Walter Crane's pictorial cover for *A Floral Fantasy in an Old English Garden* (1899) captures the essence of an old-fashioned garden, with its hedged enclosure, spade-shaped tubbed trees of improbable height, and topiary peacocks.[10] A sundial and a simple garden gate complete the scene.

Billowing hedges and fanciful clipped topiaries were emblematic of old English gardens. Topiaries took many inventive forms, from cakestands and spirals to hatted heads and chessmen, each identified with a specific garden, such as Levens Hall and Montacute. The historic topiary gardens at Levens Hall, in Cumbria, which date to the late seventeenth century, are probably the most outstanding examples of their kind. "Near the house," according to a description in 1884, "are pyramids with balls at top and bastionettes fashioned in their angles, arbours impenetrable to sun or rain or peering eyes, tall mushrooms on slender stalks, and other quaint devices."[11] In 1905, Jekyll praised the gardens at Levens as perfect complements to the house, "growing with it into a complete harmony of mellow age."[12] The impeccably maintained gardens at Levens Hall continue to enthrall visitors today.

Brickwall, in Northiam, East Sussex, is an equally remarkable green garden, with origins dating to 1680, when it was laid out by the Frewen family. In 1873, Devey remodeled the timber-framed Jacobean house, adding a new front with half-timbered gables overlooking the garden.[13] Nearly thirty years after Devey's addition had been allowed to mellow, Jekyll commented that Brickwall was a "delightful example, both as to house and garden, of these old places of the truest English type . . . the garden [being] laid out to view, almost as a picture hangs on a wall, in the very best position for the convenience of the spectator."[14] The garden consists of two major sections separated by double flower borders filled with plants that Jane Frewen might have selected in the late seventeenth century. A long line of pyramidal yews frame the view to the house from the nearer compartment, which once featured a long reflecting pool. Jekyll praised the simplicity of the clipped yews, observing that they are best kept to one form or shape rather than a medley of forms, as found in other places.

Great Fosters, in Egham, Surrey, boasts some of the best topiary gardens created in the early twentieth century. Now a country house hotel, the core of the building is formed by a U-shaped Elizabethan manor house that once served as a royal hunting lodge. While the manor was undergoing renovations in 1918, the architect W. H. Romaine-Walker (1854–1940) created elaborate gardens that harked back to the time when the property was once part of Windsor Great Park. His scheme included clipped yew hedges, a knot garden, and an archery pavilion set within the medieval moat and grounds. In the 1970s, when

BELOW
H. Inigo Triggs, *Examples of Topiary Work*, line drawing, 1902 (Triggs, 1902)

BOTTOM
Topiary gardens at Levens Hall, Kendal, Cumbria

29

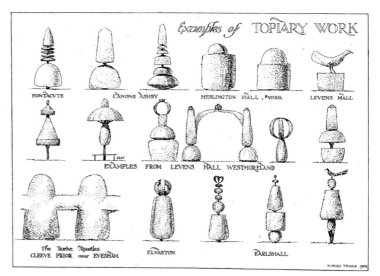

George S. Elgood, *Levens*, watercolor (Elgood and Jekyll, 1904)

TOP
George S. Elgood,
Brickwall, Northiam,
watercolor (Elgood and
Jekyll, 1904)

ABOVE
Pyramidal yews at
Brickwall, Northiam,
East Sussex

OPPOSITE
H. Inigo Triggs, *A Plan
of the Gardens at Brick-
wall,* line drawing, 1902
(Triggs, 1902)

the London M25 Orbital Motorway sliced through the main axial avenue, the period gardens were ingeniously screened, while later additions and a comprehensive restoration program by Kim Wilkie Associates have served to preserve these unique gardens.

A necessary adjunct to topiary gardens is a wide bowling green lined with clipped hedges, and beyond, a tree-shaded walk and perhaps wild parkland. At Berkeley Castle, a twelfth-century battlemented castle not far from the Severn River in Gloucestershire, a long bowling green is banked by ancient yew hedges on three sides. "The yews, still clipped into bold rounded forms, may have formed a trim hedge in Tudor days, and the level space of turf . . . lies cool and sheltered from the westering sun by the stout bulwark of their ancient shade," wrote Jekyll, who was a frequent visitor to the castle.[15] Dense flower borders filled with hardy English plants form a foil for the dark green hedges and the smooth lawn as captured in Ernest Rowe's watercolor.

The garden design ideas of Sedding's and Blomfield's books left no question in Muthesius's mind that the geometric garden should replace the landscape garden. "It is inconceivable that anyone in England today with a genuine concern for art could question its rightness," he asserted.[16] But these books drew the wrath of William Robinson, the era's most vocal horticulturist and promoter of the gardenesque approach to garden design. In *Garden Design and Architects' Gardens* (1892), Robinson took both books and their authors to task. His subtitle, "Two reviews, illustrated, to show, by actual examples from British gardens, that clipping and aligning trees to make them 'harmonise' with architecture is barbarous, needless, and inartistic," passionately expressed his heartfelt disdain for architects' gardens. Both books, he claimed, were "made up in great part of quotations from old books on gardening—many written by men who knew books better than gardening." In short, they contributed nothing to the "beautiful art of

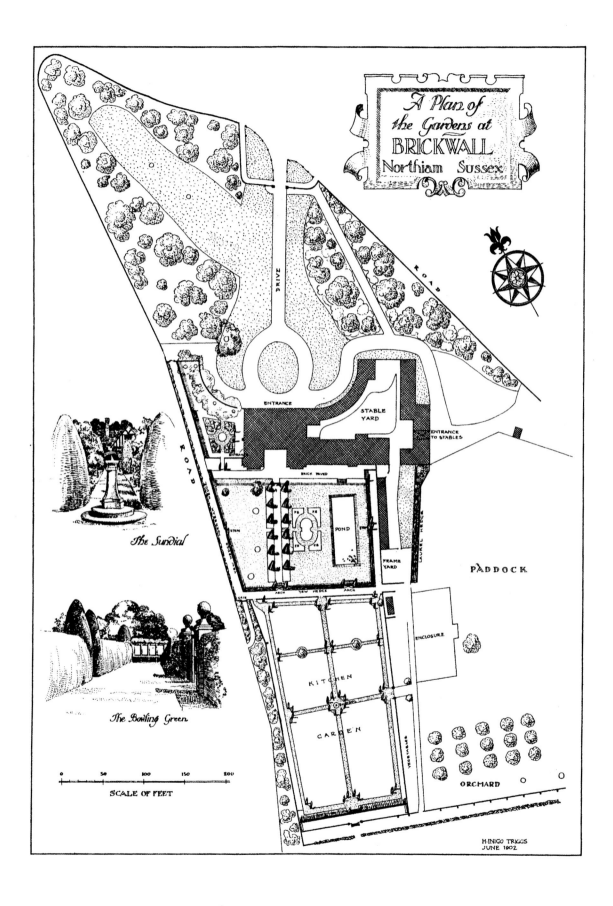

A Plan of
the Gardens at
BRICKWALL
Northiam Sussex

ROAD

DRIVE

ROAD

ENTRANCE

STABLE
YARD

ENTRANCE
TO STABLES

BRICK PAVED

POND

FRAME
YARD

LAUREL HEDGE

PADDOCK

YEW HEDGE

ARCH   ARCH

GATE

ENCLOSURE

KITCHEN

GARDEN

VEGETABLES

ORCHARD

The Sundial

The Bowling Green

0   50   100   150   200

SCALE OF FEET

H·INIGO TRIGGS
JUNE 1902

gardening or garden design." [17] He singled out Sedding's *A Garden Enclosed* as a book devoted to "vegetable sculpture [written by someone] without any knowledge of plants, trees, or landscape beauty." [18]

Beyond the heat of the moment—and the controversy simmered for years—was the reasonable viewpoint that hardy plants in naturalistic settings were the foundation of any garden. Robinson, who was known as the Father of the English Flower Garden, took up the cause for Englishness in garden design and in choice of plants in the 1870s, long before the voices of either Blomfield or Sedding were

heard. Robinson championed the same native English plants that William Morris used in his wallpapers and textiles. Robinson's numerous books favoring naturalistic groupings of hardy perennials were far more popular among gardeners than either Sedding's or Blomfield's books.

Though informal flower borders and naturalistic sweeps of woodland plants were important considerations, most of the gardens associated with the Arts and Crafts Movement were architectural, rather than horticultural, in concept. These gardens owe their greatest debt to traditional designs as extolled by Sedding and

ABOVE
Ernest Arthur Rowe, *Bowling Green, Berkeley Castle*, watercolor, 1908

ABOVE LEFT
W. H. Romaine-Walker, topiary garden at Great Fosters, Egham, Surrey

his followers. Their compartmentalized spaces and structural frameworks based on enclosing hedges or walls served as prototypes for small country house gardens designed by a younger generation of imaginative architects, some of whom had been pupils in Sedding's office. They opted for old-time accessories, such as sundials and armillary spheres, rather than classically inspired fountains and the stiff formality typically found in Victorian gardens.

Arts and Crafts gardens, distinguished by their exceptional architectural detailing, exemplary craftsmanship, emerald-green lawns, exquisite flower borders, and neatly clipped hedges, provided inviting, yet secluded outdoor spaces adjacent to the house. In their purist form, these gardens were designed by architects—some of whom had little knowledge of horticulture—rather than by horticulturists. Every architect, according to Muthesius, "considers it his duty to design the garden in conjunction with the house and to steep himself in the principles of garden design as in those of the art of furnishing a room."[19]

OPPOSITE
Beatrice Parsons, *Bluebells at Stansted, Kent*, watercolor, 1901

37

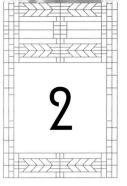

WILLIAM MORRIS'S EARTHLY PARADISE

WILLIAM MORRIS WOULD BE SURPRISED to learn that he played a considerable role in house and garden design dynamics of the early twentieth century. His first biographer, J. W. Mackail, observed that although Morris always prided himself on his knowledge of gardening, he doubted whether "he was ever seen with a spade in his hands."[1] A poet, calligrapher, manuscript illuminator, printer, embroiderer, entrepreneur, conservationist, utopian thinker, lecturer, writer, and, above all, pattern designer, Morris accomplished more in his lifetime than ten men, dying in his early sixties from sheer exhaustion. Gardens never strayed far from his mind. His two country homes—Red House and Kelmscott Manor—as well as his workshops at Merton Abbey abounded with the flowers, fruits, and birds that formed the core of his firm's famous wallpapers, textiles, and tapestries. Morris's gardens were a testament to his fascination with the Middle Ages and among the earliest examples of the rage for old-fashioned gardens. Morris, in fact, dedicated his life to medieval times, from its romance and visual imagery to the traditional handcrafts and medieval-inspired guilds

OPPOSITE
William Morris, *Pome-
granate*, wallpaper, 1866

PREVIOUS
William Morris, *Lark-
spur*, wallpaper, 1872

that made them. Drawing on the ideas of Gothic Revival architect Augustus
Welby Pugin, who suggested that the ills of society could be rectified with the
spirituality of Gothic art and architecture, Morris embraced medievalism as the
model for his life's work.

William Morris (1834–96) spent an idyllic childhood in the country, on
the edge of Epping Forest in Essex, where he developed a lifelong passion for all
aspects of nature. In the early 1860s, he began designing wallpapers, choosing
as his vocabulary the garden and meadow flowers, fruits, and vines he knew as a
youth. The names he chose for his patterns, *Blackthorn, Daisy, Eyebright, Honeysuckle, Larkspur, Pomegranate*, and scores of others, attest to his devotion to the
natural world.[2] Upon entering Exeter College, Oxford, in 1853, Morris formed
important friendships with Edward Burne-Jones, Dante Gabriel Rossetti, and
other artists associated with the Pre-Raphaelite Brotherhood. He also came under
the influence of John Ruskin, whose book, *Stones of Venice*, ignited his interest
in architecture. During a brief apprenticeship with the architect G. E. Street,
Morris met Philip Webb, who soon became an influential friend and collaborator.
Morris's newfound fascination with the Arthurian legend opened up a world of
medieval lore and soon found him writing poetry epics, such as *The Defence of
Guenevere* (1858), *The Life and Death of Jason* (1867), and *The Earthly Paradise*
(1868), the latter a three-volume narrative poem that firmly established his reputation as a poet. In all, he wrote dozens of volumes of prose and poetry.

In 1861 Morris founded the firm Morris, Marshall, Faulkner and Co. to
produce simple, yet elegant home furnishings such as hand-printed wallpapers,
fabrics, furniture, and decorative arts as an antidote to the machine-made,
overly ornate Victorian pieces—vestiges of the Great Exhibition of 1851—that
he abhorred. Located at first in London's Red Lion Square and later at 449
Oxford Street, the company's showrooms offered commercial wares designed by
Burne-Jones, Webb, Ford Madox Brown, William De Morgan, and other artists.[3]
Morris's frustration at finding acceptable furnishings for his own home sparked
his idea for artists, designers, and craftsmen to work together harmoniously to
produce attractive decorative products. Morris's vision centered on transforming
prevailing ideas about decorating houses with overwrought goods to simpler,
well-designed objects that harked back to England of the Middle Ages. His dictum—"Have nothing in your houses that you do not know to be useful or believe
to be beautiful"—became the guiding light of his personal mission.[4] The fledgling firm's commission in 1867 to decorate the Green Dining Room at the South
Kensington Museum (now the Victoria and Albert Museum) in London set them
on their way. In its heyday, the firm produced an exhaustive range of wallpapers,
fabrics, tapestries, carpets, furniture, tiles, stained glass, and metalwork, all with
characteristic medieval-inspired floral designs.[5] The venture eventually foundered due to the harsh realities of business economics. In a letter to an American

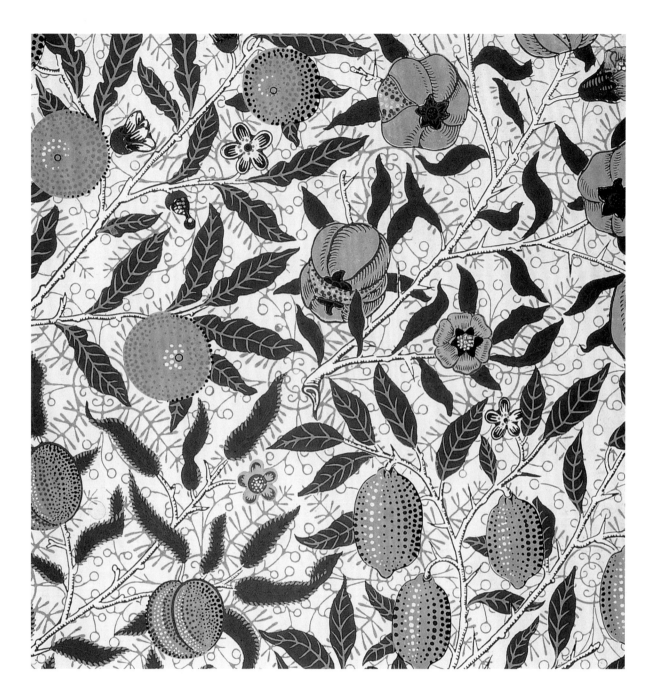

admirer in 1884, Morris acknowledged that even though the manner of work done in the Middle Ages was the *only* way, reality proved that it was impossible "in this profit-grinding society."[6]

In later years, Morris turned his energies to socialism, becoming a passionate advocate and lecturer, much to the astonishment of his friends and family. His utopian romance, *News from Nowhere*, describing his beloved home and garden at

Kelmscott Manor, was published in 1891, the same year that Morris founded his final enterprise, the Kelmscott Press. Named after Kelmscott House, his home in Hammersmith, Kelmscott Press published some fifty books, designed and produced by the leading artists of the day and still considered the apogee of book arts. The sumptuous *Works of Geoffrey Chaucer* was published in 1896, the same year that Morris died.

In the end, Morris's legacy as a pattern designer outlasted his reputation as a poet and socialist; many of the individual patterns remain in production today. His reverence for old buildings, traditional crafts, and the beauty of the English countryside inspired generations of followers, among them Gertrude Jekyll, Ernest Gimson and the Barnsley brothers, Robert Lorimer, C. F. A. Voysey, and M. H. Baillie Scott, who would form the nucleus of the Arts and Crafts Movement. Each designer would leave his or her own distinctive mark upon architecture and garden design of the period.

Morris's thoughts on gardens and flowers can be found in some of his writings, and not surprisingly he had strong opinions. He railed against the popularity of florists' flowers, with all their natural traits bred out of them. "When the florists fell upon the rose [which Morris regarded as the queen of flowers] . . . they strove for size and got it, a fine specimen of a florist's rose being about as big as a moderate Savoy cabbage." They "improved" the scent, but "missed the very essence of the rose's being. . . . they threw away the exquisite subtlety of form, delicacy of texture, and sweetness of color."[7] He also cautioned against double flowers and other tokens of artificiality, such as carpet-bedding ("an aberration of the human mind"), as well as the misuse of plant curiosities that were more appropriate for botanical gardens than home gardens. He also had definite ideas about the use of color in gardens. "Flowers in masses are mighty strong color, and if not used with a great deal of caution are very destructive to pleasure in gardening," he wrote. Some flowers, such as scarlet geraniums and yellow calceolaria, were simply "bad" and when planted profusely showed that "even flowers can be thoroughly ugly."[8]

Writing in 1879, Morris presaged ideas later promoted by other reformers, notably William Robinson and Jekyll. Morris's ideas about the essence of a garden, rather than his thoughts about flowers, provided a credo for garden design theory that spilled over into the early 1900s. In *Hopes and Fears for Art*, Morris wrote

Large or small, it should look both orderly and rich. It should be well fenced from the outside world. It should by no means imitate either the wilfulness or the wildness of Nature, but should look like a thing never to be seen except near a house. It should, in fact, look like a part of the house. It follows from this that no private pleasure-garden should be very big, and a public garden should be divided and made to look like so many flower-closes in a meadow, or a wood, or amidst the pavement.[9]

43

Morris's ideas about domestic architecture, interior design, and gardens coalesced at Red House, his country home near Bexleyheath, Kent. Designed by Webb in 1859, it was the architect's first independent architectural commission and a new home for Morris and his bride, Jane Burden, whom Morris and Rossetti "discovered" in Oxford. A brooding beauty, with masses of dark, wavy hair, Jane was immortalized in Rossetti's paintings. The couple lived at Red House for only five years before Morris was forced to sell it after running into financial difficulties that jeopardized his firm.

Today Red House symbolizes the values that Morris honored most: honesty and beauty. It is also considered the first modern country house, representative of a new approach to house and garden design. Sited in an orchard and meadow, the house and garden are inseparable. "Red House garden, with its long grass walks, its midsummer lilies and autumn sunflowers, its wattled rose-trellises inclosing richly-flowered square garden plots, was then as unique as the house it surrounded," wrote Mackail in 1899.[10] Fiona MacCarthy, Morris's modern biographer, has suggested that the garden was even more influential than the house.[11] May Morris, the Morrises' younger daughter, remembered "the garden

BELOW
Walter Crane, *Tea at Red House*, watercolor, 1907

OPPOSITE
Philip Webb, Red House, Bexleyheath, Kent

44

that graced this pleasant home [as] characteristic, so happily English in its sweetness and freshness, with its rose-hedges and lavender and rosemary borderings to the flower-beds, its alley and bowling green, and the orchard-walks among the apple-trees."[12] Another observer described the garden as "vividly picturesque and uniquely original . . . divided into many squares, hedged with sweet-briar or wild rose, each enclosure with its own particular show of flowers."[13]

This medieval-inspired pleasure garden, filled with gnarled old fruit trees and a subtle selection of simple flowers, was a far cry from the typical parterre gardens of late-Victorian-era estates filled with the vividly colored annuals that Morris loathed. In contrast, the garden at Red House harked back to a flowery medieval *hortus conclusus*, with enclosure hedges or trellises, straight paths, and profusions of traditional herbs, flowers, and fruits. Such gardens served as a source of inspiration for the firm's renowned tapestries with their minutely detailed floral backgrounds. Morris's garden was basically a large square, subdivided into four spaces surrounded by wattle fence, similar to those depicted in medieval illuminated books. It was an earthly paradise, an oasis meant for practicality, enjoyment, and seclusion, rather than ostentatious display.

BELOW
Well house at Red House

BOTTOM
Edmund Hort New, *Red House, Upton*, line drawing (Mackail, 1899)

OPPOSITE
William Morris and Philip Webb, The Trellis, wallpaper, 1864

Red House was profoundly influential in its time, inspiring Jekyll, for example, in the design of the interiors of her home at Munstead Wood nearly forty years later. Hermann Muthesius stated that Red House stood "at the threshold of the development of the modern English house," while Rossetti thought it more of a poem than a house.[14] A picturesque Gothic cottage, built of red brick laid in English Bond, with a steeply sloping roof and pointed gables, the exterior belies its light and airy interiors. Behind the small-paned windows lay whitewashed walls, exposed brick, red-tiled floors, plain rush-seated chairs, painted cupboards, and all the handmade furnishings that would inspire the formation of Morris's firm. In all, it was living proof of his insatiable thirst for design reform in the domestic arts.

Red House is also remarkable because the house and garden were conceived as an integrated unit. A romantic retreat, the house nestles into a surrounding orchard with hedged enclosures demarking the boundaries of the garden. As Mackail remarked, "The building had been planned with such care that hardly a tree in the orchard had to be cut down; apples fell in at the windows as they stood open on hot autumn nights."[15] Roses clambered up the side of the house, and Webb's fanciful well house with its conical red-tiled roof, which gives so much character to Red House, solidified the relationship between the house and garden.[16] Surrounded by trellises covered with roses, white jasmine, and honeysuckle, the well court became a fragrant enclosure where family and friends could enjoy their afternoon tea. Webb's detailed drawing of the trellis in the original plans for Red House may have inspired Morris's earliest wallpaper design, *The Trellis*, in November 1862, for which Webb drew the birds.[17] Even though the outlines of Morris's garden and some of the original fruit trees still survive, the essence of his paradise garden can best be appreciated in the company's legacy of pattern designs and tapestries.

After leaving Red House, followed by years of living in smoke-choked London, Morris was again able to satisfy his yearnings for a summer place in the country. In 1871 he found an old house about thirty miles (fifty kilometers) from Oxford on the upper reaches of the Thames that would become synonymous with his ideals. Located in a tiny village near Lechlade, Kelmscott Manor is a late-sixteenth-century Tudor manor house built of gray limestone, with roofs covered in heavy stone slates and a picturesque farm enclosure replete with a dovecote.[18] He acquired the lease in June that year but never actually owned the house.[19] It has been said that Morris wanted the house as a love nest for

his wife and her lover, Rossetti. Nonetheless, Morris reminisced lovingly about Kelmscott in 1895, remarking on what went into the making of an old house "grown up out of the soil" and the lives of those who lived there before him. He extolled the "sense of delight of meadow and acre and wood and river . . . a liking for making materials serve one's turn . . . and a little grain of sentiment."[20]

In his pithy comments about gardens, Morris observed that "Many a good house both old and new is marred by the vulgarity and stupidity of its garden, so that one is tormented by having to abstract in one's mind the good building from the nightmare of 'horticulture' which surrounds it." Not so at Kelmscott, where "the garden, divided by old clipped yew hedges, is quite unaffected and very pleasant."[21] In a letter to his mother, Rossetti spoke of the garden as "a

BELOW
Marie Spartali Stillman,
Kelmscott Manor, water-
color, ca. 1890

OPPOSITE
Kelmscott Manor,
Lechlade, Gloucestershire

perfect paradise."[22] The walled garden was filled with flowers familiar from his pattern designs, and beyond there was a meadow filled with bluebells, apple blossoms, and birdsong; rooks in the elm trees; blackbirds in the garden; and doves on the roof.

The most memorable evocation of Kelmscott is in the closing chapters of *News From Nowhere*, when the wayfarer journeys by riverboat from Hampton Court to Kelmscott:

> *my hand raised the latch of a door in the wall, and we stood presently on a stone path which led up to the old house. . . . My companion gave a sigh of pleased surprise and enjoyment . . . for the garden between the wall and the house was*

redolent of the June flowers, and the roses were rolling over one another with that delicious super-abundance of small, well-tended gardens which at first sight takes away all thought from the beholder save that of beauty.[23]

The garden was to be savored from both inside and outside the house. From one of the rooms of Kelmscott, one could "catch a glimpse of the Thames clover meadows and the pretty elm-crowned hill over in Berkshire."[24] From another place in the house, one could admire the sharp turn of the gables (the house has seventeen), the stone barn, sheds, and the dovecote. Today those same amenities await the visitor at Kelmscott Manor, although the interiors are not arranged as they were in Morris's day; they were, in fact, quite spartan. Morris thought that Kelmscott embodied the best of England, its countryside, architecture, and gardens.

Morris, who died in October 1896 from "simply being William Morris," is buried nearby in the Kelmscott churchyard. One hopes that the house and garden brought him much pleasure in his lifetime. His workshops at Merton Abbey, on the River Wandle in Surrey, had equally pleasant surroundings. "His factory [was] a scene of cheerful, uncramped industry, where toil looks like pleasure, where flowers are blooming in windows, and sunshine and fresh air brighten the faces of artist and mechanic." Roses climbed the ruined abbey walls and a kitchen garden was filled with wild strawberries and plants used for dyes for his textiles.[25] But Red House and Kelmscott Manor above all laid the foundations for the Arts and Crafts approach to home and garden making, namely the essential relationship between house and garden and the reverence for vernacular building arts.

ABOVE LEFT
Walled garden at Kelmscott Manor

ABOVE RIGHT
Charles March Gere, Kelmscott Manor, line drawing (Morris, News from Nowhere, 1891)

OPPOSITE
Joseph Pennell, The Enchanted Doorway [Merton Abbey], ink drawing, 1886

51

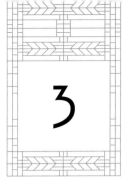

3

THE LURE OF THE COTSWOLDS

THE COTSWOLDS, A REGION IN THE WEST COUNTRY noted for its hidden valleys and the distinctive soft, gray limestone used in its buildings, is still a mecca for the Arts and Crafts Movement. Because the Cotswolds were both remote and economically depressed after the removal of its once-flourishing wool industry to the north, its sleepy villages and trove of medieval and Tudor stone buildings remained undisturbed, only to be rediscovered in the nineteenth century. William Morris, whose Kelmscott Manor was situated just on the edge of the Cotswolds, reveled in the region's old buildings, traditional crafts, and natural beauty. He, in turn, inspired several architects and designers to move to the Cotswolds to set up workshops practicing some of the local crafts.

In 1884, Morris encouraged Ernest Gimson (1864–1919), a young man from Leicester who had attended one of his lectures, to become an architect. Armed with a letter of introduction from Morris, Gimson went to work in John Sedding's London office, and while there he met fellow architect Ernest Barnsley (1863–1926), from Birmingham, as well as his younger brother, Sidney Barnsley (1865–1926), who was in

ABOVE
Sapperton Vale from
Cotswold Farm

PREVIOUS
Ernest Barnsley, winter
garden and troughery
at Rodmarton Manor,
Rodmarton, Gloucestershire

Shaw's office. They became fast friends, sharing living quarters in London and imbuing themselves in the world of Arts and Crafts, with Morris and Company's showrooms next door to Sedding's office.

According to Gimson's biographer, Norman Jewson, his gospel was that of Morris, "of healthy employment for all in making useful and beautiful things or productive agriculture, giving everyone an intelligent interest in their work, time to do it as well as might be, with reasonable leisure time for other interests." [1] Following Morris's recommendation to learn manual skills, Gimson began making rush-seated ladderback chairs, which became a staple of his later workshops.

Gimson also became interested in reviving the long-lost art of plasterwork, studying examples in old manor houses. True to Gimson's style, he adapted, rather than copied, antique examples, using floral elements, such as roses, honeysuckle, dianthus, lilies, strawberry plants, and, in later years, his signature squirrels and oak leaves.[2] The Barnsley brothers took up cabinetmaking and woodworking, and all three routinely exhibited their work at the annual venues of the Arts and Crafts Exhibition Society in London.

After several years devoted to travel (Sidney Barnsley toured Greece in 1888 with Robert Weir Schultz, another important Arts and Crafts architect) or building houses in the Midlands, they became gripped by the romantic notion of living and working in the country.[3] With their families in tow, they removed to the Cotswolds in 1893 to begin earning their livings along the lines dictated by Morris. They were among the first of Morris's disciples to set up workshops in the country. In 1902, Charles R. Ashbee's (1863–1942) Guild of Handicraft, founded in London in the 1880s as a result of the Arts and Crafts Exhibition Society, moved to Chipping Campden, where it continued to produce its distinctive metalwork and furniture until 1907, when it foundered due to competition from companies such as Liberty's.[4]

Gimson and the Barnsleys specialized in a new type of furniture and decorative arts that drew heavily on traditional country models without replicating them. They were renowned for their high level of craftsmanship and their exclusive use of native woods. In workshops first at Pinbury Park and later at Daneway House in Sapperton, most of the wares were executed by local cabinetmakers. In addition to their furnishings, which were much in demand, Gimson and the Barnsleys also undertook select architectural commissions ranging from repairing old buildings to designing new cottages.[5] Their architectural work, which was characterized by a respect for vernacular traditions, use of local building materials, and an affinity for the surrounding landscape, elicited much praise. As one critic wrote in 1909, they "are among the leaders of the school that is seeking to create an original and living style in architecture."[6]

Their fledgling efforts caught the eye of Lord Bathurst, who leased them his summer home at Pinbury Park, with magnificent views over the Sapperton Vale, provided they would repair the old Jacobean house. From 1894 until 1901, the families lived together at Pinbury, where they established the first of their furniture-making workshops. Under Ernest Barnsley's direction, they added a wing to the house, Gimson plastered the ceiling, and they made other improvements to the property. At the same time, they refurbished two terraced gardens, one near the house and enclosed by a low dry-stone wall, and the other on a lower level, adjacent to an ancient yew allée. They added a simple, yet elegant, stone summerhouse in one corner of the enclosure and lined the garden with clipped topiaries.[7] They would adapt all these elements in their later, more renowned, work. When Lord

Bathurst returned to take up residence in the newly improved Pinbury Park, he generously gave each of the families land in Sapperton on which to build their own houses. Each house was a highly individualistic expression of its designer.

Ernest Barnsley, who was the most outgoing of the three personalities, selected an old cottage dating from approximately 1800, up a steep lane from the village church and commanding a breathtaking view over the vale. Naming it Upper Dorvel House, he added two wings to the cottage, carefully marrying the new with the old by adhering to local Cotswold building traditions. Furnished throughout with products of their workshop, the house has a main hall embellished with Gimson's plasterwork ceiling and decorative friezes in floral motifs. Meandering, low stone enclosure walls define the confines of the property, and nestled between the entry drive and the house is a small formal garden terrace. Laid out as a rectangular room, an extension of the house, the terrace features neatly clipped boxwood shrubs and simple flower beds. As H. Avray Tipping, *Country Life*'s architecture critic, wrote, "the charm of the little garden makes us pause without. It at once gives the impression that it is right; that it fulfils the

particular requirement; that it is of the shape, size, material and construction needed at this special spot. . . . This enclosure . . . is the requisite semi-formal link between the straight lines of the building and the tumbled Cotswold landscape."[8] What Barnsley achieved at Upper Dorvel House—the simple configuration, use of local materials, and intimate relationship with the house—was the essence of an Arts and Crafts garden that would be emulated by many other designers.

Gimson built himself a new L-shaped cottage, named Leasowes, with rough stone walls and a thatched roof. His house, which reflects his exacting requirements and the effects he wanted to produce, is conspicuous for its absence of ornamentation, an austerity that marks his furniture designs. Described as "a thinker, an explorer, a teacher," Gimson was the more reflective of the three and passionately committed to the ideals of the Arts and Crafts Movement, embracing simplicity, utility, and respect for materials in all of his work.[9] In the living room, a plain whitewashed ceiling with oak beams, thick stone walls, and a large open hearth provide an atmosphere that one critic called "a temple of elegance and refinement."[10] Like Upper Dorvel House, the grounds are enclosed by low

OPPOSITE
Pinbury Park, Sapperton, Gloucestershire

BELOW
Ernest Barnsley, Upper Dorvel House, Sapperton, Gloucestershire

57

BELOW
Frederick L. Griggs, *Leasowes*, engraving, 1922

OPPOSITE TOP LEFT
Sidney Barnsley, dovecote
at Beechanger, Sapperton,
Gloucestershire

OPPOSITE TOP RIGHT
Ernest Gimson, Leasowes,
Sapperton, Gloucestershire

OPPOSITE BOTTOM
Sidney Barnsley, long
border and summerhouse at
Combend Manor, Elkstone,
Gloucestershire

dry-stone walls, with an extraordinary stone dovecote at the entry gate. The finely crafted rubblestone wall and towering dovecote caught the eye of *Country Life*, and a photograph of it is included in Lawrence Weaver's *Small Country Houses of To-Day* in 1912. The dovecote's rustic charm symbolizes the creativity of architectural detailing during the Arts and Crafts era. Jekyll and Weaver praised Gimson's naturalistic pool at Stoneywell Cottage, near Leicester, where the margin carefully followed the natural contours of the ground. "Mr. Gimson," they wrote, "has shown an appreciation of the character of the site by making the pool accord in its rough simplicity with the attractive, roughly-built cottage." [11]

Sidney Barnsley, who was more apt to work on his own rather than provide designs for furniture to be made by craftsmen, built himself a small, rustic stone cottage with thick stone slabs on the roof. Like Gimson's cottage, Barnsley's Beechanger has an extraordinary dovecote rising from the stone wall like a lighthouse looming up at sea. Barnsley was involved in architectural work on two old Cotswold manor houses, both with noteworthy gardens. In the 1920s, he remodeled Combend Manor, a seventeenth-century house in Elkstone, and laid out a garden, loosely configured in a series of terraces near the house, and a naturalistic pond garden farther away near the orchard. Characteristically, the terrace gardens were enclosed by low dry-stone walls, with a stone summerhouse in one corner and several archways, one with a dovecote at the top.

In July 1925, Jekyll prepared planting plans for the pond garden and the herbaceous borders at Combend Manor. Her introduction to Sidney Barnsley may have come from their mutual friend, the architect Robert Weir Schultz.[12] Jekyll, who was then eighty-one years old, sent detailed planting plans for the garden, based primarily on the survey plan provided by Barnsley. The pond garden, with drifts of ferns, shrub roses, and naturalized groupings of bulbs in the grass, did not go forward, although there is a similar water garden there today. Her recommendations for the herbaceous borders leading to the summerhouse are thought to have been implemented. At this time in her life, Jekyll worked almost entirely from her exhaustive memory of plants, providing her signature, but predictable, groupings of favorite perennials. Her mind was still exceptionally acute in sounding out overall design improvements, but a number of her recommendations for architectural embellishments for Barnsley's plan, including a pergola to frame the view across the valley, were nixed by the architect.[13]

At Cotswold Farm, a seventeenth-century house in Duntisbourne Abbots, not far from Cirencester, Sidney Barnsley added two wings in 1926 for Sir John and Lady Birchall. After Barnsley's death later that year, Norman Jewson (1884–1975), who originally came to Gimson's office in 1907, made further improvements to Cotswold Farm. He laid out extensive terraced gardens on the hillside in 1938, replete with a characteristic stone summerhouse in the lower garden. His stone terraces, connected by a series of steep staircases, gave architectural bones to the garden. In later years, the Birchalls' daughter-in-law transformed Jewson's garden into a horticultural paradise, with the introduction of rare trees, shrubs, and herbaceous perennials in the best tradition of English garden making. On the upper terrace, overlooking the unspoiled valley, a group of columnar box topiaries lend the house and garden its unmistakable Cotswold character.[14]

Jewson, who chronicled the work of Gimson and the Barnsleys in his autobiographical memoir, *By Chance I Did Rove*, worked in the traditional Cotswold manner, refurbishing a number of manor houses. Jewson set up his own practice in 1919 after working briefly for Gimson; he was known for his exceptional craftsmanship, respect for traditional building techniques, and conservation efforts. As he modestly observed, "I hoped that my buildings would at least have good manners and be able to take their natural place in their surroundings without offence."[15] In 1925, he purchased Owlpen Manor, a Tudor manor house near Uley, of medieval origin, with sixteenth- and seventeenth-century additions. Jewson spent the next several years carefully repairing it. The interiors are embellished with modeled plasterwork

BELOW LEFT
Summerhouse at
Cotswold Farm

BELOW RIGHT
Terrace garden at
Cotswold Farm

OPPOSITE
Sidney Barnsley and
Norman Jewson,
Cotswold Farm,
Duntisbourne Abbots,
Gloucestershire

61

BELOW
Owlpen Manor, Uley,
Gloucestershire

OPPOSITE
Simon Dorrell, Owlpen
Manor, line drawing, 2003

by Jewson and Gimson, as well as furnishings designed by all and made by teams of local craftsmen.[16] Three asymmetrical bays, each dating from a different era, overlook a rare intact old garden in the foreground and a beautiful valley in the distance. Owlpen folds so naturally into the hill that it gives new meaning to the symbiotic relationship between house and surrounding landscape. The name Owlpen (which apparently has nothing to do with owls) implies enclosure.[17]

The old garden had been admired by many travelers, among them Jekyll, Vita Sackville-West, and Geoffrey Jellicoe. As Jekyll and Weaver wrote in *Gardens for Small Country Houses*, plans and photographs can never convey "the wealth of incident crowded into an area of little more than half an acre" or "with what modesty the house nestles against the hillside and seeks to hide itself amidst regiments of yews." [18] The yews, in fact, are one of the distinguishing features of the garden. The square Yew Parlour, in Jekyll's day nearly twenty-five feet (about seven meters) high and varying from six to ten feet (two to three meters) wide,

was probably planted in the early eighteenth century when the medieval garden was refurbished. The site, which slopes dramatically to the south, is edged with rows of massive yews on the upper slope and along the main garden path to the south. This dramatic view has been memorialized in a Gothic-inspired etching by Frederick L. Griggs, an important artist and sometime architectural associate of Jewson's. In 1927, an American architect commented that the garden "is one of the finest and most satisfying things of its kind anywhere [with] whimsical conceits, such as peacocks and dragons in yew."[19] Although the garden is not large in size, its form and planting is straightforward, yet dramatic.

In 1908, Gimson began work at the Drakestone estate near Stinchcombe, with its incomparable views over the Vale of Berkeley and the Welsh marshes. He got no further than constructing two stone cottages before his clients, Walter and Mabel St. John-Mildmay, replaced him with Oswald P. Milne (1881–1967), a young architect who had been a pupil in Lutyens's office.[20] Drakestone, which

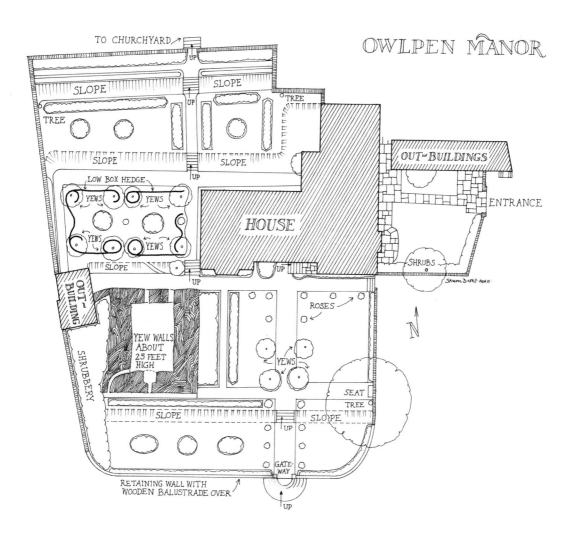

Frederick L. Griggs, Owlpen
Manor, etching, 1931

nestles into the hill, is the quintessence of an Arts and Crafts family house. It is
built of local golden stone, with a stone roof that was a traditional feature of the
region. Milne also designed a stone terrace, with walls and stairways leading to the
garden, where a double-stairway, built over an arch with a Lutyens-inspired pool
underneath, offers an enchanting view to the house. Weaver praised Drakestone
as a "good example of the success which comes from the right handling, in the
simplest way, of materials beautiful in themselves."[21]

In the mid-1920s, Milne designed a charming holiday house and garden at
Coleton Fishacre for the Rupert D'Oyly Carte family. The house, which lies deep
in a Devonshire combe, was built entirely of local materials, including blue-gray
shale. At the edge of the quarry, Milne built a stone belvedere, and closer to the
house, stone terraces and water features, including a rill garden. Lady Dorothy
D'Oyly Carte, however, was responsible for the marvelous shrub gardens and
glades that drift casually down to the sea. As Christopher Hussey wrote in

Country Life in 1930, "If houses may be endowed with personalities, Coleton Fishacre is a gentleman. It is completely at ease here, and it puts the landscape at ease no less than the visitor."[22] The house and garden are now one of the treasures of the National Trust.

Around 1909, Ernest Barnsley received a commission that would bring a new dimension to the Art and Crafts philosophy of planning a house and garden. After visiting Rodmarton Manor in 1914, Ashbee exclaimed, "The English Arts and Crafts movement at its best is here—so are the vanishing traditions of the Cotswolds."[23] Claud Biddulph, who had probably spotted the *Country Life* article on Barnsley's own house in April 1909, asked Barnsley to design a "cottage in the country" that would be at once substantial in size and offer employment to the many local people. His plan was to spend no more than £5,000 per year, but his undertaking took until 1929 to complete.[24] During these years, the project grew from a small country house to a large manor house. It has

TOP LEFT
Oswald Milne, Drakestone
Manor, Stinchcombe,
Gloucestershire

TOP RIGHT
Garden staircase at
Drakestone Manor

ABOVE LEFT
Oswald Milne, Coleton
Fishacre, Kingswear, Devon

ABOVE RIGHT
Recessed pool at Coleton
Fishacre

been owned by three generations of the same family and, unusually, is in unaltered condition today.

No doubt Biddulph was drawn to Barnsley because of Barnsley's own house (just four miles, or six-and-a-half kilometers, from Rodmarton), but also for the furnishings produced in the Sapperton workshops. Rodmarton was painstakingly built by hand from local materials—stone from a local quarry and timber felled on the estate—by local laborers and furnished throughout with decorative furnishings designed by the Barnsleys that were made in their workshops or on-site. Jewson designed most of the decorative leadwork, featuring flora and fauna motifs. Conceived to look like a series of cottages on a village street, with five gables on the front and five on the garden side of the main house, Rodmarton gives a nod to the old, but avoids line-by-line imitation.

Barnsley provided the overall garden plan, laid out as a series of outdoor rooms, each enclosed by low stone walls or clipped hedges, leaving most of the details to the head gardener, William Scrubey. The ingenious series of

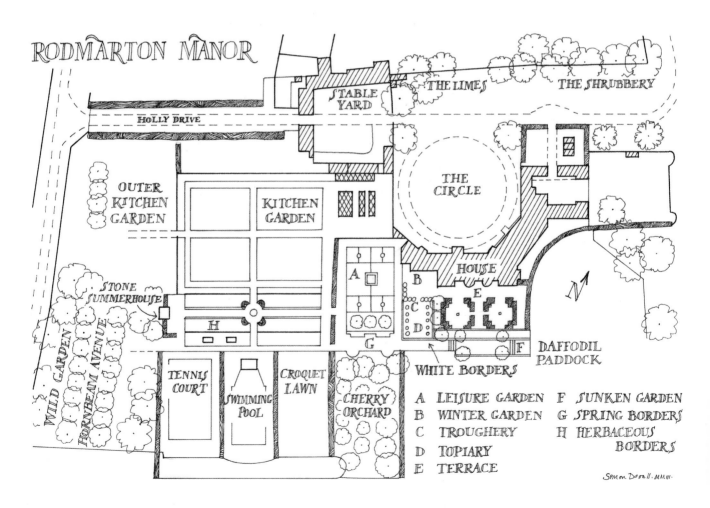

RODMARTON MANOR

THE LIMES   THE SHRUBBERY

STABLE YARD

HOLLY DRIVE

THE CIRCLE

OUTER KITCHEN GARDEN   KITCHEN GARDEN

HOUSE

STONE SUMMERHOUSE

A   B   E   C   D

DAFFODIL PADDOCK

WHITE BORDERS

F

WILD GARDEN   HORNBEAM AVENUE

TENNIS COURT   SWIMMING POOL   CROQUET LAWN   CHERRY ORCHARD

H   G

A   LEISURE GARDEN   F   SUNKEN GARDEN
B   WINTER GARDEN   G   SPRING BORDERS
C   TROUGHERY   H   HERBACEOUS
D   TOPIARY   BORDERS
E   TERRACE

SIMON DORELL. MMIII.

interconnecting gardens, ranging from formal near to the house to informal farther afield, is based on the theories set forth in Sedding's *Garden-Craft Old and New*. This is not surprising, as Ernest Barnsley initially trained with Sedding in London. The gardens encompass most of the dominant theories of garden design at the time, from Robinson in the wilder parts to Jekyll in the more formal areas.

The gardens to the west of the house have been designed to maximize the view across the Marlborough Downs from the south façade. The terrace on the south face is treated as the most formal garden room, with clipped yew hedges and Portuguese laurels.[25] Adjacent rooms include a troughery and topiary garden, lined with stone feeding troughs collected from the farm and planted with alpines, and a winter garden, now planted with a pleached lime allée. Below the terrace and abutting the meadow is a rustic stone pergola covered in flame-red *Vitis cognettiae* (crimson glory vine) in the autumn. On axis with the terrace gardens is one of the most dramatic sequences of the garden, a double-bordered

BELOW
Sunken garden at Rodmarton Manor

OPPOSITE
Simon Dorrell, Rodmarton Manor, line drawing, 2003

Summerhouse and borders
at Rodmarton Manor

BELOW
Lawrence Johnston,
topiary birds at Hidcote
Manor, Hidcote
Bartrim, Gloucestershire

OPPOSITE
White Garden at
Hidcote Manor

walk enclosed by high hedges, with a stone summerhouse to denote the end of the vista. From the summerhouse, visitors can gaze across the borders to the house.

The thirteen-foot-wide (four meters) borders are planted in large drifts reminiscent of Jekyll's style. A large kitchen garden lies behind one side of the borders, while on the other are a series of enclosed areas, including a tennis court and a swimming pool, each suitably enclosed with high hedges. Even the wilder components of the garden—a rockery, croquet lawn, and orchard—are carefully delineated within geometric confines. The hornbeam allée, underplanted with wild cow parsley and combining formality and informality, is just one of the many incidents in the garden. The gardens at Rodmarton have only increased in their beauty as they have matured. At once there is a sense of privacy, enclosure, subtlety, and an inordinate attention to detail, just as in the house. In many ways Rodmarton stands as the supreme example of the vision of Ernest Gimson, the Barnsleys, and their associates in the Cotswolds.

By contrast, the gardens at Hidcote Manor, arguably the most famous in the Cotswolds (if not Britain), are the work of a rarefied connoisseur, rather than an

70

architect. In 1907, American-born Lawrence Johnston began creating a complex garden from bare ground that eventually enveloped the modest manor house. Guided by books and his far-flung travels (he was an expert horticulturist and a dedicated plant collector), he created a masterpiece that draws millions of visitors today. Tipping credited Johnston with "cultural knowledge and faultless taste. . . . We get the botanical range of a John Tradescant or a William Robinson combined with the grasp of design of an André Le Nôtre or a Harold Peto."[26] Over the decades, Johnston, who had the benefit of a generous budget (albeit managed by his mother), expanded and fine-tuned his grounds with both formal and naturalistic features, drawing inspiration from gardens around the world. The inner core of garden rooms—the Stilt Garden, Pillar Garden, Circle, and White Garden—skillfully offset the naturalistic areas, such as the Stream Garden and the Wilderness. The Long Walk slices through the composition in one direction and the Theatre Lawn in the other. Although Hidcote is a grand creation that takes its inspiration in part from the Arts and Crafts philosophy, it goes well beyond its tenets of intimacy and simplicity.

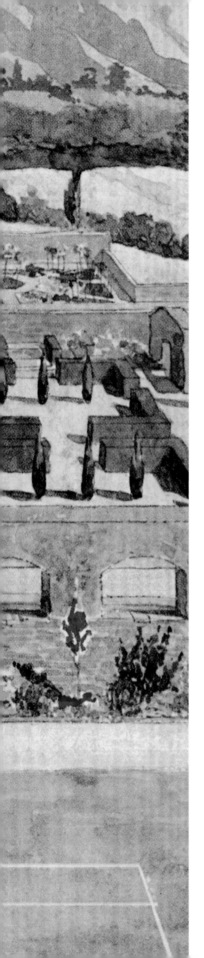

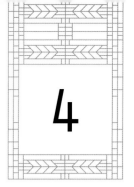

4

ARCHITECTURAL GARDENING

MORE THAN ANY OTHER PUBLICATION of the period, *The Studio* magazine reveals how artists and architects actually envisioned gardens. Founded in 1893 by Charles Holme, an art connoisseur and latter-day owner of Morris's Red House, *The Studio* celebrated the new approach to art and design that emerged at the end of the nineteenth century.[1] It appealed to the younger generation of art lovers and artists who had tired of the late Victorian era's stale academic approach to art and embraced the current House Beautiful aesthetic.[2] Adopting the motto "Use and Beauty," the magazine was singular for recognizing applied art and craftsmanship as the equal of fine art. Its coverage included jewelry, metalwork, embroidery, photography, and book arts as well as domestic architecture, interior decoration, and garden design.[3]

In addition to its unparalleled coverage of all the arts, *The Studio* was successful because of its exceptional illustrations. Its covers—the initial one designed by Aubrey Beardsley and others by C. F. A. Voysey—lent a distinctive graphic identity to the magazine. Early issues included facsimiles of lithographs made especially for the magazine by James McNeill Whistler and other fashionable artists. *The Studio*'s

ABOVE
C. F. A. Voysey, cover for
The Studio, 1893

OPPOSITE
Percy B. Houfton, *House
at Barnsley*, perspective
(*Studio Yearbook of Decorative Art*, 1907)

PREVIOUS
W. H. Ward, *Garden at
High Moss, near Keswick*,
perspective (*Studio
Yearbook of Decorative
Art*, 1908)

reviews of the Arts and Crafts Exhibition Society's annual venues and its sponsorship of design competitions appealed to up-and-coming architects, artists, and designers. Extensive coverage of trends in Europe and America gave birth to *The International Studio*, for many years a mainstay of art schools abroad. *The Studio* also published volumes devoted to individual artists and themes, annual yearbooks of decorative arts, gardening annuals, and a formidable range of books, including *The Gardens of England*, edited by Holme.[4]

The Studio's appealing color renderings of houses and gardens encapsulated the versatility and creativity of garden design from the architectural viewpoint. Even though many of these renderings were romanticized visions of gardens, they were always rich in imagination and detail. A rendering of High Moss, near Keswick, Cumbria, is an excellent example of the type of designs that architects were producing at the time. Designed in 1900 by William Henry Ward (1865–1924), who worked briefly for Lutyens, the garden at High Moss, a storybook double-gabled, whitewashed cottage, is somewhat fanciful.[5] The walled enclosure, anchored by twin garden houses, with paved and topiary gardens surrounded by high, clipped hedges, is more suited to a small Elizabethan manor house than a vernacular-style Lakeland cottage.[6] A rendering for a proposed house in Barnsley depicts a linear hedge with arched openings separating the front lawn from the geometric garden enclosures. Parterres, planted with rose or peony standards and clipped yews in one area and a sundial garden in the other, offer pleasant, but undistinguished outdoor spaces.

The Studio was among the first to champion Voysey (whose work was featured in the first issue), Baillie Scott, Charles Edward Mallows, Charles Rennie Mackintosh, and other architects associated with the new art. Most of the architects hailed by *The Studio* were largely ignored by *Country Life* magazine, founded four years later in 1897 to promote upper-class country living. *Country Life* championed architects such as Edwin Lutyens and Robert Lorimer, whose clients sought houses steeped in vernacular traditions, rather than the artistic homes favored by *The Studio*.

The Scottish architect Charles Rennie Mackintosh (1868–1928) was one of the most original architects to emerge in the mid-1890s. He was described by Hermann Muthesius as "an architect to his fingertips [with a] strong architectural sense" that prevailed in his idiosyncratic buildings and furnishings.[7] Although Mackintosh's early sensibilities were founded in the Arts and Crafts philosophy, his work rapidly transcended the insularity of his English contemporaries.

Mackintosh and his circle, including the Macdonald sisters (Margaret and Frances) and Herbert MacNair (all based at the Glasgow School of Art), gave birth to the Glasgow style in their revolutionary display at the Arts and Crafts Exhibition Society in 1896.[8] The group's distinctive embroideries, metalwork, posters, and furniture, later shown in international exhibitions, would have a far-reaching influence on modern design.[9] The Macdonald sisters' highly stylized flowers and elongated female figures in their gesso panels and stained glass formed the decorative base in their numerous Glasgow commissions, including interiors for four tearooms designed by Mackintosh.

Mackintosh's architectural work was widely applauded abroad. His entry for the 1901 German-sponsored *Haus eines Kunstfreundes* (House for an Art Lover) competition signaled his unusually fertile approach to design. The Glasgow School of Art and several of his country houses are considered masterpieces. His passion for decoration, whether flower studies, landscapes, or textiles painted in his last years when his architectural commissions diminished, all attest to his unique vision.[10]

Along with the Glasgow School of Art, Hill House is his best-known and best-preserved work. He received the commission from the prominent Glasgow publisher Walter Blackie in 1902, shortly after being made partner in the architectural firm Honeyman, Keppie, and Mackintosh. Mackintosh's charge was to design a country house in Helensburgh, Dunbartonshire, on the top of a hill overlooking the Firth of Clyde. When Mackintosh handed Blackie the plans, he wrote, "Here is the house. It is not an Italian villa, or English Mansion House, Swiss Chalet, or a Scotch Castle. It is a Dwelling House."[11] His design was vaguely Scottish Baronial, but the light gray stucco exterior, with unadorned gables and chimneys and asymmetrical windows with minimal dressings, signaled a revolutionary approach. The interior spaces are dramatic and unconventional, with stark, dark-stained wood on the main floor and ethereal white bedrooms with elegant rose- and lavender-colored fittings upstairs. The decorations, designed in collaboration with his wife, Margaret Macdonald Mackintosh, ranged from his signature geometric furniture to striking metal-and-glass light fixtures. More than one hundred years later, the house is still awesome, rising up like a phoenix on a hillside among more conventional homes.

The garden is rarely mentioned, but Mackintosh's perspectives of the house show how he linked indoor and outdoor spaces through geometry. There are low terrace walls, with espaliered shrubs of impossible form and glittering fruit trees that seem to be on the verge of bursting, and a baronial-style dovecote

anchored in one corner. The semicircular entry drive is lined with square-shaped rose standards. U-shaped spy holes on the boundary walls frame the appropriate viewpoints to the house. The garden plan echoes the square motifs used in the furniture and light fixtures in the house. The terrace, divided into nine squares, resembles an outdoor gameboard for tic-tac-toe, or one of Mackintosh's ebonized tables or metal lighting fixtures.[12]

The contemporary Glasgow architect John James Joass (1868–1952) was the first to address the history and lore of garden design in the pages of *The Studio*. Joass made a case for seventeenth-century formal gardens in Scotland as worthy prototypes for new gardens. Referring to the lengthy debates about the "relative function of the architect and the horticultural artist in regard to garden design," Joass argued that since the Renaissance period, architects had shown themselves quite capable of designing gardens. The moderate scale of seventeenth-century Scots gardens were excellent models "for everyday application when the pleasaunce is becoming again a part of the English dwelling."[13] Old Scots garden enclosures (or pleasaunces), with their characteristic walls, ornamental detailing, and garden buildings, provided inspiration and vocabulary for Arts and Crafts gardens.

Barncluith, a steeply terraced garden overhanging the River Evan in Lanarkshire, is sheltered by long enclosure walls and has fanciful bird topiaries in yew and box, as well as traditional summerhouses. "It is quite unlike anything else,"

BELOW
Charles Rennie Mackintosh, *The Hill House, Helensburgh*, line drawing, 1903 (*Studio Yearbook of Decorative Art*, 1907)

OPPOSITE LEFT
Charles Rennie Mackintosh, Hill House, Helensburgh

OPPOSITE RIGHT
Ornamental dovecote at Hill House

77

wrote another Scotsman, Robert Lorimer. "It is the most romantic little garden in Scotland."[14] Stobhall, in Perthshire, overlooking the River Tay, is another romantic garden, with a seventeenth-century topiary garden and dwellings dating to the same century. As envisioned by L. Rome Guthrie, an Arts and Crafts architect who supplied illustrations for H. Inigo Triggs's *Formal Gardens in England and Scotland*, the elegant central sundial and exaggerated yews provide a perfect match for the old house.

Although he was not the first to write about garden design in *The Studio*, Edward Schroeder Prior (1852–1932) summed up the magazine's approach to the decorative aspects of a garden. An important Arts and Crafts architect, Prior "was the most eccentric, intellectual and original pupil in the Shaw office," according to historian Margaret Richardson.[15] A founder member of the Art Workers' Guild and secretary of the Arts and Crafts Exhibition Society, Prior was known for his highly original blending of building materials in two extant projects, The Barn,

Edward Schroeder Prior,
Voewood (Home Place),
High Kelling, Norfolk

in Exmouth, Devon, and Home Place, High Kelling, Norfolk.[16] Prior began work at Home Place (now known by its original name, Voewood) in 1903 for the Reverend Percy Lloyd. After the construction of several outbuildings, including thatched cottages for the gardeners, Prior set to work on the main house, designed in a butterfly plan with distinctive colors and patterning of the textured wall surfaces. In contrast to the house's eccentrically patterned exterior, the interiors consist of plain whitewashed walls and untreated timbers, taking their cue from Philip Webb's Red House for William Morris and Lutyens's house for Gertrude Jekyll at Munstead Wood. The sunken garden (formerly a flat turnip field) was reached by stone steps leading down from the terraces flanking the two wings of the house. A water garden and pergolas completed the scheme. In their book, *Gardens for Small Country Houses*, Jekyll and Weaver pronounced the stepped scheme "a counsel of perfection."

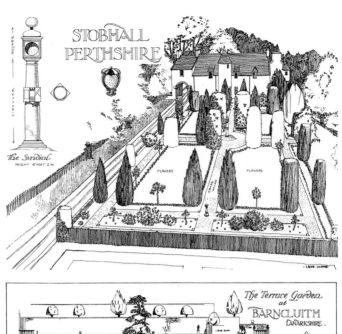

Prior addressed his articles to "garden-makers as artists," outlining the principles, practice, and materials that one needed to grasp. "The garden's immediate connection with the house is manifest," he wrote, reiterating much that had been said earlier by John Sedding.[17] Prior was critical of the improper use of materials and referred to the "nastiness of the materials of garden-design" and "the present-day vulgarities of commercial material [which need] to be taken into account by the garden-maker."[18] He recommended the creation of an enclosure with hedges or walls, the use of stone for edging paths, and straight lines for flower bed layout. "Of course in practice irregular slopes and irregular boundaries are the common lot, but let not the garden-maker be discouraged. Out of such material his art grows," he concluded.[19]

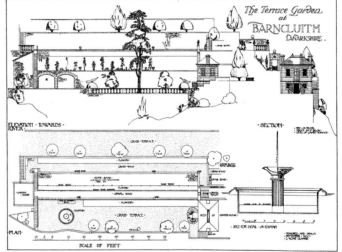

Among *The Studio*'s writers, Charles Edward Mallows (1864–1915) had the most significant impact in defining the essential guidelines of good garden design for Arts and Crafts architects. Mallows possessed an artist's eye for composition and appropriateness, and regardless of the size of the houses he designed, they always appeared unpretentious. Although little remains of Mallows's built work, his

TOP
L. Rome Guthrie, *Stobhall, Perthshire*, line drawing (Triggs, 1902)

ABOVE
L. Rome Guthrie, *The Terrace Garden at Barncluith, Lanarkshire*, line drawing, 1902 (Triggs, 1902)

renderings for schemes, both real and imaginary, distill the essence of architectural gardening at its best.[20] Above all, he is best remembered as a skilled pencil draftsman and perspective artist.

Jekyll and Weaver praised Mallows in *Gardens for Small Country Houses*, singling out one of his houses for the "close connection of house and garden," the underlying premise of their book.[21] His schemes typically employ a simple sunken garden, sometimes with a central pool, and architectural devices such as covered archways to connect house and garden. Brackenston, in Pembury, Kent,

designed for the Reverend R. F. W. Molesworth, has a straightforward layout of terraces, with low walls and a simple pergola enclosing the garden, as shown in a rendering published in 1907. He possessed an unusually observant eye for paving, steps, pergolas, and other architectural detailing, all designed to good scale. Together with his pupil, F. L. Griggs, Mallows wrote numerous articles on architectural gardening for *The Studio* between 1908 and 1910 that introduced the nuances of garden design to the younger generation. They served as a forum for Mallows's own work and theories.

Charles E. Mallows, *Design for Brackenston, Pembury, Kent*, pencil drawing by Frederick L. Griggs, 1904

A COTTAGE DOOR AND GATE   DESIGNED AND DRAWN BY F. L. GRIGGS

Frederick L. Griggs,
*A Cottage Door and
Gate*, line drawing (*The
Studio*, March 1909)

Frederick Landseer Griggs (1879–1938), who was known for his brooding etchings of rural cottages and the English countryside, was another leader of the Arts and Crafts Movement.[22] Associated with the Cotswold School, he counted Charles Ashbee, Philip Webb, Ernest Gimson, and the Barnsley brothers among his friends. Although he trained as an architect, it was his talent as an architectural draftsman and etcher that brought him considerable renown. His etchings of imaginary medieval buildings form the core of his artistic talent, but he also illustrated numerous books, including garden memoirs.[23]

In their articles for *The Studio*, Mallows and Griggs captured the essence of the symbiotic nature of gardens and architecture in both words and pictures. "The happy union of house and garden in architectural design," they wrote, emerged in sixteenth-century England as the result of designers considering "reasonableness and order" as necessary components to all good architecture. Mallows paid tribute to Sedding, whose principles of twenty years earlier had finally seen the demise of the "landscape man" in favor of architectural gardening.[24] Flagged walks flanked by high hedges and other equally simple devices inspired by old manor house gardens could be used to great effect in new gardens for smaller houses, he advised, echoing the words of Sedding. But even the best of garden planning, they argued, could be spoiled by the faulty arrangement or lack of scale in the detailing. Decorative features, such as lead figures, sundials, and balustrades "should always be judged on the site and never left to be settled by designs on paper, however carefully they may be worked out."[25] In general, their recommendations for garden design were sensible, if not self-effacing.

Mallows's 1909 scheme for remodeling a small homestead known as Crocombe in Happisburgh, on the Norfolk coast, is simplicity itself. As Jekyll and Weaver wrote, "The essence of the planning is the protection of the garden from the fierce and frequent winds that blow from north and east."[26] This is achieved with a hedged recess near the house and a sunken flower garden in the old farmyard with flagged paths and steps surrounding it. For additional shelter from the winds, Mallows proposed several schemes in *The Studio*, ranging from a long, open pergola to a more rustic covered arcade. In all, it was typical of his simple, yet elegant, approach to garden design that was devoid of the eccentricity shown by some of his better-known colleagues.

The two most complete examples of Mallows's work are Craig-y-Parc in Pentyrch, near Cardiff, and Tirley Garth, both of which bring to life his ideas about garden planning. Designed in 1913 for Thomas Evans, a colliery owner in Wales, Craig-y-Parc is a double-gabled house, with a cloister court connecting the two wings, overlooking a formal terraced garden. A small rose garden adjacent to one wing and a lily garden on the other serve as outdoor rooms. From the long flight of steps leading down to the lawn enclosed by low stone walls is a grand view of the countryside of rural South Wales. Woodland gardens on the entrance side of the house provide the requisite balance between informality and formality. It is now a private school.

Tirley Garth, near Taporley, Cheshire, is a gracious country house, originally commissioned by Bryan Leesmith in 1906, when it was called Tirley Court. It was not completed until 1912 when Richard Prestwich, a Manchester textile industrialist, asked Mallows to finish the building. The house, built around a central courtyard, with an enclosed cloister walk serving as part of the terrace, is a grander version of Craig-y-Parc. The site was selected to take advantage of the superb view across the Cheshire plain.[27] Tirley Garth also has an outstanding

Charles E. Mallows, *A Seaside House and Garden at Happisburgh, Norfolk*, line drawing (*The Studio*, March 1909)

Charles E. Mallows,
Tirley Garth, Taporley,
Cheshire

Charles E. Mallows, *The Garden Entrance, Tirley Court [Tirley Garth]*, line drawing (*The Studio*, October 1908)

garden, conceptualized for the first client, but not built until 1912. Mallows's sketches, first published in *The Studio*, show a strong architectonic conception. When the project finally went forward, Mallows consulted with the landscape architect Thomas Mawson for recommendations for the plantings.

Mallows made skillful use of the different levels of the hillside site, with a circular vegetable garden encompassing an acre in size at the uppermost elevation, and a long, linear axis connecting the circular garden with a semicircular rose garden on axis with the house. The rough slate paving, steps, and other architectural detailing defining each level and garden area are tributes to Arts and Crafts sensibilities of utility and beauty as well as an example of "the happy union of house and garden." Mawson provided planting plans for the borders and the surrounding landscape.[28] Tirley Garth still retains Mallows's remarkable hardscaping, along with Mawson's horticultural elements, including impressive sweeps of mature rhododendron plantations. But it is Mallows's visionary perspectives that bring the garden alive as it was in the Arts and Crafts era.

Simon Dorrell, *Tirley Garth*, line drawing, 2003

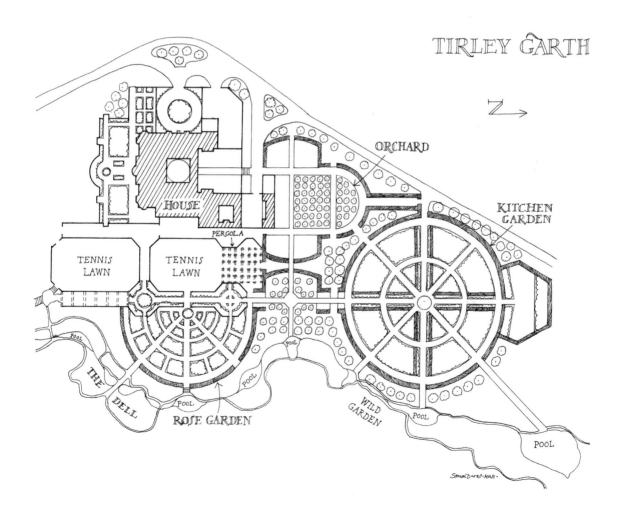

TIRLEY GARTH

ORCHARD

KITCHEN GARDEN

HOUSE

PERGOLA

TENNIS LAWN

TENNIS LAWN

POOL

THE DELL

POOL

POOL

ROSE GARDEN

POOL

WILD GARDEN

POOL

POOL

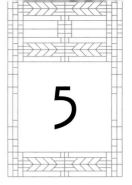

5

INDIVIDUALITY AND IMAGINATION

OF THE MANY ARCHITECTS WHO CREATED innovative houses and gardens during the Arts and Crafts era, C. F. A. Voysey and M. H. Baillie Scott stand out for their highly identifiable styles and fertile imaginations. *The Studio* hailed Baillie Scott as "one of the most individual architects of the present day," and Voysey's philosophy was set forth in a tract entitled *Individuality*.[1] Early in their careers, their approaches to architecture and design were shaped by the ideals of the Arts and Crafts Movement. They furnished their houses with wallpapers, fabrics, and decorations of their own designs and provided appropriate gardens for them. Both architects appealed to middle-class clients with artistic leanings, such as artists, writers, and publishers. Baillie Scott had a longer, more successful career than Voysey, attracted an international following, and was able to adapt long after the Arts and Crafts Movement had been eclipsed. Voysey, whose ironclad principles never wavered, saw the demise of his architectural career when he failed to grasp the changes wrought by World War I. Today he is hailed for his imaginative houses and charming pattern designs that evoke the carefree, childlike world of a bygone era.

BELOW
C. F. A. Voysey, *The Orchard, Chorley Wood, Hertfordshire,* line drawing (*The Studio Special Number,* 1901)

PREVIOUS
C. F. A. Voysey, *The House That Jack Built,* chintz, 1929

Charles Francis Annesley Voysey (1857–1941) grew up in an unusual household in rural Yorkshire, where his father, the Reverend Charles Voysey, was expelled from the Church of England for questioning church doctrine. Voysey's personal ideology, which suffused all his work, was an odd combination of the puritanism of John Wesley (one of his ancestors) and the Gothic revivalism of architect Augustus Welby Pugin. John Betjeman, the witty poet laureate and editor of *The Architectural Review,* wisely observed that Voysey interpreted in stone and color what the Reverend Voysey had preached.[2] Voysey was articled for five years to the ecclesiastical architect John Pollard Seddon; his later experience in Devey's office quickened his approach to domestic architecture. After he launched his own practice in the late 1880s, commissions were slow to materialize. He then turned to pattern design at the suggestion of Arthur Heygate Mackmurdo, a well-known designer and founder of the Century Guild. Voysey continued to design wallpapers and textiles well into the 1930s, when, as a disillusioned and somewhat bitter man, these activities provided him with a source of income during lean years. In the 1890s, he built some of his best-known houses: Broadleys, Moor Crag, Greyfriars, and New Place.[3]

Known for his idiosyncratic architectural vocabulary of roughcast houses with low, projecting eaves, green slate roofs, and massive buttresses and chimneys,

PLANS FOR THE HOME

HOUSE FOR JVLIAN STVRGIS ESQᴿᴱ AT PVTTENHAM NEAR GVILDFORD SVRREY

HOUSE AT PUTTENHAM, GUILDFORD, SURREY

REPRODUCED FROM A WATER-COLOUR DRAWING

C. F. A. Voysey, Architect

Voysey was one of the most original architects of the era. His houses were economical and efficient—his personal motto was "keep it simple." As Baillie Scott wrote in 1907, just as Voysey's career was beginning to fade, "If one were asked to sum up in a few words the scope and purposes of Mr. Voysey's work, one might say that it consists mainly in the application of serenely sane, practical and rational ideas to home making."[4] Edwin Lutyens praised his originality, "the 'hearted shutters,' the client's profile on a bracket, the absence of accepted forms, the long, sloping, slate-clad roofs, [and] white walls clear and clean! No detail was too small for Voysey's volatile brain."[5] A caricature of one of his houses appears in his nursery chintz, *The House That Jack Built*, designed in 1929.

C. F. A. Voysey, *House at Puttenham, Guildford, Surrey [Greyfriars]*, perspective (Sparrow, 1904)

The Orchard, Voysey's own modest house, best symbolizes his ideal home. "Untrammelled by the intervention of a client," as one critic remarked, the architect did just as he pleased.[6] Located in Chorleywood, in suburban Hertfordshire, it was within easy reach of his London office on the Metropolitan Railway line.[7] The exterior is whitewashed roughcast, with towering chimneys and a green slate roof, while the interiors were predominantly white, with slate floors and turkey-red curtains. Voysey designed every detail, from the carpets and wallpapers to the furniture and the metal fittings on the doors. The overall impression was one of lightness, simplicity, and purpose. Only twenty feet (six meters) from the village road, the front door to the house was approached through a straight path bordered by yew hedges. The welcoming doorway, glimpsed through the hedges, had his signature heart-shaped letter box. Surrounded by a two-acre orchard filled with old apple trees, walnut trees, hollies, and a large cherry tree, The Orchard also had a flower garden filled with roses and birds, which dominate his wallpaper and textile patterns.

Fundamental to an appreciation of Voysey is his duality as an architect and a designer. As a fledgling architect, he presented himself as an artist, wearing clothing of his own design (such as cuffless trousers and jackets without lapels) and donning artistic-looking hats. In his architectural work, he adopted a limited palette of colors, primarily black, white, pale green, and deep red accents. An active member of the Art Workers' Guild, Voysey frequently exhibited his wallpapers, textiles, metalwork, and furniture at the Arts and Crafts Exhibition Society's annual exhibitions in London. His evocative pattern designs and the quaint simplicity of his houses

91

quickly caught the public's attention. In an 1893 interview in *The Studio*, Voysey held the Morrisian line that artists should work in healthy environments and sweep ugliness away (although Voysey disliked Morris personally because of his atheism), but his theories about ornamentation were more specific. "The danger to-day lies in over-decoration," he said; "we lack simplicity and have forgotten repose, and so the relative value of beautiful things is confounded."[8] Perhaps as a rationale for not building houses at the time, he observed that wallpaper could help disguise the ugliness of bad furnishings that he found so prevalent. Although he was an exceptional wallpaper designer, his preferred treatment for walls was, in fact, wood paneling, either stained or polished; in most of his houses, wallpaper was generally confined to the bedrooms.

C. F. A. Voysey, *Bird and Bramble*, wallpaper, 1901

Voysey's patterns portray an imaginary world of birds, trees, animals, and flowers reduced to symbols, unlike Morris's more flowing, detailed patterns. Some of Voysey's designs reveal a darker side to his personality, with a recurring demon figure that also appears in his tiles, gate latches, and sundials, as well as menacing birds and other unsavory characters. His gargoyle depicting a demon was hailed for its "delightfully grotesque quality . . . suggestive of the medieval craftsman" by Jekyll and Weaver.[9] Most of his patterns depict a happy world of songbirds, flowers, berries, and fruits, an idealized Garden of Eden, with columnar evergreens interspersed with fruit trees clipped into heart-shaped standards. *The Squire's Garden* wallpaper is a medieval *hortus conclusus* enclosed by vine-covered trellises and ornamented with potted trees, trees clipped into pyramidal shapes, a dovecote, a sundial, peacocks, and garden birds.

Although Voysey is not known as a garden designer, he provided simple layouts for grounds and gardens in the course of his work, crossing paths with Gertrude Jekyll and Thomas Mawson, who designed gardens for several of his clients. Typically Voysey specified enclosure walls, usually roughcast, as well as garden houses, dovecotes, gates, sundials, and other components that harmonized with the style of the house. These were practical as well as ornamental features—especially dovecotes, which attracted the all-important birds into the garden.[10]

92

Watercolor perspectives of Voysey's houses, some prepared by the architect himself, depict lush settings that blend simple flower gardens with more naturalistic areas. His perspective for Broadleys, for example, includes a small sunken garden on the south side of the house that exists today. Built in 1899 as a summer house for Helen and Arthur Currer Briggs of Leeds, Broadleys is an L-shaped roughcast house with three prominent bays overlooking Lake Windermere in the Lake District. At the turn of the twentieth century, this area of outstanding natural beauty, extolled in earlier years by William Wordsworth and John Ruskin, was ripe for development. The sunken garden at Broadleys, with a central sundial, stone paths, flower borders, and other typical Arts and Crafts features, may have been designed by Mawson, who was working nearby at Moor Crag at the same time. Today the steep incline to the lake is covered with naturalistic drifts of rhododendrons and other ornamental shrubs and trees that were typical of Mawson's style.

For Oakhurst (now Ropes and Bollards), in Fernhurst, Sussex, Voysey chose a view of the house across a green Robinsonian meadow filled with carpets of scillas and daisies. The long, low house is atypical in form for Voysey, but replete with all his signature details. A stone wall along the embankment accommodates the grade change, while low, clipped hedges with topiaries mark the entrance to the garden.

C. F. A. Voysey, Broadleys, Windermere, Cumbria

C. F. A. Voysey, *Design for Oakhurst [Ropes and Bollards], Fernhurst, Sussex,* watercolor, 1901

C.F.A. VOYSEY. INV·T ET DEL·T AR

An arch in the back hedge takes its curve from the eyebrow recess over the garden gate and doorway. The cheerful garden inside the enclosure is filled with climbing roses, hollyhocks, and rose standards, all improbably blooming at the same time as the meadow flowers. The scarlet color serves to highlight the red curtains in the windows and the tile detailing on the house. The garden is a fantasy not unlike those depicted in Voysey's wallpapers and textiles.

The garden at New Place, near Haslemere, Surrey, is a rare survival of one of his gardens. Designed in 1897 for Sir Algernon Methuen, founder of Methuen Publishing and an alpine fancier, the house and garden are considered one of Voysey's most successful designs. "The mind and heart of the owner," wrote one critic about New Place, "are plainly traceable in the perfect way in which the formal gardens next to the house gradually merge into the informal and wild parts further down the slope."[11] Voysey's initial plan for the grounds carries the notations, "flowers big and tall," "high yew and holly hedge," "briars, blackthorns, and other wild shrubs," and "wood left more or less wild."[12]

The formal garden enclosures are arranged on four ascending levels to accommodate the steeply sloping site and enclosed with low brick walls. A sunken garden

BELOW
C. F. A. Voysey, *Proposed House [New Place] at Haslemere*, watercolor, 1897

OPPOSITE
Simon Dorrell, *New Place*, line drawing, 2003

on the lowest level, adjoining the main drawing room, has junipers in each corner and a central sundial. The main garden borders, filled with *Abutilon vitifolium* and other perennials in soft shades of blue and cream, lead to a hedged enclosure with a sheltered seat. An arched opening in a hedge leads to a bowling green and arbor. Several thatched-roof summerhouses, designed to harmonize with the main house, are placed at axial points along the paths to afford both shelter and architectural interest in the garden.[13] In all, it was a good, solid plan. In 1901, Lady Methuen asked Jekyll's advice about turning one area into a rose garden, having disliked Voysey's idea of waves of blue rue. Following a visit to New Place the next spring, Jekyll recommended dwarf rose bushes in each of four beds, with half-standards in the center of each.[14] The gardens at New Place continued to evolve over the years, with the addition of a Japanese garden and water and rock gardens, but Voysey's framework for the grounds has remained undisturbed.

At first glance, the early architecture of Mackay Hugh Baillie Scott (1865–1945) bears a strong resemblance to that of Voysey, with whitewashed stucco houses, exaggerated gables, and low, swooping rooflines. Like many architects of his generation, Baillie Scott was first exposed to Voysey in *The Studio*. Though

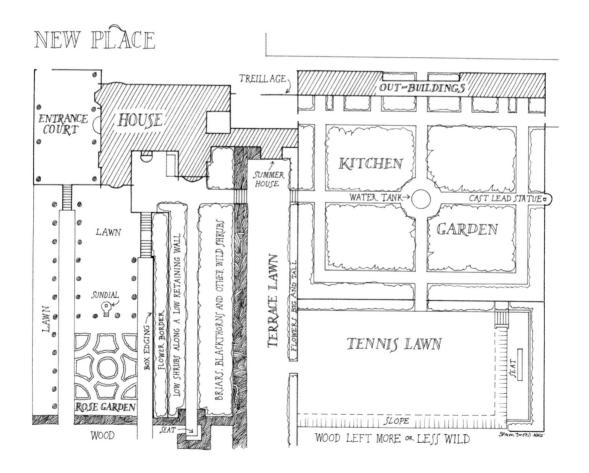

not as well known or appreciated as Voysey is today, Baillie Scott ran a highly successful practice, specializing in suburban houses with richly decorated interiors. He shared Voysey's disdain for the ugliness of Victorian era furnishings, but his interiors were more ornate than Voysey's, with inlay panels and a range of furniture with intricate floral motifs, as well as wallpapers, textiles, metalwork, and stained glass.

Blackwell, located on the hillside above Broadleys in Bowness-on-Windermere, is one of his grandest houses and the most complete example of his work today. Designed in 1898 for Sir Edward Holt, a wealthy Manchester brewery owner, Blackwell was a holiday retreat with generous, yet informal, rooms for family gatherings. Similar to Voysey's houses, Baillie Scott's Blackwell responds to the local Lakeland vernacular, with roughcast whitewashed walls and steeply pitched slate roofs. At the same time, it is strikingly modern in appearance. Decorated throughout with furniture, tiles, wall coverings, carved woodwork, metalwork, wood carvings, and stained glass in floral motifs, Blackwell is a fitting tribute to the full capabilities of this pioneer of the Arts and Crafts Movement.[15] On the exterior, the grounds that were originally laid out by Mawson in 1902 have long since disappeared, and the original plans no longer survive. Today a pleasant grass terrace surrounds the house. Blackwell is now a fully furnished museum of international significance.

Baillie Scott is a somewhat enigmatic figure, whose appearance resembled "an unassuming countryman," as Betjeman described him, rather than an artist or a businessman.[16] Born in Kent to an affluent family, he was originally slated for life as a farmer in Australia, where his family owned sheep ranches. After studying scientific farming at the Royal Agricultural College, he had a change of heart and decided to become an architect. In the 1880s he was articled to an architect in Bath before moving to the Isle of Man, where he practiced architecture for twelve years. He began experimenting with different styles, particularly Tudor half-timbering, and also came under the influence of the famed Manx silversmith, Archibald Knox, whose distinctive Celtic-inspired style resurfaces in Baillie Scott's interior decorations.

The key to Baillie Scott's successful career lies in his artistic approach to domestic architecture, coupled with his affinity for craftsmanship as exemplified at Blackwell. His early articles for *The Studio*, in which he spelled out the necessity for "simplicity and homely comfort," brought him commissions in England and Europe, including one from Grand Duke Ernest-Ludwig of Hesse to redecorate the Ducal Palace in Darmstadt.[17] In 1901, he also entered the famous House for an Art Lover competition that Charles Rennie Mackintosh had entered, winning a coveted prize. Few of his original drawings exist, as his Bedford office was destroyed by fire in 1919 and the London one suffered bomb damage in 1941. Fortunately, his book, *Houses and Gardens*, as well as his articles for *The Studio* provide a record of his work.

Baillie Scott was more articulate than Voysey and most other Arts and Crafts architects, with the exception of Robert Lorimer, on matters relating to garden design. The opening lines of his 1906 book acknowledge the importance of gardens. "One of the most prominent features in the literature of the last few years has been the garden book, and so numerous have these publications become that every one may learn how a garden should be formed and how maintained," he wrote. "All the gardens described in these books are necessarily attached to houses, and the house as an appendage to the garden meets with a certain degree of attention."[18] This approach was certainly at odds with most architects of the time, who viewed the garden as an appendage of the house. By 1933, when he issued

BELOW
Wall covering at
Blackwell

OPPOSITE
M. H. Baillie Scott,
Blackwell, Bowness-
on-Windermere,
Cumbria

99

BELOW
M. H. Baillie Scott,
cover of *Houses and
Gardens*, 1906

OPPOSITE TOP
M. H. Baillie Scott,
Heather Cottage,
perspective (Baillie
Scott, 1906)

OPPOSITE BOTTOM
M. H. Baillie Scott,
*Proposed House [Under-
shaw], Guildford, Surrey*,
perspective (*The Studio*,
May 1909)

100

the second volume of his work, Baillie Scott's ideas about gardens had matured. "Every architect is necessarily interested in the design of the garden which surrounds the house he has built, just as a painter is interested in the pattern of the frame for the picture he had painted," he wrote. "The garden should, after all, constitute a kind of out-door extension of the building, and may consist of a number of open air apartments connected by corridors which in some cases link themselves with those of the house, so that the house and garden together form a complete arrangement of indoor and outdoor rooms."[19]

Because Baillie Scott designed modestly scaled suburban houses, his ideas were most pertinent to the homeowner who could not afford elaborate upkeep. "The function of the garden is to grow fruit and vegetables for the household, and also to provide outdoor apartments for the use of the family in fine weather," he stated simply. For a small garden, however, the stiff lines between the kitchen and pleasure gardens needed to be blurred. "The grey-green foliage and great thistle-like heads of the globe artichoke, the mimic forest of the asparagus bed, and the quaint inflorescence of the onion have each a distinctive beauty of their own which would be more widely recognized if these plants were not used for food," he wrote. Some of his ideas, such as the incorporation of a small orchard ("the trees, once planted in grass, will require but little attention") or a woodland copse ("demands absolutely no labour"), were somewhat naïve.[20]

For Heather Cottage, one of the houses featured in *Houses and Gardens*, he proposed blending the natural stands of heather with a formal garden near the house. "On sunny hills, where purple heather grows, purple heather shall be the dominant note," he advised.[21] The long, low white house, with a swooping red-tiled roof, sits comfortably in the heath, with hills of heather rising in the background. How different Baillie Scott's perspectives, with their soft, romantic gardens, were from Voysey's more dramatic views, with flowers reduced to decorative elements.

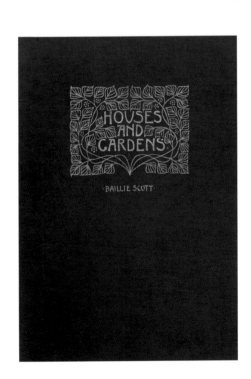

Baillie Scott's recommendations for architectural features in his gardens, such as a seat or a summerhouse at the end of a vista, a dipping well for watering the garden, dovecotes ("a homely note"), and arbors and pergolas, were always practical. "A garden," he wrote, "should be full of mystery, surprises, and light and shade. One of its most attractive features [is] the pergola, with its paved walk checkered by the shadows of the climbing plants which form its walls and roof." At Heather Cottage, a long pergola serves to screen the drive from the lawn, providing an important architectural component.

Pergolas also serve to link the house with the garden, as seen in Baillie Scott's rendering of the rose-laden chalk pergola at Undershaw, in Guildford (published in *The Studio* in 1909). The

ABOVE
M. H. Baillie Scott, *Garden at St. Catherine's Court Near Bath*, perspective (Baillie Scott, 1906)

OPPOSITE TOP
Simon Dorrell, *Snowshill Manor*, line drawing, 2003

OPPOSITE BOTTOM
M. H. Baillie Scott, Armillary Court at Snowshill Manor, Snowshill, Gloucestershire

102

tile-roofed, half-timber and brick cottage with an informal flagged walk has sunken gardens on either side of the pergola, an excellent example of "open-air compartments connected by corridors." The garden is awash with candybox groupings of delphiniums, lilies, lupines, dianthus, and other cottage-garden flowers. Echoing the words of Jekyll, whose books Baillie Scott considered infallible guides to garden planning, he advised massing flowers in informal clumps, planted so that "at each season of the year something is in bloom there, and in blooming forms a well-studied arrangement of colour."[22]

Unlike Voysey, Baillie Scott was equally at home restoring old manor houses or designing new houses. His evocative pastel rendering of the garden at St. Catherine's Court, near Bath, shows a small terrace with twin pillars of yew and other Arts and Crafts elements. At Runton Old Hall, Baillie Scott collaborated with Jekyll, one of three projects he worked on with her.[23] Jekyll's introduction to Baillie Scott came in 1907, when he wrote to her on behalf of a client: "We are anxious to have some good perennial borders and a good selection of roses for a rose garden and pergola," he wrote. "I have always had such a great appreciation of your books on gardening."[24] The following year, she assisted with the gardens at Runton Old Hall, located near the sea in Norfolk, where the manor house had suffered from recent disfigurements by a ruthless modern builder, according to Baillie Scott.[25] He restored the flint-and-brick house, added a new wing, and planned a garden to complement the house. He devised a series of paved courts set with cobblestones in patterns, brick-and-flint walls to subdivide the garden into spaces and reduce the effect of the seaside winds, and archways for the main vistas. "The final touch to this garden scheme," he wrote, "was added by Miss Jekyll, who arranged the flowers to secure well-thought-out schemes of colour at all seasons." Even though Baillie Scott credited the client, Bertram Hawker, for his artistic sensibilities, Hawker rejected so many of Jekyll's ideas that one plan marked "thrown out" betrays her irritation.[26] Little survives of Jekyll's plantings, but Baillie Scott's thoughtful layout remains intact. The flint-and-brick archways and walls, as well as the patterned stone paths in the courts, provide an exceptional example of how a garden could be designed to relate to the house architecturally.

Snowshill Manor, an old Cotswold manor house in a tiny village near Broadway, in Gloucestershire, reveals Baillie Scott's ingenuity in garden planning. Dating to 1500, with numerous later additions and dependencies, the manor house was desolate and surrounded by a sea of wilderness in 1919, when architect and antiquarian

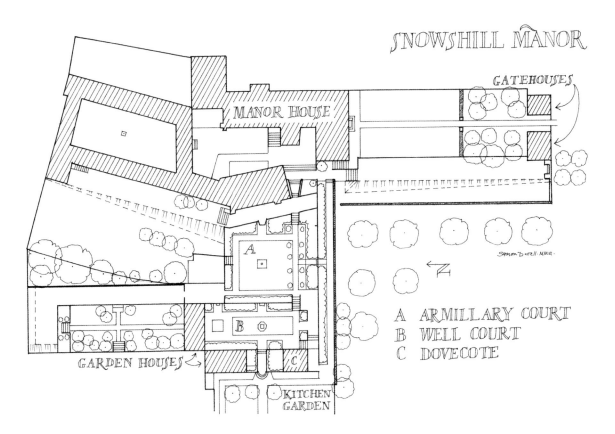

SNOWSHILL MANOR

GATEHOUSES

MANOR HOUSE

GARDEN HOUSES

KITCHEN GARDEN

Symon Dorrell · MMXI ·

A ARMILLARY COURT
B WELL COURT
C DOVECOTE

Charles Paget Wade rescued it, devoting much of his life to restoring the house and amassing a large collection of antiques, artifacts, and whimsies. Wade's winning entry in a competition for a small garden organized by *The Studio* bears a striking resemblance to the arrangement at Snowshill, with a series of courts and long vistas.[27] Until recently, it was assumed that Wade had designed those gardens, but plans have surfaced bearing Baillie Scott's name.[28] Most likely, Wade conceived the basic layout and Baillie Scott provided the technical expertise.

Wade and Baillie Scott successfully merged the different levels and outbuildings—the land slopes steeply to the south where the derelict farmyards once stood—into one cohesive unit with informal regularity. From the top terrace, one looks down on the various walled enclosures and across to the fields in the distance; from the Armillary Court below, one can glimpse the stone manor house through columnar yews. "The design was planned as a series of separate courts,

sunny ones contrasting with shady ones and different courts for different moods," Wade wrote. "The plan of the garden is more important than the flowers in it. Mystery is most valuable in garden design; never show all there is at once. Plan for enticing vistas with a hint of something beyond."[29]

The dovecote and farm sheds that Wade had restored were skillfully tied into the plan so that each structure retained its individuality while complementing the others. Changing levels, vistas, and architectural features throughout give the garden its uniqueness. In addition to an armillary sphere, columns, a sundial, an ancient well, and all manner of statuary, Wade further embellished the garden with his favorite color, turquoise, which he thought a good foil for the green grass and foliage. In Wade's day, Snowshill was an architect's garden with little emphasis on flowers, but today it is filled with many beautiful plantings and is a splendid example of Baillie Scott's planning principles.

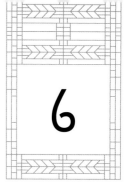

THE ART AND CRAFT
OF GARDEN MAKING

BY THE EARLY 1900S, WRITING ABOUT garden design in Britain advanced from the theoretical to the practical. With the publication of two outstanding books, *The Art and Craft of Garden Making* (1900) and *Gardens for Small Country Houses* (1912), garden design became an identifiable entity, rather than an adjunct of architecture. Many books covered the details of horticulture and planting design, but few explored the practicalities of designing and laying out small properties from the homeowner's viewpoint. John Sedding, Reginald Blomfield, and their followers had enlightened people about the proper attitude regarding garden design, but it fell to Thomas Mawson and Gertrude Jekyll to demonstrate exactly how to execute these ideas.

One of the few designers who was not an architect by training, Thomas Hayton Mawson (1861–1933) successfully bridged the gap between horticulture and architecture. Mawson referred to himself variously as "garden architect," "landscape gardener," and "landscape architect," thus revealing the inexactitude of the profession in its formative years.[1] Although Mawson was primarily associated with his

BELOW
Formal garden at
Graythwaite Hall

BOTTOM
Thomas Mawson,
Langdale Chase, Wind-
ermere, Cumbria

PREVIOUS
Thomas Mawson,
Graythwaite Hall,
Ulverston, Cumbria

native Cumbria and Yorkshire, in later years he had one of the largest British and international practices of his generation.[2] Although an exceptionally competent designer, especially in the realm of site planning and architectural detailing, Mawson lacked an easily identifiable style.

The key to his successful career was the combination of his exceptional knowledge of practical horticulture and his expert technical skills. Early in his career, he worked in a family nursery business and attended a technical school, where he learned drawing and drafting, an experience that coalesced when he and his brother Robert established Lakeland Nurseries in Windermere in the Lake District. Robert managed the horticultural side of the business, while Thomas designed the grounds for their clients. Mawson's first significant client was Colonel Thomas Myles Sandys, who commissioned him to lay out six acres of grounds at Graythwaite Hall in Ulverston, Cumbria, in 1889. At Graythwaite, the assignment required extensive earth-moving and grading to take advantage of the picturesque quality of the grounds and give definition to the house. Mawson designed a sweeping drive, stone terraces, and a formal garden filled with yew topiaries, and he specified landscape plantings throughout the property.

At Graythwaite, he met the architect Dan Gibson (1865–1907), who subsequently worked for him for two years before establishing an independent architectural practice. "He exercised a great influence on the work of the office," Mawson recalled, "and set up as high an ideal for the architectural section of our work as I had striven for in landscape expression."[3] Gibson, whose work was lauded in Jekyll's book *Garden Ornament*, excelled in the design of sundials, gates, and garden houses, which added cachet to Mawson's practice.[4] In 1899, Mawson crossed paths again with Gibson at Brockhole, the summer home of William Gaddum in the increasingly fashionable Lake District. For the spectacular thirty-acre site, Mawson designed a series of terraces ranging from formal to informal that slope down to the shores of Lake Windermere.

Although Mawson's career is heralded today for its international scope, it is his early work in the 1890s as a regional Lakeland garden designer that reveals his commitment to the Arts and Crafts Movement. Surprisingly, a number of his early projects, such as Graythwaite Hall, Brockhole, and Langdale Chase, survive, although the latter two are no longer private residences. Brockhole, with its extensive grounds still intact, has been repurposed as a regional visitor center, and Langdale Chase is now a luxury hotel. The commission for Langdale Chase came in 1894 from Edna Howarth, an avid yachtswoman who wanted a comfortable place to entertain guests. Mawson's solution for the steep site, not unlike that at nearby Broadleys, was informal groupings of azaleas and rhododendrons, with an expertly executed series of stairs leading down to the shore. It probably commands the best view of Lake Windermere of all the projects. By 1901, Mawson opened a London office (next door to Edward Mallows's office) in addition to the one in Windermere. Of all his clients, his greatest was Sir William Lever (later Lord Leverhulme), who commissioned four significant gardens, including Mawson's masterpiece, the classically inspired garden at The Hill, Hampstead, London, with its extraordinary range of pergolas.[5]

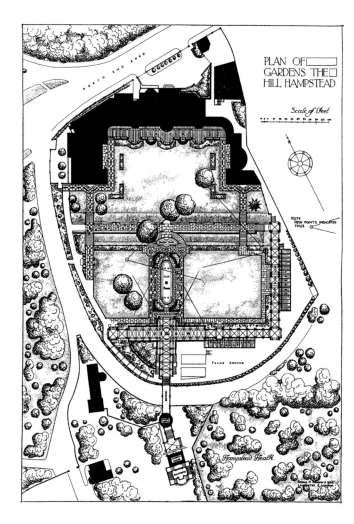

Thomas Mawson, *Plan of Gardens, The Hill, Hampstead,* line drawing (Mawson, 1901)

In addition to his gardens, Mawson's greatest legacy is his book *The Art and Craft of Garden Making,* first published with his own funds in 1900. Literally an overnight success, one reviewer hailed it as a worthy successor to Blomfield's book ten years earlier.[6] A second edition appeared the next year, followed by three more; the final edition of 1926, written in collaboration with his son, E. Prentice Mawson, is considered the definitive work on Mawson's career. Today the book is regarded as the first modern work to address the extent of responsibilities entailed in landscape architecture. Dedicated to his first client and mentor, Colonel Sandys, Mawson also acknowledged his indebtedness to Mallows, Frederick Griggs, and others who provided illustrations for his book. Later editions include color plates by artists Ernest Albert Chadwick and Ernest Arthur Rowe, whose illustrations regularly appeared in *The Studio.* Between the first and second editions, the book grew by leaps and bounds from a quarto size to a heavy folio of more than 400 pages.

ABOVE
Thomas Mawson, cover
of *The Art and Craft of
Garden Making*, 1901

OPPOSITE TOP
Thomas Mawson,
*Gardens at Bailrigg, Near
Lancaster*, perspective by
Ernest Albert Chadwick
(*Studio Yearbook of Deco-
rative Art*, 1908)

OPPOSITE BOTTOM
Thomas Mawson,
*Water Pavilion and Per-
gola at Shenstone Court,
Lichfield*, perspective by
Ernest Albert Chadwick
(*Studio Yearbook of
Decorative Art*, 1908)

110

Mawson's book clearly made a case for both the art and the craft of garden making. Written in plain language, with appealing illustrations, it blended theory with practical details of design and planting. It was addressed to potential clients to help them understand the scope of what a garden designer does and to provide them with sample solutions, whether an overall plan of the grounds or details of the architectural embellishments and garden furnishings in which his firm specialized. Mawson's book also brought a new dimension to the professional rendering of landscape plans that included topography, elevations, and sightlines as opposed to romanticized visions of gardens on paper.

On a visit to the offices of the Olmsted Brothers in Brookline, Massachusetts, the leading landscape architecture firm of its day, Mawson was impressed by the thoroughness of their approach and their working methods. "In the matter of office organization we in England have much to learn [and] their survey and contour work, which formed the basis of every plan, was done with a thoroughness seldom attempted at home," he wrote. "The method of preparing the plans by regular stages, ending with the work of the men who take out the quantities for trees and shrubs required, all carefully noted on the plans, was a revelation to me."[7] Because Mawson was able to define and illustrate the role of a landscape architect in a way that had not been done before, *The Art and Craft of Garden Making* was hailed by academic institutions in America, where the landscape architecture profession was just blossoming with the establishment of a program at Harvard University in 1900. As a result, Mawson received speaking engagements at Harvard, Cornell, and Yale universities on landscape architecture.

Foremost among Mawson's theories was the Arts and Crafts dictum of integrated house and garden, or as he expressed it, "garden design in its relation to the house and its architectural character."[8] *The Art and Craft of Garden Making* attests to the practical methods for ensuring this essential harmony, illustrated with examples drawn exclusively from his own work. In essence, Mawson regarded garden design as an art, in which the style of the house dictates the configuration of the garden. He held formality at arm's length, however, preferring to enhance the natural character of the landscape rather than forcing the issue. Whenever possible, he used local materials and vernacular detailing in his architectural components. His work benefited greatly from his collaboration with architects such as Gibson, Mallows, M. H. Baillie Scott, and C. F. A. Voysey.[9]

As shown in his book, Mawson's responsibilities ranged from laying out new gardens to reconfiguring old ones by other designers. Little Onn Hall, in Church Eaton, Staffordshire, is an excellent example of Mawson's ability to conceptualize a comprehensive scheme for improvements where an earlier landscape was already

GARDENS of BAILRIGG near
LANCASTER for
HERBERT·STOREY·ESQ
THOMAS·H·MAWSON F.R.I.B.A.
GARDEN·ARCHITECT

PLAN·

in place. The original Victorian hall, built in the 1850s by Colonel Ashton on the site of an ancient moated house, had fallen into disrepair by the time of his death. His daughters approached Mawson in the early 1890s about improving the extensive grounds that still retained remnants of the ancient watercourse. Designed in collaboration with Gibson, Little Onn Hall must have pleased Mawson, who included the project in each edition of his book.

Foremost in his mind was providing the low-lying Tudor-style hall with an "architectural support," as he called it.[10] As the ground was fairly level, he felt the need to introduce some architectural character into the site. His plan shows how he achieved this with an arrangement of terraces for a rose garden and flower borders that linked with an existing kitchen garden and, farther afield, a moat garden. The surrounding grounds were enhanced with plantations of rhododendrons, azaleas, lilacs, yews, and holly trees to complement mature oak, elm, and sycamore trees. To provide more architectural form to the terraces, he planted Irish yews clipped into squares and pyramids. As he wrote, "the architectural details have a great influence on the scheme as a whole."[11] He designed a charming summerhouse (indicated as a water pavilion on his plan) overlooking one end of the moat. The rose garden, opposite the front courtyard, was planted with masses of old-fashioned varieties, such as China roses, damask roses, and York and Lancaster roses; the enclosure walls were covered in tea and noisette roses. Mawson built two pavilions in the corners of the rose garden. Little Onn Hall combines the best of old and new, with a delicate balance between architectural and horticultural elements.

Thomas Mawson, *The Gardens at Little Onn Hall, Staffordshire*, line drawing (Mawson, 1901)

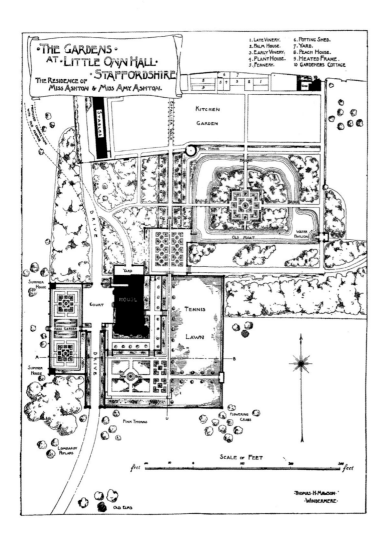

Dyffryn Gardens near Cardiff, South Wales, is one of Mawson's best surviving gardens and fully encapsulates his design philosophy.[12] The site is in a sheltered valley, with undulating pasture lands and picturesquely timbered forested areas. In 1906, Mawson received the commission from philanthropist John Cory to extend the existing gardens, which had been laid out in 1893 when the house was built. After Cory's death four years

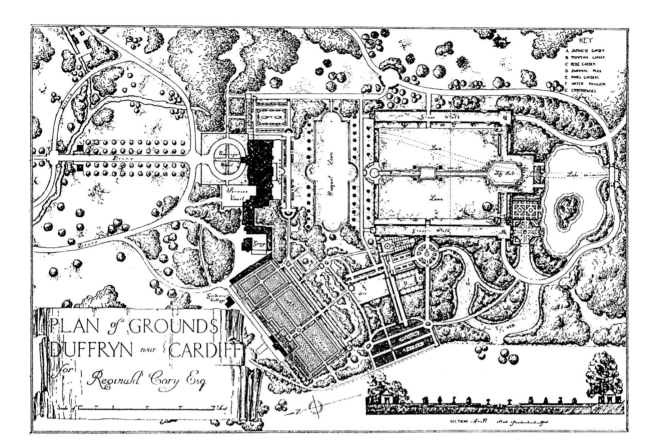

later, Mawson's extensive plans were implemented by his son, Reginald Cory, a well-known horticulturist and plant collector who proved to be an ideal client.[13] Mawson did not include a discussion of the project until the final edition of his book, perhaps to preserve the privacy of his client.

In his plan for the fifty-five-acre property, Mawson added a great lawn to the south front of the sprawling Victorian house to "provide a restful base to the house." To enhance the setting, he added a long axial canal and lily pond extending from the balustrade near the house to the lake in the distance. In contrast to the serenity of the south front, Mawson, encouraged by his client's passion for gardening, created a riot of special gardens—rock gardens, rose gardens, a Pompeiian garden, terraced gardens, pond gardens, herbaceous borders, and "most important of all, the pinetum and experimental gardens"—on the east and west sides. The result, he wrote, was one of "startling contrasts and surprises [and because] each garden is enclosed in its own screen of architecture or foliage, it seldom clashes with its neighbour."[14]

Two midcareer garden commissions in 1909, both in the Lake District, show how Mawson's style had solidified with terraces, ornamental pools, flights of stone steps, and other architectural features drawn directly from his book. At Rydal Hall, which had been in the Le Fleming family since the sixteenth century (with

Thomas Mawson, *Plan of Grounds, Duffryn [Dyffryn], Near Cardiff,* line drawing (Mawson, 1926)

Thomas Mawson,
Dyffryn Gardens,
Cardiff

many subsequent improvements), Mawson laid out an Edwardian-style terrace garden that is largely unchanged today (it was restored in 2005). From the upper terrace, a flight of steps leads down to two main parterres with flower beds and a central pool and fountain. His addition of two small pergolas along the outer wall adds interest to an otherwise conventional layout. Steps lead down to the lower level with further beds along the balustrades. All the construction materials, which were locally acquired, were restored. In all, it is a classic Mawson garden that works perfectly with the old hall. At Holker Hall, now one of the most famous gardens in the Lake District, Mawson's charge was to design a walled rose garden in an extensive twenty-five-acre site, ranging from formal gardens to woodland walks with champion trees developed by generations of the Cavendish family. In the 1990s, Mawson's rose garden was replaced by an elliptical garden, part of a scheme that included development of new gardens, such as a labyrinth and Kim Wilkie's turf amphitheater.

Influential as Mawson's book was, *Gardens for Small Country Houses* by Jekyll and Weaver probably had a greater impact than any book of the era on the practical issues of garden design for the average homeowner. First published in 1912, it served as a companion volume to *Country Life*'s popular *Small Country Houses of To-Day* series, which spotlighted recent work by Arts and Crafts architects. The

ABOVE
Thomas Mawson,
Holker Hall, Cark-
in-Cartmel, Cumbria

OPPOSITE
Thomas Mawson,
Rydal Hall, Ambleside,
Cumbria

authors noted in the preface to their book that it "filled a place hitherto empty, on the bookshelves of the garden-loving public."[15] Unlike Mawson's book, theirs was aimed primarily at owners of moderate-sized houses in affluent communities, but it also had a wide appeal among professional garden designers and architects alike, especially in America. For years it was considered the bible of formal garden design principles, and even today, more than one hundred years after its publication, it is still a major resource for garden designers, landscape architects, and architects.

The Arts and Crafts approach to garden making, with its emphasis on practicality and ingenuity, unfolds in the pages of *Gardens for Small Country Houses* through schemes by many of the key architects of the day, including Robert Lorimer, Edwin Lutyens, Mallows, and Voysey. The heart of the book is the well-honed selection of *Country Life*'s incomparable photographs, Jekyll's delightful plans, and the authors' insightful commentary. The book's topics are similar to those included in Mawson's book, but it is not nearly as encyclopedic. Its success lies in its broader focus on both new and historic gardens, rather than on the work of a single designer.

Unlike earlier manifestos by Blomfield and others, *Gardens for Small Country Houses* is a far cry from pompous historicism and rigid rules. The advice offered is always inspirational, yet practical. "Our noble English yew is nearly always beneficial in the garden landscape," the authors wrote. "Whether as a trimmed hedge or

as a fast-growing tree, its splendid richness of deepest green, and, indeed, its whole aspect is of the utmost value."[16] The prose may be somewhat flowery, but the advice is always solid, without a shred of romanticism. What also distinguishes the book is its expert selection of gardens suited to various small sites. Examples of the work of Lutyens and Jekyll abound, but others, such H. Inigo Triggs's own garden, Little Boarhunt, in Liphook, are equally skillful in their planning. They included it as an example of "how the qualities that make the beauty of the historic formal gardens may be reproduced . . . for houses of moderate size."

BELOW
Edwin Lutyens, half-moon steps in the sunken garden at Folly Farm, Sulhamstead, Berkshire, 1922

OPPOSITE
H. Inigo Triggs, Little Boarhunt, Liphook, Hampshire, ca. 1912

Whether King John actually ran a boar through the grounds at Little Boarhunt is a matter of dispute, but Triggs captured some of the romance of a bygone era in his well-considered scheme for a sunken parterre in the former farmyard. The enclosure nestles into the L-shaped house, with the other two sides framed by brick pergolas and a garden house in one corner, "inexpensively built a single brick thick, with its faces cemented." A long water rill runs the length of the enclosure, with a central rectangular pool that serves for watering the garden. A figure of a boy with a fish rises from a slender brick column in the center of the pool, and a brick dovecote anchors the north wall. "The sunk garden itself is an admirable example of the wealth of interesting detail that can be employed in a small space without creating any feeling of overcrowding."[17] Thanks to their exposure in *Gardens for Small Country Houses*, the water rill, garden house, and dovecote at Little Boarhunt soon became much-imitated features in British and American gardens, just as the work of Lutyens and Jekyll held wide appeal among landscape architects worldwide.

119

Along with layouts that worked so naturally with their houses, Arts and Crafts gardens were renowned for their detailing, which both books describe. Steps and paving, summerhouses, pergolas, arbors, and water features all fell into this category. Mawson concurred with Jekyll and Weaver that "nothing imparts character to a garden, and gives more interest, than well designed and carefully executed architectural details."[18] The stone steps and paving that seem technically correct in Mawson's work burst into life in a playful manner in Lutyens's designs, where the paving has just the right

BELOW
Edwin Lutyens, Rotunda
Pool at Hestercombe,
Cheddon Fitzpaine,
Somerset, 1908

OPPOSITE
Edwin Lutyens, tile-
built pergola at Marsh
Court, Stockbridge,
Hampshire, 1913

120

amount of irregularity, and his signature half-moon steps, such as those at Folly Farm, provide a pleasing method of connecting changes in levels. "Although stairways are among the most useful elements in garden design, and give just opportunity for conscious architectural treatment" wrote Jekyll and Weaver, "it is not always desirable to force the note of formality."[19]

One of the most ancient ways of defining outdoor spaces is through the use of hedges, or living greenery. They serve as a background for flower borders, a neat enclosure for a bowling green, or an ornamental device to be clipped and pruned into decorative shapes; in short, they offer architectural interest. Used by nearly every Arts and Crafts architect, hedges not only provide drama in perspective renderings, but also work well on the ground. Mawson recommended yew and holly hedges to enhance the effect of flowers against their dark background, but he advocated simpler forms of clipped hedges. "The simpler forms . . . are the most satisfactory because they express their purpose without any show or pretense, [but] it is well to avoid heads clipped to the forms of wild beasts, peacocks, etc., unless to express some symbolic meaning."[20]

Enclosure walls of brick or stone not only ensure privacy and shelter, but they can extend the parameters of the house. Arched openings offer easy access from one area to the next. If these are covered with vines, they should not smother the walls and obliterate their beauty—one of Jekyll's pet peeves. Low retaining walls, typically in rough stone of the region, can be enhanced with careful plantings of alpines in the wall joints and a judicious selection of small shrubs and rambling roses at the foot. Jekyll thought that such low walls were enhanced by plantings on the top, rather than at the foot.

Formal water features, such as long canals, waterlily ponds, reflecting pools, and small fountains, add immeasurably to small gardens. Mawson even questioned whether a garden was complete without water, whether a small reflecting pool or an architecturally treated pond with fountains and cascades derived from the great European gardens. Jekyll and Weaver recommended that the water, whether set in turf or in a paved court, "should be kept at its proper level, which is as high as possible. The nearer it is to the kerb of the pool, the wider and more beautiful will be the reflections."[21]

One of the most important elements of gardens of the Arts and Crafts era were

small structures, such as sturdy pergolas, informal gazebos, thatched pavilions, stone summerhouses, or romantic dovecotes. Their success, advised Jekyll and Weaver, depends as much on skillful placement as upon their form and materials. A small structure was usually integrated into the scheme either at the end of a long walk or at the corner of a garden wall, but most importantly, its style should reflect the architecture of the main house and it should be built of local materials. Mawson, Jekyll, and Weaver had their points of dispute about what was best and how to achieve it, but in the end their recommendations have proved timeless.

7

AT HOME WITH TWO MASTER GARDENERS

ARTS AND CRAFTS GARDENS MIGHT HAVE BEEN little more than a curious trend had it not been for William Robinson (1838–1935) and Gertrude Jekyll (1843–1932). Near contemporaries, their careers ran along parallel lines. Each possessed an exceptional knowledge of horticulture and each wrote more than a dozen important books, but their backgrounds and personalities were entirely different. Born in Ireland of unconventional parentage, Robinson was a shrewd businessman, while Jekyll, who was born in the more genteel environment of London's Mayfair, was an artist at heart. Like William Morris's Red House, their homes expressed their individuality and the fruits of their labors. Robinson's Gravetye Manor was Elizabethan in origin and at one time surrounded by a thousand acres of bucolic fields and woodlands; Jekyll's Munstead Wood was a more modest affair, fifteen acres of grounds enveloping a modern cottage designed by Edwin Lutyens.

Robinson was considered the prophet of wild gardening and an unswerving advocate for the cultivation of hardy plants at a time when bedding-out with tender annuals was the accepted practice in British gardens. Jekyll's reputation rests equally on her writings and her practical work as a garden designer, while Robinson's legacy lies primarily in the incomparable array of publications he either wrote or edited.[1] His two most important books—*The Wild Garden* (1870) and *The English Flower Garden* (1883)—were perennial favorites among many generations of gardeners, and the various magazines that he edited held a wide appeal to amateur and professional gardeners alike.[2]

The Wild Garden, which cautioned that unmanaged wilderness was not the same as landscapes enhanced by carefree perennials, opened many readers' eyes to the natural beauty of indigenous plants. Jekyll consulted *The Wild Garden* when she developed her gardens at Munstead Wood in the 1880s and 1890s, and many Americans acknowledged their indebtedness to the book in their landscape planning. Wilhelm Miller, an influential American editor and horticultural writer, formulated a style of landscape design suited to the American Midwest based directly on Robinson's books. *The English Flower Garden*, compiled mainly from articles published in *The Garden*, a journal that Robinson edited for decades, was one of the first modern-day compilations of cultural information and design advice aimed at home gardeners. Sprinkled with line drawings by artists and pithy commentary on design matters, it was an immensely popular book. Fifteen editions of the book were published in Robinson's lifetime, and it has been continuously in print since its initial publication in 1883.[3] When Miller visited Gravetye after reading these books, he gasped at the "luxurious abandon" of its plantings and the "glorious scale" with which wild gardening was being carried out.[4]

In comparison with Jekyll's worldwide renown today, Robinson's reputation pales somewhat as a result of his dogmatic personality. Although his publications were revolutionary in their day, they lack the elegant writing style that sets Jekyll's books apart and consequently are appreciated primarily by specialists. Robinson, however, was a master of marketing his knowledge through books and journals. More cosmopolitan than Jekyll, he visited Europe and the United States, where he met the leading botanists, horticulturists, and designers of the day. In 1870, for instance, his visit to Central Park and Mount Auburn Cemetery (known for its splendid trees and ornamental shrubs) fanned his interest in public gardens, while Horatio Hollis Hunnewell's famed pinetum (pine arboretum) near Boston left him in awe of American gardeners.

In the 1880s, when Jekyll was just beginning to write gardening pieces for *The Garden*, Robinson was firmly established in the field. After the publication of Jekyll's first book, *Wood and Garden*, in 1899, it quickly became apparent that her talents went far beyond mere horticultural knowledge. To her books and to the hundreds of gardens she designed, Jekyll brought the full panoply of her multiple skills as artist, craftswoman, antiquarian, architectural connoisseur, and horticulturist. *The Studio* noted that she had "the trained eye of an artist as well as the eloquent pen of the ready writer," something that could not have been said of Robinson, who was basically a reporter.[5] By the time *Colour in the Flower*

Garden was published in 1908, both the author and her garden at Munstead Wood were world famous, whereas Gravetye Manor was known only to Robinson's inner circle of friends.

In 1885, when he bought Gravetye Manor in Sussex, Robinson had already written ten books and founded at least five periodicals, of which *The Garden* and *Gardening Illustrated* were the most successful. Originally built in 1598, Gravetye Manor is ideally situated in the rolling countryside of the Weald of Sussex, with easy access by rail to Robinson's editorial offices in London. The large stone manor house stands midway on a hill, the north side protected from the winds and the south front overlooking the expansive view. Over the years, he transformed both house and garden, publishing a detailed record of his yearly progress in *Gravetye Manor, or Twenty Years' Work Round an Old Manor House.*[6] For the interior renovations and additions to the manor house, he turned to the architect George Devey, whose work there greatly displeased Robinson.[7] He then engaged Ernest George of the London architectural firm George and Peto, whose most famous pupil was Edwin Lutyens. Lutyens, who later designed a boathouse on one of the lakes at Gravetye, found Robinson exasperating, boring, and full of contradictions. Jesting with Reginald Blomfield one day, Lutyens suggested "cutting a statue of W. Robinson in yew as a monument to all he has done for gardening."[8]

BELOW
Alfred Parsons, *South Terrace, Gravetye Manor*, watercolor, early 1900s

PREVIOUS
Beatrice Parsons, *Spring Woods, Gravetye, Sussex*, watercolor, early 1900s

125

ABOVE
Gravetye Manor,
East Grinstead,
West Sussex

OPPOSITE
Simon Dorrell,
Gravetye Manor, line
drawing, 2003

Referring to the still-simmering controversies initiated by John Sedding and Blomfield, Robinson snapped in one of his regular columns for *Country Life*, "There is so much phrasemongering in matters of garden design and art that it is better to deal with actual work."[9] Gravetye's garden and landscape entailed a tremendous amount of work, including massive earthmoving and the building of walls, terraces, and pergolas. In addition to the garden and pleasure grounds, there were hundreds of acres of fields, meadows, and naturalistically planted woodlands. The pleasure grounds were initially conceived along gardenesque lines, but Robinson several years later changed the naturally sloping grade near the house to flat stone terraces that exemplified Blomfield's stance, which Robinson had vehemently rejected not long before. Unlike Blomfield, however, Robinson dealt with the greater landscape beyond the immediate house. He wrote, "There is no reason why the garden, which in our country is so often the foreground to a beautiful landscape, should not itself be a picture always."[10]

Initially the flower gardens consisted of simple beds close to the house and filled with tufted pansies, self-colored carnations, and roses, with the emphasis on the plants themselves rather than on the design of the borders. "I am a

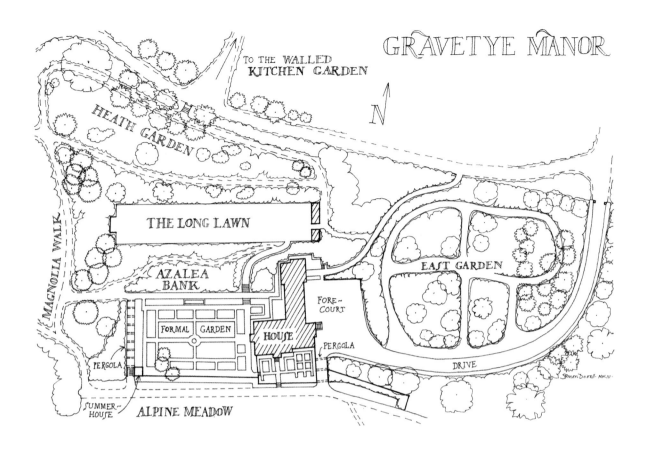

GRAVETYE MANOR

TO THE WALLED
KITCHEN GARDEN

HEATH GARDEN

THE LONG LAWN

AZALEA
BANK

MAGNOLIA WALK

FORMAL GARDEN

FORE-
COURT

HOUSE

PERGOLA

EAST GARDEN

DRIVE

PERGOLA

SUMMER-
HOUSE

ALPINE MEADOW

flower gardener," he wrote, "and not a mere spreader-about of bad carpets done in reluctant flowers." A garden should contain "the greatest number of favourite plants in the simplest way." With that in mind, he "threw the ground into simple beds, suiting the space for convenience of working and planting, not losing an inch more than was necessary for walks."[11] Henry James left a memorable record of Gravetye's gardens when he wrote, "Few things in England can show a greater wealth of bloom than the wide flowery terrace immediately beneath the gray, gabled house, where tens of thousands of tea-roses . . . divide their province with the carnations and pansies [and] the medley of tall yuccas and saxifrage."[12]

While Robinson was fine-tuning his flower gardens, he was assiduously buying up neighboring farms and woods until he had amassed nearly a thousand acres. His great love was Gravetye's carefully managed woodlands, planted with native plants, along with sweeps of thousands of daffodils. *Home Landscapes*, a companion volume to *Gravetye Manor*, eulogizes his woodlands. The rolling terrain of his estate soon resembled the naturalistic beauties of an eighteenth-century picturesque landscape, replete with a herd of pedigree Sussex cattle whose deep red color provided a perfect foil for the verdant countryside.

As his passion for plants consumed him, Robinson's collection of flowers, fruits, shrubs, and trees (some of which came from America) grew to substantial proportions. His water gardens, for instance, included one of the largest collections of waterlilies in Europe, including a special tank devoted to rare specimens acquired from the French breeder Latour-Marliac. Pergolas were festooned with hundreds of varieties of his world-famous clematises. His walled kitchen garden, built in 1896, housed an unsurpassed collection of vegetables and fruits, some of which were espaliered on the walls. He paved the small garden flanking the south porch with old flagstones from London, filling the beds with plants in shades of lilac, purple, pink, and silver. On higher ground, near the north face of the manor house, he developed an azalea bank and, higher still, a garden devoted exclusively to heathers, separated by a traditional bowling green. On the south side of the manor house, a large alpine meadow was planted with masses of naturalized scillas, daffodils, anemones, and fritillarias. The east garden, off the entry court, was devoted to magnolias and other ornamental trees and shrubs, including a rare specimen, *Davidia involucrata* (dove tree), first introduced from China in 1904.

For many, the most breathtaking part of Gravetye was the west paved garden, brimming with tea and China roses and surrounded by pergolas, arbors, and trellises. In its heyday, the garden was given over to nearly thirty beds of roses and their companion plants, such as dianthus, violas, pansies, forget-me-nots, and carnations, whose colors were chosen to complement the gray stone manor house. In the northwest corner stands a stone summerhouse designed in 1900 by Ernest George, who also designed the pedestal for the central sundial, placed at the crossing of the two main paths paved with old stones from London rather than high-maintenance gravel. In later years, when Robinson was confined to a wheelchair, some of the paths were remade as stone ramps.

Robinson considered the west and south flower gardens, which open out directly from doors in the house, as "a larger living-room" and "in intimate relation to the house," the stance taken by the formalists in the 1890s. "The real flower garden, where all our precious flowers are," he commented, should be

"in close relation to the house, so that we can enjoy and see and gather our flowers in the most direct way. . . . Going for a half a mile to get to the flower garden, as happens in some Scotch places, or scattering garden flowers in all directions, is not the right way," he concluded.[13]

In the belief that his gardens were "full of pictures," Robinson invited many noted landscape painters to paint them. "I have worked long and hard to prove that the garden, instead of being a horror to the artist, may be the very heart of his work," he commented.[14] Among his favored artists were Henry G. Moon, a botanical illustrator for *The Garden* who was renowned for his exacting depictions of flowers and his sensitive Corot-inspired landscape paintings, and Alfred Parsons, who illustrated many of Robinson's publications and was a garden

ABOVE
Ernest George, summerhouse at Gravetye Manor

OPPOSITE
Beatrice Parsons, *West Paved Garden, Gravetye Manor,* watercolor, early 1900s

Beatrice Parsons,
West Paved Garden,
Gravetye Manor, water-
color, early 1900s

Beatrice Parsons
Gravetye Manor

designer of some note. Moon's drawings, which were simply executed and full of life and character, appealed to Robinson the most. His landscape paintings of Gravetye's woodlands still hang in Gravetye Manor today.[15]

At Robinson's death in 1935, Gravetye was left to the Forestry Commission, with the stipulation that there be no lectures or technical instruction, because "the trees, woods, and landscape shall be the only teachers."[16] After lying derelict for years, the manor house and thirty acres were leased in 1958 to restaurateur Peter Herbert, who proceeded to transform Robinson's home into one of the leading country house hotels in Britain. The initial clearing of the garden took more than two years.[17] All the main garden areas were refurbished, and the once-dense central flower beds in the west garden were replaced by a smooth, green lawn. More recently, the gardens have been fully revitalized in "luxurious abandon" by head gardener Tom Coward, who studied at Great Dixter, one of England's most important gardens and a mecca for Arts and Crafts enthusiasts. Today Gravetye is a monument to Robinson's ideals. As he said when he launched *Flora and Sylva* (a short-lived luxury journal with color plates by Moon), "I married Flora to Sylva, a pair not far apart in Nature, only in books." The same could be said of Gravetye.

OPPOSITE
Munstead Wood,
Godalming, Surrey

BELOW
Summer borders at
Gravetye Manor

132

Jekyll's home, Munstead Wood, can be considered the perfect expression of the symbiotic nature of house and garden. It became renowned during her lifetime through the many books and articles she wrote about it as well as through personal visits paid by admirers from around the world. Few houses better express their owner's character than Munstead Wood, which resulted from the happy combination of a skilled architect and a determined client. The gardens did not follow a prescribed plan but evolved over time and were nearly fully developed before the house was built. When Robert Lorimer visited Munstead Wood in 1897, just six days after Jekyll moved into her new home, he commented that she had laid out

BELOW
Henry G. Moon,
*Flower Border at
Munstead [House],*
watercolor, ca. 1896

OPPOSITE
Helen Allingham,
*October Michaelmas
Daisy Borders,* water-
color, early 1900s

134

all the gardens first and "left a hole in the centre of the ground for the house."[18] It was the architect Edwin Lutyens's ingenious design that inextricably married the house with the garden.

Prior to moving to Munstead Wood, Jekyll had lived nearby with her family at Munstead House, where her keen knowledge of horticulture and unique approach to planting design quickened. The lessons she learned there later paid off at Munstead Wood.[19] Robinson, whom she had first met in 1875, visited in 1880 to confer about her garden and perhaps advise on how to lay it out. Two years later, *The Garden* published an article about her garden, praising the long border: "Never before have we seen hardy plants set out so well or cultivated in such a systematic way."[20]

Jekyll began gardening at Munstead House in 1878, while she was studying various arts and crafts, but by 1883 she had clearly run out of space. That year, she was able to acquire fifteen acres nearby, mostly of "the poorest possible soil."[21] Nonetheless, she used what natural advantages she found there, developing the former Scots pine plantation into woodland gardens and the poor field into her working gardens, reserving the central chestnut copse for the site of her house, which was not built until 1897. In the woodland gardens, Jekyll followed Robinson's suggestions, underplanting areas with masses of rhododendrons or azaleas, and giving each path a specific interest, whether ferns and bracken or lilies, to complement the selected groupings of birches, chestnuts, or oaks. She planted rivers of daffodils along ancient packhorse tracks and established an area devoted to native heaths. Where the lawn met the woods, she planted clumps of lilies, ferns, asters, and other shrubbery edge plantings, an idea gleaned from Robinson.

As she fully explained and illustrated in *Colour in the Flower Garden*, Jekyll established a number of ornamental gardens devoted to flowers of one season. These included a spring garden, a naturalistic primrose garden, a June cottage garden, and September borders of perennial asters, among other flowers. Her October Michaelmas daisy borders, arranged with mounds of soft blues and purples, provided a "garden picture" in cool months that was not far from the house. Perhaps her most widely acclaimed creation was the main flower border, 200 feet (61 meters) long and 14 feet (4 meters) deep, backed by a high sandstone wall that separated it from the spring garden.

The border's complex and intricate color scheme was based on harmonious color relationships, inspired perhaps by one of J. M. W. Turner's paintings. In the large central portion, fiery reds faded to orange and deep yellow. The colors continued to fade to paler yellow and pink, culminating at both ends with blues and lilacs in a ground of gray foliage. The whole arrangement was actually an elaborate piece of *trompe-l'oeil*. To reach the border, one strolled down a shaded nut walk from the house and through a pergola, emerging into bright sunlight to face a carefully arranged river of color and texture. The whole picture was clearly visible from the lawn, "the cool colouring at the ends [enhancing] the brilliant warmth of the middle and [each section] a picture in itself." [22]

Two acres of Munstead Wood were given over to working gardens, including a kitchen garden, a nursery, and a large orchard, which visitors rarely saw. There were numerous cottage-style borders and hedged compartments filled with

BELOW
Helen Allingham,
*In Munstead Wood
Garden [Main Flower
Border]*, watercolor,
early 1900s

OPPOSITE
Simon Dorrell,
Munstead Wood, line
drawing, 2003

136

drifts of China roses, irises, hollyhocks, and her own strain of lupines in special colorations that complemented the gray clapboard barn.[23] Jekyll's large nursery supplied plants for her garden design commissions, while the kitchen garden kept the house supplied with fruits and vegetables. Next to the potting shed and greenhouses, Jekyll devoted a special garden to pansies. In the garden yard she raised lily of the valley and narcissus, which were sold at Covent Garden. Reserve gardens not only filled the house with flowers but provided valuable seeds that Jekyll sold to commercial nurseries in England and France.

In Edwin Lutyens (1869–1944), Jekyll found an architect who shared her vernacular sensibilities for homebuilding and could create a house worthy of her gardens. Lutyens hailed from a small village not far from Munstead. After studying at the South Kensington School of Art (where Jekyll had studied years earlier) and working briefly in the office of Ernest George, he had just set himself up as an architect when he met Jekyll in 1889. They liked one another immediately and soon were scouring the countryside, under Jekyll's direction, looking at old cottages and studying traditional building methods, which they avidly discussed and debated. Jekyll's influence on the young architect is legend; when she asked him to design her house in 1892, they embarked on a fruitful collaboration that resulted in dozens of houses and gardens.

Jekyll's love of simple materials and excellence in craftsmanship extended to the planning and building of all aspects of Munstead Wood, not only the house. One colleague extolled her "passion for matters concerning domestic architecture that almost equals [her] interest in plants and trees."[24] This love of local customs, artifacts, and buildings was recorded in minute detail in her 1904 book, *Old West Surrey.* Before settling on a design for the house, Lutyens built two small cottages on the site, one for Jekyll's head gardener and the Hut, where she lived for two years while her main house was under construction. Guided by the main requirements for her house, "serenity of mind" and "the feeling of a convent," the resulting design in 1896 brought together everything that she desired. Built of local bargate stone and timber felled on her own property, it "does not

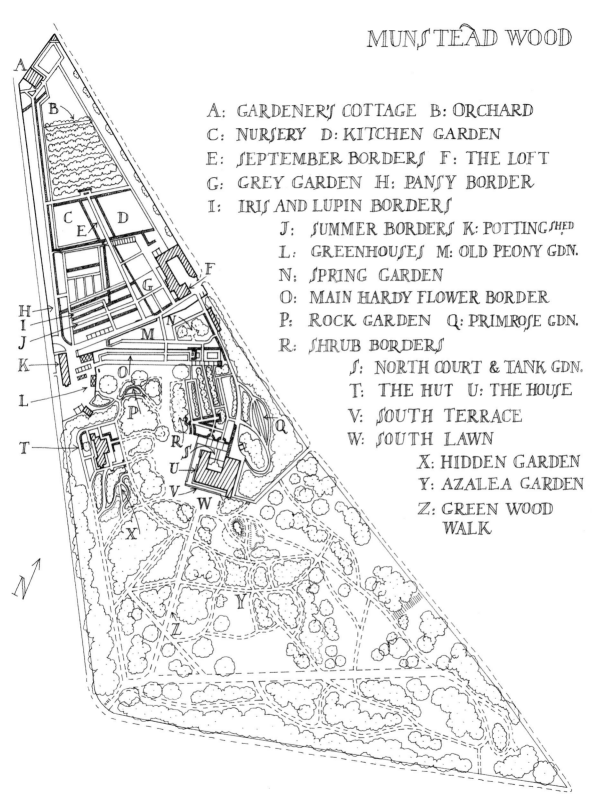

MUNSTEAD WOOD

A: GARDENER'S COTTAGE   B: ORCHARD
C: NURSERY   D: KITCHEN GARDEN
E: SEPTEMBER BORDERS   F: THE LOFT
G: GREY GARDEN   H: PANSY BORDER
I: IRIS AND LUPIN BORDERS
J: SUMMER BORDERS   K: POTTING SHED
L: GREENHOUSES   M: OLD PEONY GDN.
N: SPRING GARDEN
O: MAIN HARDY FLOWER BORDER
P: ROCK GARDEN   Q: PRIMROSE GDN.
R: SHRUB BORDERS
S: NORTH COURT & TANK GDN.
T: THE HUT   U: THE HOUSE
V: SOUTH TERRACE
W: SOUTH LAWN
X: HIDDEN GARDEN
Y: AZALEA GARDEN
Z: GREEN WOOD WALK

N

SIMON DORRELL · MM III.

Thomas H. Hunn,
*The Pansy Garden,
Munstead Wood,*
watercolor, ca. 1910

stare with newness," as Jekyll commented in *Home and Garden*, nor was it a copy of an old building.[25] Lutyens married a small Tudor-style manor house with a highly personal interpretation of local vernacular style. The house was at once quirky and contrived, but simple, elegant, and eminently comfortable.

Jekyll's study of numerous crafts and appreciation for local customs influenced the furnishing of her house as well as its craftsmanship. The house is steeped in the regional Surrey vocabulary, with half-timbering, deeply hipped roofs, and plain plastered walls. Like those of Morris's Red House, the corridors are timber-lined, with whitewashed walls and oak doors. The furnishings were simple Jacobean chests and tables, and the decorations and ornamentations were mostly Jekyll's own handiwork. In the end, Munstead Wood may have been a large house for a single woman, but it was unpretentious and extremely suited to her.[26]

The character of Munstead Wood was lost after Jekyll's death in 1932, but her many books, articles, and photographs serve to keep its significance alive today. When it went out of family hands in 1948, Munstead Wood was divided up into several parcels. Both the Hut and the gardener's cottage survive, and sections of the original working gardens have been restored. The house, principal gardens, and woodlands have been in sympathetic hands for many years. The gardens were substantially rehabilitated in the 1990s, based on a vast store of visual and written information available about the property, and they continue to be refreshed. Jekyll's shrubbery borders, main flower border, spring garden, and seasonal color borders bloom once again.

CLOCKWISE FROM LEFT
Katharine Montagu Wyatt, *North Court, Munstead Wood*, watercolor (Gloag, *A Book of English Gardens*, 1906)

North Court at Munstead Wood

October Michaelmas Daisy Borders at Munstead Wood

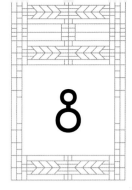

A PERFECT HOUSE
AND GARDEN

THE COMPATIBILITY OF THE IDEAS of Edwin Lutyens with those of Gertrude Jekyll led to a fruitful partnership that resulted in some of the most celebrated houses and gardens of the early twentieth century. Having a Lutyens house and a Jekyll garden was the ultimate emblem for Britain's new wealthy elite. Even though Jekyll designed hundreds of gardens in her lifetime, those she designed with Lutyens best encapsulate the Arts and Crafts approach to garden making. While Jekyll's planting style remained static—in the 1920s she continued to rely on the formulas she had developed in the 1890s—Lutyens's meteoric career quickly advanced from the Surrey Vernacular style of Munstead Wood to High Georgian in a matter of years. Despite the range of architectural styles represented in his country houses, his gardens associated with Jekyll are firmly entrenched in Arts and Crafts methodology.

Deanery Garden, in Sonning, Berkshire, is one of their best collaborations. Designed in 1899 for Edward Hudson, founder and managing director of *Country Life*, Deanery Garden established the standard for the intimacy of house and garden. Jekyll, who wrote gardening notes for the magazine, is thought to have introduced Lutyens to Hudson, a

ABOVE
Edwin Lutyens and
Gertrude Jekyll, water
rill at Deanery Garden,
Sonning-on-Thames,
ca. 1902

PREVIOUS
Edwin Lutyens and
Gertrude Jekyll, garden
front at Goddards, Abin-
ger Common, Surrey,
ca. 1903

rather shy and inarticulate man who had much in common with Lutyens. Both men expressed themselves in their passions rather than in words: Lutyens in buildings and Hudson in his appreciation of country houses that his publications made famous.[1] They enjoyed a lifelong friendship, with Hudson commissioning four projects from Lutyens and publishing accounts of all Lutyens's principal buildings in *Country Life*.[2]

Lutyens's biographer Christopher Hussey called Deanery Garden "a perfect architectural sonnet, compounded of brick and tile and timber forms, in which [Lutyens's] handling of the masses and spaces serve as rhythm: its theme, a romantic bachelor's idyllic afternoons beside a Thames backwater."[3] Hudson's busy schedule led him to sell Deanery Garden a few years after its completion. The starting point for Deanery Garden was the vestiges of the old site, once the house of the Dean of Salisbury. Old brick walls running between the river and the village defined the property outlines, and an aging apple orchard provided the romantic setting. Lutyens designed a brick house tight against the wall behind the busy village street, with the principal entrance through a door in the wall into a chalk-vaulted cloisterlike passageway (perhaps a nod to the site's ecclesiastical origins) that leads to a formal courtyard enclosed on three sides. Another doorway in the wall opens onto a path with a vine-covered pergola leading to the garden, a trick Jekyll used to great effect at Munstead Wood. Lutyens reused the idea for entrances in a high wall at Millmead.

The gardens are a series of enclosures that hug the house on different levels, each with vistas to the distant orchard. "House and garden are a single interpenetrating conception," wrote Hussey. In his opinion, the design and execution of Deanery Garden, with "Jekyll's naturalistic planting wedded [to] Lutyens's geometry," settled the steaming controversy between Blomfield and Robinson of formal versus naturalistic garden design.[4] Though Hussey's comments, written in 1950, give equal credit to Jekyll, an anonymous *Country Life* article of 1903 omits any reference to her: "Mr. Lutyens never designed a more perfect house or a more charming garden."[5] In *Houses and Gardens of E. L. Lutyens*, Lawrence Weaver acknowledged Jekyll's work with Lutyens in "producing effects of singular richness."[6]

Deanery Garden has many of Lutyens's trademark features, such as his signature radiating half-moon steps, linear water rills, semicircular pools, spouting masques, and pergolas with alternating round and square piers, that appear in later gardens. One of the focal points, and the most imitated by other designers, is the long rill, with circular pools (referred to as "tanks" by Jekyll) at both ends and a square pool in the center of the rill. Here Lutyens's fascination with geometry is at its most playful: a path with square stepping stones arranged at alternating angles on the lawn bisects the central square pool; one circular pool is elevated, while the other one is recessed under a bridge-walkway that leads from the house to the orchard; square steps alternate with round ones; and so on. The rill is flanked by wide grass panels with pale-toned flower borders; closer to the house a bowling green runs parallel to the rill garden. The formality of these upper gardens and others near the house fades into the natural element, the orchard.

Deanery Garden was designed for roses, one of Hudson's hobbies. Jekyll's favorite rose, 'The Garland', rambles in the old apple trees and spills out from the tops of the retaining walls throughout the garden. These walls have been planted with dianthus, stonecrops, and other wall-loving plants described in Jekyll's book *Wall*

Simon Dorrell, *Deanery Garden*, line drawing, 2003

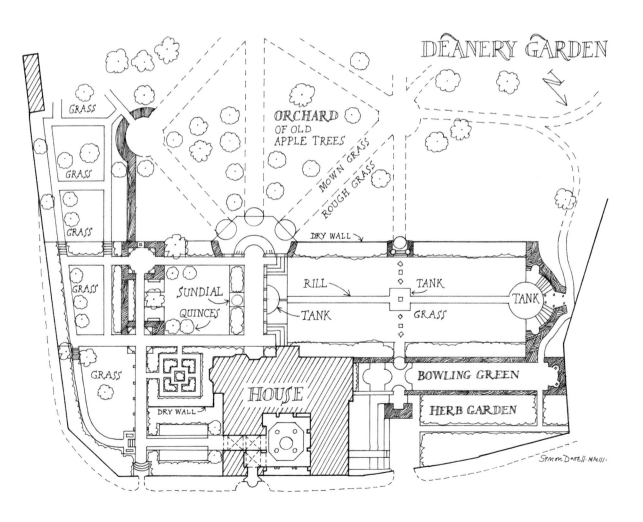

BELOW
Garden front at
Goddards

OPPOSITE
Edwin Lutyens and
Gertrude Jekyll, Marsh
Court façade, Stock-
bridge, Hampshire, 1912

144

and Water Gardens. "The garden is rich in delightful detail," whether in the flower borders or the ornamental figures in bronze and stone. It is a "remarkably beautiful and charming garden," wrote Jekyll and Weaver.[7] Deanery Garden provides a perfect balance of old elements with new ones. It also balances the architectural detailing found in the pavers and hedging with the informality of the plantings. With its various compartmentalized outdoor rooms, Deanery Garden is an exceptional example of how to achieve a harmony between house and garden as well as the marriage of formality with informality.

Goddards, along with Orchards and Munstead Wood, is one of Lutyens's most important and original early houses. Located in Abinger Common, Surrey, Goddards is a homespun version of some of his grander confections. The fanciful house, built entirely from local stone and oak with light-colored roughcast walls, jaunty red brick mullions and window surrounds, and a tile roof, provided a perfect setting for a small, enclosed garden court designed by Jekyll. Originally designed in 1898 as a holiday home for working women from the East End of London, it was enlarged and converted to a year-round country house in 1910 for Frederick Mirrielees, the owner. With its twin gables, tall brick chimneys, and distinctive detailing, it is still an unusually well-preserved house.[8] Goddards is also one of the first examples of what would become one of Jekyll's most consistent planting themes: a quiet, welcoming front entrance contrasted with the principal garden in the back, hidden from view of the street.

The focal point of the garden court, nestled between the two splayed wings of the house, is the stone well, around which are grouped low-growing plants "like sea anemones lying on a rock," noted Weaver.[9] This garden court undoubtedly took its inspiration from the North Court at Munstead Wood, designed only two years earlier, with millstones in the pavement adding a decorative element. The

paving, with pockets in the irregular flagstones for sun-loving plants with gray and silver foliage, identifies its function as a terrace rather than as a traditional flower-filled pleasure garden. In her choice of plantings, Jekyll may have considered the institutional or low-maintenance nature of the garden, as the house was originally intended to be used in summer only. A low stone wall encircles the well and another marks the outer parameters of the terrace. The linear theme is extended with low, clipped yew hedges that define the outer limits of the garden.

Marsh Court, designed in 1901 for Herbert Johnson, is a far grander and

more whimsical house than Goddards, with an architectural garden that looks impressive in photographs; in reality, it may not have been very welcoming for actual use. Located in Hampshire, overlooking the River Test, Marsh Court is built from brilliant white chalk with sharply contrasting red brick chimneys and irregular patches of red tiles and black flint decorating the walls. The checkerboard theme is carried out in the terrace paving, in the jagged paved paths, and in the sundial, which matches the exterior of the house. The last of Lutyens's houses modeled after a Tudor manor house, Marsh Court was "Lutyens in his gayest mood," wrote Weaver.[10]

The sunken pool garden is the focal point of the scheme. From the elevated point of the water garden (below which lies a pergola), one can gaze back at the architectural fantasy of the house. Conceived as an outdoor room, the garden functions as an arm of the H-shaped house. A long rectangular pool, surrounded by high balustraded walls, is sunk into the multiple folds of low, broad steps. As in some of Lutyens and Jekyll's subsequent work, the paths and landings for the

BELOW
Sundial at Marsh Court

OPPOSITE
Lily pool and sunken
garden at Marsh Court,
1932

steps are constructed from York pavers with panels of herringbone-patterned brickwork. Bisecting the pool, a tiny water rill runs from lead cisterns in one high wall to the other. Stone planters are embellished with seahorses spouting water from their muzzles, and lead tortoises are arranged along the edges of the pool. These sculptures were made by Lady Julia Chance, whose house, Orchards, had been designed by Lutyens in 1899 and whose work appears in a number of Lutyens and Jekyll gardens.

"Water takes its highest place in garden architecture when it determines the complete design of an enclosed space, such as the pool garden at Marsh Court," wrote Jekyll and Weaver in *Gardens for Small Country Houses.* "No scheme contrived within so small a compass could exceed in richness of effect this combination of steps, paving, pool, and balustrade."[11] Lutyens and Jekyll created many variations on Marsh Court's water garden in their later work, including Hestercombe, Folly Farm, and Gledstone Hall.

By 1905, Lutyens was the most fashionable architect in the country, with many houses already built or underway. Millmead, completed that year, showed "how perfect a thing a little country house on a tiny plot of ground can be, and how a 'sordid half acre' can be transformed into an earthly paradise."[12] Jekyll had

146

spotted the vacant lot in Bramley, Surrey, where some old cottages had been demolished several years earlier, and she saw the possibilities of building "the best small house in the whole neighborhood."[13] What struck her about the spot, despite years of rubbish accumulation and overgrown weeds, was that it was within sight of the woods of her childhood home in Bramley, where she had spent many carefree days romping. The site, less than half an acre in size, was long and narrow (75 feet by 400 feet, or 23 meters by 122 meters) and sloped rather awkwardly down to a marshy millmead and brook. She engaged Lutyens to design the house, while she busied herself with designing a garden. The house that Lutyens designed was no longer in the Surrey Vernacular style of Munstead Wood and Orchards, but in a Georgian style, "rather over-windowed," according to architectural critic H. Avray Tipping.[14]

The modest L-shaped house took up almost the entire width of the site, and because it was located on a busy village street, they decided to build a high enclosure wall. Like the wall at Munstead Wood, it was constructed of local bargate stone with tile

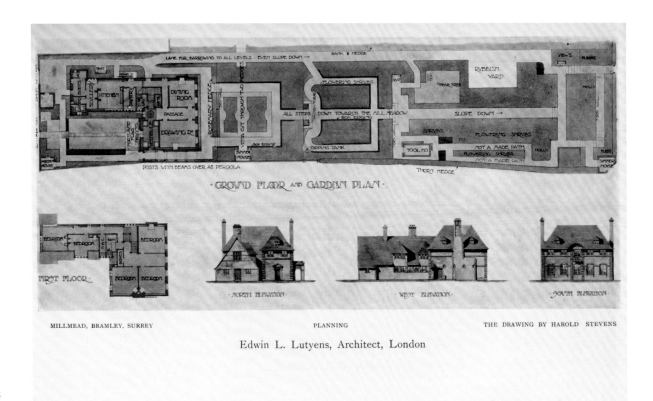

GROVND FLOOR AND GARDEN PLAN.

FIRST FLOOR.

NORTH ELEVATION.

WEST ELEVATION.

SOVTH ELEVATION.

MILLMEAD, BRAMLEY, SURREY   PLANNING   THE DRAWING BY HAROLD STEVENS

Edwin L. Lutyens, Architect, London

coping. Where the wall ends in the back, at the edge of the steeply sloping site, yew hedges continue the high enclosure. An opening in the wall on the street leads to a small forecourt, and a paved walk leads to the front entrance. A narrow, five-foot-wide (one-and-a-half meter) walkway between the west side of the house and the enclosure wall provides access to the main garden on the sunny south side of the house. "The planting in the forecourt is kept rather quiet, with plenty of green foliage," wrote Jekyll and Weaver. "The flowers are of a modest type, such as columbines and campanulas, [the intention being] green and quiet in anticipation of a riot of bright blossom in the main garden on the sunny side of the house."[15]

Jekyll divided the long, sloping garden into four terraces, starting with the relatively level area nearest to the house, with a rose garden and a central sundial, and ending with the thicket at the bottom near the millstream. Jekyll admitted that the problems of the ground being a long strip required "judicious management of each succeeding level, so that each should have individuality and distinctive interest, and yet that there should be a comfortable sense of general cohesion."[16] Each compartment was delineated with low dry-stone walls and profusely planted with fragrant, sun-loving plants such as lavender, with gentle steps leading from one level to the next. The largest area, near the bottom, was

LEFT
Edwin Lutyens and
Gertrude Jekyll, sum-
merhouse at Millmead,
Bramley, Surrey, ca.
1912

OPPOSITE
Harold Stevens, *Ground
Floor and Garden Plan,
Millmead, Bramley,
Surrey*, drawing (Spar-
row, 1909)

149

given over to ebullient flower borders and ornamental fruit trees, so that from
the bottom of the garden one could view the house through an impressionistic
blur of flowers and foliage. Even though the property is relatively modest in size,
it includes three summerhouses, the most impressive of which is located on the
upper garden terrace on axis with the sundial in the rose garden. From here one
can enjoy the distant views of Jekyll's childhood woodlands. She never lived in
this house, as it was built as a speculative venture, but Millmead is an excellent
example of Jekyll's skillful planning on a challenging site, encompassing both formal elements and informality, in the true spirit of the Arts and Crafts Movement.

In many ways, Folly Farm, located in Sulhamstead, Berkshire, represents the
culmination of the Lutyens and Jekyll partnership, for many of the ideas that
they had experimented with for years matured here. Folly Farm also represents a
transition from the Arts and Crafts to the Modern movements in garden design,
presaging Sissinghurst and other complex gardens in its series of compartmentalized outdoor rooms. It successfully combines vestiges of the "old" and the "new"
and "newer," and like many gardens of the early twentieth century, it represents
a continuum linking it to the present day. Folly Farm has had a variety of owners
(but only one architect), each of whom left an imprint. It is considered one of the

BELOW
Simon Dorrell, *Folly Farm*, line drawing, 2003

OPPOSITE TOP
Edwin Lutyens and Gertrude Jekyll, Dutch canal garden at Folly Farm, Sulhamstead, Berkshire, ca. 1921

OPPOSITE BOTTOM
Dutch canal garden at Folly Farm

150

best examples of the Lutyens and Jekyll collaboration in private ownership, and a recent refurbishment by the renowned garden designer Dan Pearson has injected a dazzling new life into these extraordinary gardens.

Folly Farm started out as a modest timber-framed farmhouse with ancillary barn buildings. In 1905, H. H. Cochrane asked Lutyens to design an addition to convert it into a country house. For this addition, which turned out to be far grander than the original cottage, Lutyens designed a storybook William and Mary style house, built in a soft gray brick with distinctive red-brick trim. A symmetrical H-shaped house, it is a superb example of Lutyens's "Wrennaissance" period, inspired by late-seventeenth-century buildings by Sir Christopher Wren. As part of the commission, Lutyens designed a series of courts to tie together the old and new buildings, with flagstone paths laid in a herringbone brick pattern, similar to those at Marsh Court. For these new courts, Jekyll's borders were in a feathery cottage style, with fragrant lavender, dianthus, and roses. The new entrance court, with brick garden walls and arches, called for more formality, with an emphasis on textural green foliage. Jekyll planted a rhododendron walk to separate the village street from the house and laid out traditional grass lawns flanked by flower borders on the main façade of the new building. In all it was an attractive, but not exceptional, scheme.

Today the gardens at Folly Farm owe their fame to the period of the second owner, Zachary Merton, for whom Lutyens designed another addition in 1912. His fanciful barnlike structure to the west of the brick building reverts to the architect's earlier vernacular style, with its exaggerated roofline swooping down to cover a buttressed cloister. With the exception of the barn court, the

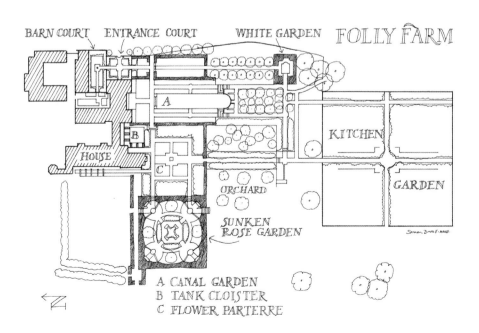

BARN COURT   ENTRANCE COURT   WHITE GARDEN   FOLLY FARM

A
B
HOUSE
C
KITCHEN
GARDEN
ORCHARD
SUNKEN ROSE GARDEN

A CANAL GARDEN
B TANK CLOISTER
C FLOWER PARTERRE

earlier gardens were replaced with a bolder theme.[17] The new scheme included three different water gardens. The first, and most dramatic, a Dutch-inspired canal modeled after seventeenth-century examples that were popular in English gardens, replaced the grass panel in front of the 1905 Dutch addition.[18] From the elevated water works and bridge at the far end of the canal, a feature derived from Deanery Garden, one could see the reflection of the house in the long pool.

A second water garden, a square tank tucked into the L of the cloistered loggia, also functioned as a reflecting pool. Jekyll planted the narrow borders along the edge with spikey water-loving plants, such as irises and arums. The third, and most dramatic, is a sunken water parterre planted with roses and "floating islands" of lavender, hidden behind high yew hedges. This garden served as the grand finale, with Lutyens's half-moon steps, curving stone paths, and herringbone brick detail. It was an architectural garden in its most ingenious configuration.

In his review of Folly Farm for *Country Life*, Hussey mused, "Probably, every man, and certainly every woman, at intervals in his life lays out gardens if only in the fertile soil of imagination."[19] Folly Farm owes its great significance to the way it was laid out as a series of interlinking rooms, each with a special vista to the house. It is also a garden of axial viewpoints in the manner of the great formal gardens of the seventeenth century. The water parterre and the canal garden are linked by a square formal garden in the middle that is surrounded by borders filled with blue and purple flowers. The main cross-axial path centered on the 1912 addition leads from this formal garden to a large walled kitchen garden. Part of the magic of Folly Farm's gardens is the network of linear yew hedges that define each room and block the view from one area to the next. The idea of compartmentalized garden rooms—progressing from one experience to the next—would become the hallmark of gardens of the Modern era.

In the 1920s and 1930s, it took six gardeners to maintain Folly Farm; in later years, the plantings were simplified or removed.[20] Dan Pearson Studio recently

TOP
Loggia and tank garden
at Folly Farm, ca. 1921

ABOVE
Blue and purple garden
at Folly Farm, ca. 1921

PREVIOUS
Loggia and tank garden
at Folly Farm

154

restored and reinvigorated the gardens with new plantings that evoke the magic of the original Lutyens and Jekyll era. The fact that plants could be changed and new areas planned owes much to Lutyens and Jekyll's brilliant scheme that reflected years of expertise. No other architect of the Arts and Crafts Movement had the benefit of such sympathetic and skillful collaboration.

Hestercombe Gardens in Somerset stands as one of the best and most lasting examples of their collaboration—one that continues to bring wide recognition to their talents. However, when Lutyens was contacted in 1903 by Edward Portman about designing a grand garden, the commission did not include a new house. Instead, his client chose to retain the banal Victorian mansion and terrace, which still stand today. Despite this setback, Lutyens produced a grand classical garden with rustic vernacular detailing. He designed an elegant classical orangery and other architectural components that enhanced the magnificent garden. In addition, he chose to create visual links between the new garden and the surrounding eighteenth-century landscape, which a lesser architect might have obliterated.

Lutyens's scheme involved a series of terraces on the sloping ground below the house to capitalize on the breathtaking views across the Vale of Taunton. A long pergola, with alternating square and round piers, provides a framework for

the garden. The centerpiece is a parterre (or plat), of 125 feet square (12 meters square), flanked by elevated water terraces that are part of an elaborate water garden. The grand plan, which developed in several phases, includes a formal rose garden, a stone rotunda, a small enclosed garden, an orangery terrace, and other features. The water system, where water drips from a lion's masque into a circular pool and runs along parallel rills before collecting in rectangular tanks near the pergola, is one of the most memorable features of the garden. Throughout the garden, local stone is masterfully blended into the various architectural components, with honey-colored ashlar used for important features. Half-moon steps define the four corners of the parterre, while stone-lined water rills, pools, paths, and steps connecting all the level changes provide added geometry.

To complement this grand plan, Jekyll used the soft gray tones of the stone as inspiration for her planting schemes, using her standard gray, pink, and white borders that were well suited to the color of the stone. The borders along the elevated

terraces and the beds in the plat are planted with a hot and cool palette that she had perfected at Munstead Wood. Edging of lambs' ears and drifts of purple- and blue-toned flowers perfectly complement the stone. The water rills are planted with arum lilies, irises, and other water-loving plants, while the elevated Dutch garden is reserved for gray foliage and fragrant plants, such as lavender, rosemary, and striking *Yucca filamentosa*. Tipping (who criticized lambs' ears as dull) found the Dutch garden "rather too much an architect's, and rather too little a gardener's, garden."[21]

After years of decline, Hestercombe was sold to the Crown Estate, and in 1973, following the discovery of a set of Jekyll's original planting plans, the gardens were restored. In more recent years, the important eighteenth-century landscape garden surrounding the Lutyens and Jekyll garden was renewed by the Hestercombe Gardens Trust, which oversees the property. Hestercombe remains one of the best and most complex examples of the Lutyens and Jekyll partnership and draws visitors from around the world.

BELOW, CLOCKWISE FROM LEFT
Water rill at Hestercombe

Dutch Garden at Hestercombe

Rotunda pool at Hestercombe

OPPOSITE
Edwin Lutyens and Gertrude Jekyll, Great Plat at Hestercombe, Cheddon Fitzpaine, Somerset

157

9

BEYOND
THE BORDERS

IN AN ARTICLE ABOUT A SCOTTISH HOUSE for *Country Life*, Lawrence Weaver remarked that "the English architectural critic, on crossing the Tweed, travels into what is almost a foreign land." [1] Nevertheless, Scotland was home to one of the most distinguished of all the Arts and Crafts architects, Robert Stodart Lorimer (1864–1929), whose houses and gardens were founded on a centuries-old tradition of Scots tower houses and their walled gardens. As with Edwin Lutyens, Lorimer's architecture was championed in the pages of *Country Life*, and both architects shared a passion for materials and a romantic vision of a garden. [2] With the exception of four of Lorimer's houses in England, for which Gertrude Jekyll designed the gardens, the architect laid out the gardens for his commissions. [3]

In Scotland, attitudes toward domestic architecture were significantly different from those in England. Whereas the English house centered on the horizontality of the hall, in Scotland it was the verticality of the tower. Most of the significant castles in Scotland owe their origins to the late seventeenth century, from which Lorimer derived his own style. Garden traditions were also different from those

ABOVE
Edzell Castle, Brechin,
Angus

PREVIOUS
Kellie Castle, Pitten-
weem, Fife

in England, mainly because of the absence of the eighteenth-century landscape movement that obliterated many older English gardens. Because Scotland's climate is varied—milder on the West Coast, which benefits from the Gulf Stream, and windy and damp on the East Coast, which faces the North Sea—Scottish gardens relied on enclosure walls and hedges for windbreaks. Kitchen gardens (with stoves inside the walls to help ripen fruit in a short growing season), topiary, and splendid examples of garden architecture were hallmarks of these gardens.

Gardening arts blossomed in Scotland in the seventeenth century, but little survives prior to that period that is the equal of England's Hampton Court. Edzell Castle, perhaps the most romantic ruin in Scotland today, has one of the earliest extant gardens. Located near Forfar, on the East Coast, it was once a wealthy Scots laird's house built in the early sixteenth century. The garden, dating from 1604, consists of a walled courtyard of approximately a half-acre, with a two-story summerhouse in one corner. Unusual rectangular recesses hollowed out in the walls are thought to resemble a heraldic *fess chequé* relating to the Lindsay family's coat of arms. These recesses provide pockets for plants, and circular openings in the walls provide nesting areas for birds. Jekyll and Weaver commented that this was a device "worthy of adoption in modern walled gardens."[4] The magnificent enclosure walls also have bas-relief sculptural panels representing the planetary deities, the liberal arts, and cardinal virtues. In all, this paradise garden played a significant role in how Lorimer configured his gardens.

Lorimer was born in Edinburgh and educated at Edinburgh University (where his father was a law professor). After training with an architect in Edinburgh, Lorimer worked in G. F. Bodley's London office for several years before returning home to establish his own practice. While in London, he discovered the Morris circle and was soon swept up in the Arts and Crafts Movement. Like Ernest Gimson and other craftsman-architects, Lorimer experimented with the allied arts, such as plasterwork and embroidery, and designed baronial-style furniture that was made by local craftsmen.

As his biographer Christopher Hussey noted, Lorimer had an extraordinary grasp of detail, a craftsman's approach to architecture, and a deep understanding of Scottish traditional architecture. "He had a rare faculty of renewing the original character of an old building and yet changing it with his own personality," Hussey observed.[5] Until the 1920s, Lorimer designed a large number of Scottish country houses with outstanding decorative interiors executed locally.

Lorimer applied Reginald Blomfield's call for formalism to the heritage of Scottish gardens, with its traditional layout, furnishings, and garden architecture freely modeled after the layout at Edzell Castle. Lorimer thought that a garden should be "in tune with the house . . . a sort of sanctuary . . . to wander in, to cherish, to dream through undisturbed . . . a little pleasaunce of the soul, by whose wicket the world can be shut."[6] His ideal garden was a walled enclosure, with "little gardens within the garden, the 'month's garden,' the herb garden, the yew alley . . . the kitchen garden [with] great intersecting walks of shaven grass, . . . borders of brightest flowers backed by low espaliers hanging with shining apples."[7] Lorimer's romantic vision is strikingly similar to William Morris's at Red House.

Lorimer's first foray into garden design came during his adolescent years at Kellie Castle, near Fife, where his family spent their summers. In 1878, Lorimer's father rescued the desolate seventeenth-century tower house, then a roofless ruin in the middle of a turnip field. To celebrate the successful remodeling of the

Simon Dorrell, *Kellie Castle*, line drawing, 2003

161

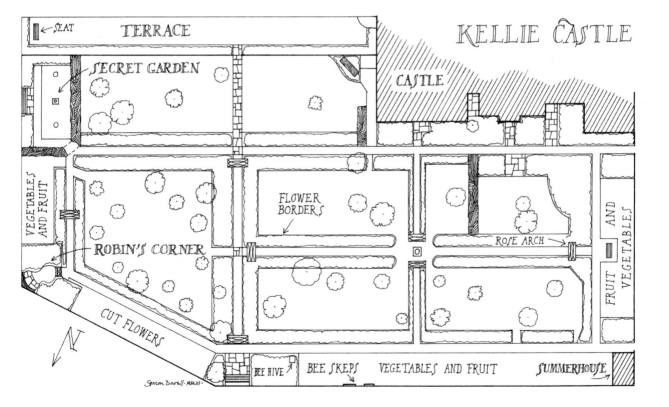

house, a Latin inscription was added over the entrance door that translates, "This mansion snatched from rooks and owls is dedicated to honest repose from labour." When the Lorimer family arrived, only the bare outlines of the one-acre garden still existed; it was seriously overgrown and the walls were crumbling. "The garden [was] still encircled by a tumbledown wall," wrote Robert's youngest sister, Louise, "a wilderness of neglected gooseberry bushes, gnarled apple trees, and old world roses, which struggled through the weeds, summer after summer, with a sweet persistence."[8] The Lorimers set out to refurbish the garden, rebuilding walls and dividing the space into compartments, with a long grass walk and a circular center for an astrolabe with a ship on top. "It converted that part, overloaded with gooseberry bushes, into an orderly and stately place."[9] Robert designed two new enclosures, including a small garden enclosed by yew hedges with topiaries and a small garden house in the northeast corner of the garth, which took on the age and appearance of the castle with the use of old slates from a farm building.

It was Louise Lorimer, Robert's mother, who was the most actively involved with the garden, planting and maintaining it for many years. Gertrude Jekyll's account of Kellie Castle in *Some English Gardens* leaves no doubt that it was an exemplary garden of roses and companion plantings. "How the flowers grow in these northern gardens," she exclaimed. "Here they must needs [*sic*] grow tall to be in scale with the high box edging [and] this is just the garden for the larger plants, [especially] single Hollyhocks in big free groups, and double Hollyhocks too."[10] Beginning in the early 1990s, the garden, now a property of the National Trust for Scotland, has been cultivated organically, with dozens of varieties of vegetables in addition to the garden flowers.[11]

One of the reasons Lorimer returned to Scotland in 1892 was that he had received his first commission to restore a ruinous late-sixteenth-century castle near Leuchars, in Fife, on the East Coast.[12] Earlshall had been purchased the previous year by Robert Mackenzie, a family friend whose interest in the Arts and Crafts Movement led him to the young architect. Lorimer completely rehabilitated the dilapidated castle,

BELOW
Robert Lorimer, topiary garden at Earlshall, Leuchars, Fife

OPPOSITE
George S. Elgood, *Kellie Castle*, watercolor (Elgood and Jekyll, 1904)

163

adding ornate interiors with paneling carved with Morris-inspired floral patterns. He also added a two-story tool house adorned with carved stone monkeys on the roof in one corner of the garden enclosure as well as a new gate lodge.

Part of Lorimer's charge was to create a garden that echoed the antiquity of the tower house. Little remained in the original enclosure, which was used for grazing livestock and surrounded by fourteen acres of parkland—a Robinsonian wild garden—that provided the ideal prelude to the garden he envisioned within the walls. "The natural park comes up to the walls of the house on the one side," Lorimer wrote, "on the other you stroll out into the garden enclosed. . . . an intentional and deliberate piece of careful design, a place that is garnished and nurtured with the tenderest care [and that] marries with the demesne that lies beyond."[13] The new gateway in the wall includes the inscription: "Here shall ye see no enemy but winter and rough weather."

A bird's-eye view of the garden shows the garden enclosed. Along the entry drive and the long grass ride that runs parallel to the west boundary wall of the enclosure, Lorimer planted a double allée of pleached lime trees. For the enclosure itself, he divided the space into five compartments, each defined by clipped holly or yew hedges. The northern section was allocated to a four-square fruit and vegetable garden, with espaliered fruit trees on the walls, wide grass walks in the center, and a line of lime trees on the eastern boundary. The southern section was divided into an orchard and bowling green or croquet lawn. A cross-axial grass walk leading to a semicircular stone arbor in the eastern wall was enclosed by high arched hedges, with ten battlemented yew alcoves filled with roses, azaleas, and fuchsias.

The main feature of the garden is the extraordinary topiary pleasaunce, positioned between the vegetable garden and the yew walk. Planted in four diagonal crosses, it was designed to be viewed from the house. To give the topiary garden a well-established appearance, Lorimer specified yews from an abandoned Edinburgh garden that were then clipped into cake stands, birds, and other traditional topiary forms.[14] The fanciful garden exuded the old-world appearance of a seventeenth-century Scottish garden, providing a worthy complement to the old house. Thus, in his first commission, Lorimer brought the tradition of old Scottish gardens back to life, and in so doing had invented a style that made his name. Earlshall represents the most enchanting, and successful, of his gardens, encapsulating all that he valued in the concept of house and garden enclosed.

Wales, separated from England by the River Severn and a boundary line meandering from Chepstow to Chester, abounds in historic parks and gardens, although most are well-kept secrets. Bodnant, Powis Castle, Erddig, and Plas Newydd are some of the better known gardens of the eighteenth and nineteenth centuries, but hidden among the hills and vales are some remarkable examples from the Arts and Crafts era.[15] In addition to Charles Edward Mallows's Craig-y-Parc and Thomas Mawson's Dyffryn near Cardiff, there are several by the architectural writer and editor H. Avray Tipping in Monmouthshire and the visionary architect Clough Williams-Ellis in North Wales.

Henry Avray Tipping (1855–1933) adopted Wales for his country homes. A man of independent means with a first in modern history from Oxford, Tipping was a connoisseur of architecture and antiques. He was also a passionate and knowledgeable gardener, having been given his first garden when he was seven years old. Most unusually for a historian, he was the author of a book about practical gardening, based on his newspaper columns. Tipping's reputation rests primarily on hundreds of definitive articles he wrote about houses for *Country Life*, beginning around 1907. Christopher Hussey observed that "Tipping brought to the writing of the articles an historical knowledge and an insistence on accuracy that gave them a new authoritativeness."[16] In addition to setting a standard for *Country Life*, Tipping compiled numerous books, including the multivolume *In English Homes*, *English Homes*, *Gardens Old and New* (with John Leyland), and one of his most popular publications, *English Gardens*.

L. Rome Guthrie, *Earlshall, Fifeshire*, line drawing, 1900 (Triggs, 1902)

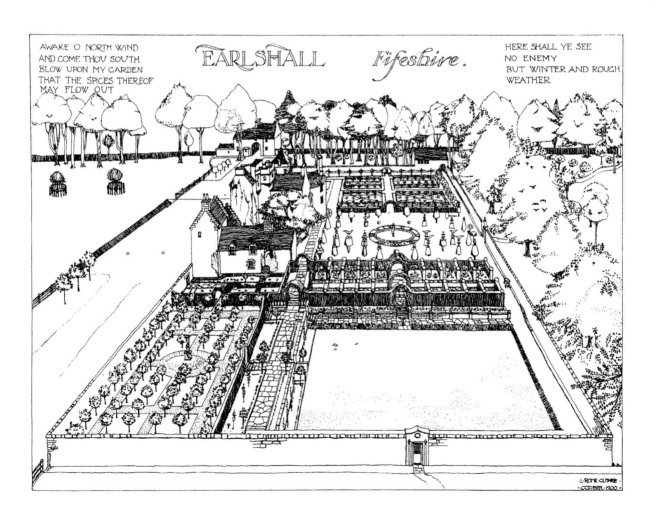

AWAKE O NORTH WIND AND COME THOU SOUTH BLOW UPON MY GARDEN THAT THE SPICES THEREOF MAY FLOW OUT

EARLSHALL   *Fifeshire*.

HERE SHALL YE SEE NO ENEMY BUT WINTER AND ROUGH WEATHER

L. ROME GUTHRIE · OCTOBER·1900 ·

Tipping's obsession with architecture and gardens played out in a succession of country homes, each of which reflected his unerring eye for design and his ability to capture a mood. When queried about the excessive costs incurred for one of them, he retorted, "You see, I do not care to keep race-horses or dancing ladies. I prefer to spend my money on walls."[17] Although he maintained a London residence, like *Country Life* editor Edward Hudson, who also had a succession of homes, Tipping yearned for the country, where he could immerse himself in architectural minutiae and gardens.

Tipping's first major home in Wales was Mathern Palace, a medieval residence in ruinous condition that had once belonged to the Bishops of Llandaff. He bought Mathern in 1894, and after carefully restoring it commented that despite the grandeur of its name, his only aim had been to create "a quiet home where the simple life may be led."[18] Unlike an architect, Tipping used a light hand in the restoration, repairing what could be saved without interfering with "the patina of age."[19] The flat site and the old farmyard enclosures provided an ideal setting for a new garden to complement the picturesque old house. Within the ancient walls he laid out a series of enclosures, with a bowling green, yew hedges, grass walks, and topiaries clipped into forms of foxes, cocks, and pheasants. "Topiary work is rather like a drink," he wrote. "Against it there are ardent prohibitionists such as William Robinson [and] outbursts of intoxicated license." He recommended the middle course of "moderate indulgence."[20] On the more sloping portion of the site, Tipping created informal rock and water gardens. In all, it was an enchanting garden, reflecting a distillation of the theories of Robinson and Jekyll.

Tipping soon became restless for another challenge, which he found nearby at Mounton House, where he began developing a naturalistic woodland garden in the steep valley and limestone gorge around 1900. A young Chepstow architect, Eric Carwardine Francis (1887–1976), a pupil of Guy Dawber and assistant to Detmar Blow, designed the house perched high on the cliff, with views of the Bristol Channel and the Mendip Hills. Together they created formal terraces around the house rivaling those at Deanery Garden in ingenuity and visual appeal. Near the house he made a long bowling green, and in another area, a reflecting pool and pergola with massive piers smothered with climbing roses and wisteria. There were more elaborate plantings in the surrounding paved gardens. To the west of the house lay the precipitous descent into the stream garden below.[21]

BELOW
H. Avray Tipping, pool and rose-covered pergola at Mounton House, Chepstow, 1917

OPPOSITE
H. Avray Tipping, Mathern Palace, Monmouthshire, 1910

167

H. Avray Tipping, High
Glanau, Monmouth,
Gwent

In 1922, Francis designed High Glanau on a site chosen for its spectacular views over Gwent. "The lie of the land," Tipping wrote, "happily suggested a dovetailing instead of a rigid boundary between the wild and the formal."[22] His design enabled the viewer to look down from the house and its formal terraces to a lily pool at the bottom of the steps or out at the view. "There is nothing really wild at Glanau," Tipping wrote. "There are woodlands . . . more or less left to native vegetation, more or less swept and garnished. It is gardening, but with nature kept in the forefront of set purpose."[23]

Luscious double herbaceous borders (or ribbon parterres), which have recently been restored by the present owners, connect the simple, low gabled house with a shelter that leads to a greenhouse beyond the wall. A second axis leads from the stone terrace, down several flights of steps, to the octagonal lily pool. The house and garden today, which look very much like the *Country Life* photographs of the 1920s, is a fine testament to Tipping's garden planning skills.

Wyndcliffe Court in Monmouthshire, built by Francis in 1922 for Charles Clay, is another example of a Tipping garden that remains largely unchanged today. The modest house, sited on a bluff overlooking the Severn estuary, is complemented by gardens that represent the impeccable planning principles of the Arts and Crafts tradition.[24] The terraces, bowling green, topiary, and sunken water garden dip deeply into Tipping's favorite vocabulary. In the topiary terrace just below the house, a semicircular pool tucked beneath the wall is reminiscent of those designed by Lutyens for Hestercombe and Deanery Garden. The bowling green on the next level down features spirals of hand-clipped yew topiaries, and a few steps below is Tipping's sunken garden, with a central pool and surrounding borders that take a cue from the pool at Hampton Court. A nicely detailed two-story summerhouse in the far corner of the sunken garden draws the eye to the distant landscape. Wyndcliffe Court is remarkable for its cozy, domestic scale, encapsulating Tipping's vision of house and garden totally dovetailed.

Clough Williams-Ellis (1883–1978) was one of the last great architects to take up the cause of the Arts and Crafts Movement. An artist by nature, he had a lifelong curiosity about architecture and boundless energy. After Trinity College in Cambridge, he trained briefly at the Architectural Association in London in 1902, but his family was skeptical of his choice of career, for architecture was thought of "as a gentlemanly hobby for the well-to-do [and] little better than plumbing as a career."[25] In particular, he was fascinated by rural cottages and old-time building methods. Like many Arts and Crafts architects, he had a fondness for regional materials, in particular the rough stone of his homeland in Wales.[26] In the Arts and Crafts tradition, he produced many beautiful watercolor perspectives and renderings for his projects, although many were lost in a fire in 1951.[27]

In 1906 he set up an office in London, where he designed model cottages and small residences in various architectural styles and remodeled old houses; after World War I, he branched out into other areas, including village design. In addition to architecture, Williams-Ellis had a lifelong passion for land conservation and preservation of the rural environment in Wales, where his family had their roots. In a curious book entitled *England and the Octopus* (1928), he wrote about urban sprawl (the octopus) encroaching on the rural countryside.[28] During his long lifetime, he developed many important friendships among architects, including Frank Lloyd Wright, who visited Williams-Ellis in 1956 on his only visit to his ancestral country.

OPPOSITE
H. Avray Tipping
and Eric Carwardine
Francis, Wyndcliffe
Court, St. Arvans,
Monmouthshire

Clough Williams-Ellis,
east terrace at Cornwell
Manor, Cornwell,
Oxfordshire

Some of his better known residential projects include a remodeling of Llangoed Hall in Powys (now a country house hotel) and Oare House in Wiltshire, for which he designed some delightful garden benches that are illustrated in Jekyll and Hussey's *Garden Ornament*, with the comment, "they are strong and simple, yet full of amusing life," which sums up Williams-Ellis's approach to architecture.[29] In 1937, he restored Cornwell village in Oxfordshire for an American client, Mrs. Anthony Gillson, who gave him carte blanche in the nine-acre garden at Cornwell Manor as well. With the exception of his own home in Wales, this is probably one of his most complete surviving gardens. He linked the village and the old manor house with a watercourse that meanders through the village and becomes more formalized in the

house grounds, widening into several pools and a long canal. He also extended the view of the house from the public road through a line of trees in the park opposite. On the terrace near the house, a small garden with clipped Portuguese laurels and a fiddler statue in the center add a note of formality in contrast to the rock and bog gardens surrounding the lower watercourse.

Williams-Ellis's most lasting contribution, where all of his diverse ideas coalesced, was the creation of Portmeirion, a model village built on the coast of Snowdonia between 1926 and 1976. Plas Brondanw, Williams-Ellis's home nearby, has one of the best-preserved Arts and Crafts gardens in Britain, one that reinforces the critical relationship of house, garden, and surrounding landscape.

Clough Williams-Ellis, Plas Brondanw, Llan-frothen, Gwynedd

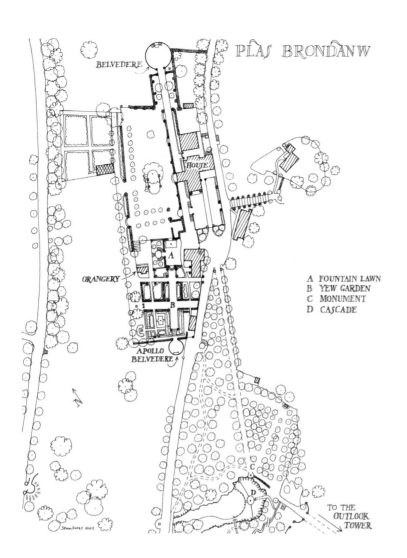

PLAS BRONDANW

BELVEDERE

HOUSE

ORANGERY

A FOUNTAIN LAWN
B YEW GARDEN
C MONUMENT
D CASCADE

APOLLO
BELVEDERE

TO THE
OUTLOOK
TOWER

174

As Hussey noted, "[It] is at Brondanw, much better than at Portmeirion, its fantastic off-shoot, that we can see the original fundamental Clough."[30] When he was twenty-five years old, and in his "antiquarian phase," Williams-Ellis received Plas Brondanw as a gift from his family. The gray stone house, dating from the seventeenth century, had long been abandoned. Over the next decades, he poured his energy and income into rehabilitating the old house and creating a garden on the steeply falling ground. Beginning in 1908, he used the local bluish-purple stone to build walls and terraces around the house and added a gate lodge and orangery around 1914. Plas Brondanw was substantially rebuilt in 1951 after a fire destroyed the home and most of Williams-Ellis's records.

The garden is ingenious for its control in providing vistas to the Snowdonia mountain range, notably Cnicht peak. Two main axes, a walkway to the northeast that terminates in the belvedere roundel overlooking Cnicht, and the other to the Apollo belvedere overlooking the quarry pool, are lined with green hedges or topiary, with little emphasis on flowers that would detract from the panoramic views. The flower garden, filled primarily with blue hydrangeas and blue-green hostas, is hidden behind the hedged compartments. A cross-axis in the yew garden looks to a carefully framed view of Moel Hebog in the distance. Delicate iron gates and stair railings are painted a special blue-green that sizzles against the green lawn. An oblong fountain pool with a statue of a fireboy by sculptor Gertrude Knoblock, benches, clipped topiaries, arched hedges, Italian cypresses, and statuary accentuate the strongly architectural layout.[31] Like the homes of other proponents of the Arts and Crafts Movement, Williams-Ellis's Plas Brondanw provides the best expression of his individuality.

ABOVE
Simon Dorrell, *Plas Brondanw*, line drawing, 2003

OPPOSITE, CLOCKWISE FROM TOP LEFT
Apollo in terrace garden at Plas Brondanw

Fireboy fountain and pool

Topiary and orangery

Staircase leading to garden

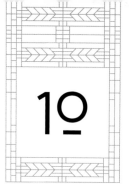

CRAFTSMAN STYLE

THE BRITISH ARTS AND CRAFTS MOVEMENT had a dramatic impact on international design, thanks to its widespread exposure in magazines and books as well as the strong presence of its founding leaders. In America, architects and designers were swept away by the Cotswolds' ideal of craftsmanship and the concept of integrated house and garden. *Country Life in America*, *House and Garden*, *House Beautiful*, and other home and garden publications regularly featured the work of British architects. In the early 1900s, when large Beaux-Arts estates were proliferating across the country, a dedicated group of architects and designers began heralding smaller, simpler houses with intimately scaled, naturalistic gardens. Built with indigenous materials with regional variations, these houses and their ancillary garden structures embraced the Arts and Crafts Movement's aesthetic of rusticity and the vernacular.

The American Arts and Crafts Movement reflected the country's melting pot of nationalities and its diverse geography, typically developing symbiotic relationships with firmly established regional traditions. In the Northeast and the South, it attached itself to the deeply entrenched Colonial Revival Movement, which harked back to colonial

BELOW
Rookwood tile in grotto
at Greenwood Gardens,
Short Hills, New Jersey

BOTTOM
Dard Hunter, *The
Peristyle of the Roycroft
Inn* (*The Roycrofter*,
January 1928)

PREVIOUS
Modern roses in the
grotto at Greenwood
Gardens

America, with clapboard houses and romantic, old-fashioned gardens and quaint garden furnishings. In the Midwest, it was linked to the Prairie School, notably in the work of Frank Lloyd Wright and his followers, and landscape architects such as Jens Jensen and Ossian Cole Simonds, who embraced William Robinson's call for wild gardening with native plants.[1] In California, where the Bungalow style reigned as the ideal Arts and Crafts home, naturalistic gardens with native plants were more appropriate than formal, English-style gardens.

Although these are only broad generalizations, the American movement was dissipated, and few houses and gardens could rival those in Britain. The Arts and Crafts Movement had a greater impact on architecture and its allied arts than it did on garden design, where its influence surfaced in details rather than overall concept. In Boston, Chicago, New York, and California, the primary hubs of the movement, Arts and Crafts communities sprang up to carry on William Morris's call for artistic reform and joy in manual work. As a result, the American Arts and Crafts Movement has come to be identified with simple oak furniture, decorative pottery and tiles, textiles, book arts, and metalwork, as well as distinctive regional architecture. One of the realms in which the American movement outshone its British mentors was in art pottery, where Rookwood, Grueby, Newcomb, Paul Revere, Batchelder, and other potteries specialized in soft, subtle glazes and simplified floral and landscape motifs. On the other end of the spectrum, Tiffany Studios became synonymous with dazzling, three-dimensional stained-glass panels and lampshades decorated with wisteria, irises, and other flowers in heavenly garden settings.

In 1906, an American writer observed that the Arts and Crafts Movement "had been necessarily somewhat slow in this country, as many have opposed its teachings. However, the strong personality of a few craftsmen has, by protest and example, shown the value of beauty of form and finish."[2] One of those strong personalities was Elbert Hubbard (1856–1915), whose Roycroft community in East Aurora, New York, was founded in direct response to Morris's example. A former soap salesman, Hubbard

realized his dream to found a craft enterprise on the premise that "life without industry is guilt—industry without art is brutality." From 1895 on, the renowned Roycroft Press produced publications ranging from utilitarian tracts such as *The Philistine* and *Little Journeys* to hand-printed volumes illustrated by the famed book designer Dard Hunter. In its heyday, Hubbard employed more than 200 artisans, or Roycrofters, who produced hand-hammered metalwork, hand-printed books, and hand-built furniture in the Roycroft shops that were sold nationwide. After Hubbard's death in the sinking of the *RMS Lusitania*, Roycroft was taken over by his son, but it foundered shortly thereafter when the appeal of such products had greatly diminished.

Gustav Stickley (1858–1942), often regarded as the "American William Morris," had an overwhelming influence on middle-class American homeowners through *The Craftsman* magazine, which reached households from coast to coast between 1901 and 1916, the peak years of the American Arts and Crafts Movement. *The Craftsman* extolled the work of English architects

VOL. XX, No. 1   APRIL, 1911   25 CENTS

THE CRAFTSMAN

"The lyf so short, the craft so long to lerne"

OUR GARDEN NUMBER

E.J.R

THE PHILOSOPHY OF GARDENS: BY WALTER A. DYER
THE GROWING INDIVIDUALITY OF THE AMERICAN GARDEN
BEAUTY AND USE OF PERGOLAS IN AMERICAN GARDENS
RUSTIC FEATURES FOR LITTLE KITCHEN GARDENS
FORTY-ONE-WEST-THIRTY-FOURTH-STREET-NEW-YORK

Cover of *The Craftsman*, April 1911

and helped translate their ideas into an American Craftsman style. Stickley also offered a line of Craftsman Homes, or inexpensive model bungalows, with regional variations from California Mission style to a mountain camp or a half-timbered cement cottage. A furniture maker, metalworker, and stone mason himself, Stickley founded a furniture workshop in Syracuse, New York, after meeting C. F. A. Voysey and C. R. Ashbee in England in 1898. Like many American artisans and architects, he subscribed to *The International Studio*, which acquainted him with Voysey, M. H. Baillie Scott, and Ashbee, and the Guild of Handicraft became a personal inspiration for him.

In 1908, Stickley embarked on Craftsman Farms, a cooperative communal venture located in northern New Jersey, joining the ranks of "American artists, reformers, writers, and architects who were seeking to remake the world," according to his biographer Mark Alan Hewitt.[3] Stickley's utopian community embodied many of the ideals of the American Arts and Crafts Movement—in particular, the virtues of the simple life, manual labor in crafts, and the nurturing of the unspoiled rural countryside—but it went bankrupt in 1915. It was here that Stickley manufactured his distinctive oak furniture for sale in showrooms in New York

City. At Craftsman Farms, he constructed a rustic house from chestnut logs gathered on the property, with a clay tile roof and a huge stone chimney. The living room, which one writer dubbed "nobly barbaric" for its massive rough-hewn posts, was furnished with products made in the workshops, and the color scheme ran to somber browns, greens, and gold.[4] Naturalistically planted boxwood, arborvitae, and barberry blended harmoniously with the log house in its rural hillside setting, and vineyards, peach and apple orchards, beds filled with gaily colored cosmos and petunias, and vegetable gardens provided a sense of self-sufficiency.

The pages of *The Craftsman* promoted the natural garden as opposed to what Stickley termed "the rich man's garden, ostentatious, spectacular, sumptuous."[5] The house, he said, should be set in the midst of the garden.

Let garden and house float together in one harmonious whole, the one finding completion in the other. . . . A garden must be spontaneous—allowed to spring from the ground in a natural way—otherwise it is devoid of that irresistible

something called style, for style is born of the shaping of use and beauty to environment. . . . Let your garden look as if it had grown of its own accord, as if Nature herself had been your architect, your landscape gardener, your designer in chief.[6]

BELOW
Flower borders at
Craftsman Farms, 1914

OPPOSITE
Craftsman Farms,
Parsippany, New Jersey

In an ideal garden, no one should be able to tell where the house ends and the gardens begin. Pergolas, he advised, were an ideal connection between the house and the healthful outdoors; they served gracefully to screen unattractive buildings, lead visitors from one area to the next, and provide outdoor living spaces and pleasant retreats. Stickley's advice was far-ranging in defining the Craftsman style of gardens.

Not far from Craftsman Farms, Baillie Scott designed The Close, a half-timbered courtyard house in Short Hills, New Jersey, in 1912.[7] A well-heeled community within commuting distance to New York City, Short Hills in the 1910s and 1920s thrived on grand houses and gardens that Stickley would have dismissed

as the "rich man's garden." The client, Henry Binsse, had spotted the article about Baillie Scott's work at Runton Old Hall in *House Beautiful* in 1911 and decided he wanted something of an old English inn for his own house.[8] It could not have been more different from Craftsman Farms, with its pale rose–colored stucco façade, half-timbering, leaded glass casement windows, and decorative lead rainwater heads. The Close is enclosed by low stucco walls, with a garden house next to the gated entry drive. The interior courtyard has simple flower borders, with a more formal treatment at the main entrance; elaborate English-style flower gardens once stood to one side of the house.

It is hard to know what Stickley might have thought of Pleasant Days, the Short Hills home of New York real-estate mogul Joseph P. Day. Now known as Greenwood Gardens, the surviving grounds provide an excellent example of regional Arts and Crafts sensibilities. The fanciful twenty-eight–room stucco mansion was designed around 1911 by William Whetten Renwick (1864–1933), a nephew of the famous Gothic Revival architect, James Renwick, Jr. William Renwick was not only a talented architect, but also a sculptor and painter who had studied at the École des Beaux-Arts in Paris. The exterior and interiors of Pleasant Days as well as the garden were enhanced with his innovative polychrome fresco-relief panels and custom-made Rookwood tiles. Renwick's distinctive metope-like bas-relief panels decorated the exterior of the once-amazing house with its distinctive undulating gray-green whaleback slate roof. The whole house was alive with decorative birds and flowers, bringing the pleasures of the summer gardens indoors.

The surviving garden structures, including a rustic stone teahouse and summerhouse, in addition to the foundation walls, water cascade, and other features, still retain their Arts and Crafts decorations. The formal gardens on the south side of the house consist of a series of grass terraces with ornamental pools and fountain figures. The Garden of the Gods is framed by a semicircular pergola enclosed by openwork trellises and polychrome herms on pedestals. Other pergolas serve to connect the house with the garden and provide pleasant walkways. Day's fortune vanished during the Great Depression,

BELOW
M. H. Baillie Scott, *House [The Close] at Short Hills, New Jersey* (*Studio Yearbook of Decorative Art*, 1914)

BOTTOM
William Whetten Renwick, *House and Garden at Pleasant Days [Greenwood Gardens]*, Short Hills, New Jersey, ca. 1924

182

and years later the crumbling house was torn down and replace with a smaller, more conventional house. The surviving gardens are an extraordinary example of the diversity and ingenuity of individual Arts and Crafts designers.[9]

Chicago was an unusually fertile area for the American Arts and Crafts Movement. Not only was it home to the Prairie School of architecture, but also the prestigious architectural publication *House Beautiful*, whose first issue in 1896 featured the work of Voysey and Ashbee. The Chicago Arts and Crafts Society, one of the oldest in the country, was established in 1897 at Jane Addams's Hull House. Frank Lloyd Wright (1867–1959), who was among the charter members, delivered his famous lecture, "The Art and Craft of the Machine," there in 1901. The society's annual exhibitions of members' work fueled many industries, such as pottery, textiles, bookbinding, jewelry, and metalwork. Ashbee's link to Chicago began in 1898, when some of his jewelry was exhibited in one of the society's exhibitions, and he personally came to Chicago two years later, the first of several trips to America.[10]

Rustic teahouse at
Greenwood Gardens

Chicago was especially renowned for its architecture, which dramatically shifted in focus from Beaux-Arts, as exemplified at the World's Columbian Exposition in 1893, to a new agenda as devised by Wright, whose organic approach to design revolutionized the American home. Wright, who was unusually verbose about his personal life and architectural goals, was in many ways a disciple of Morris. He sought harmony between architecture and the natural landscape and even recommended Gertrude Jekyll's book *Home and Garden* for its special approach to homebuilding ("It should be in every library").[11] Evocative renderings by Marion Mahoney Griffin of his early houses include lush, stylized landscapes, with swags of wisteria framing the all-important views to his buildings. Wright-designed planters overflow with trailing vines that accentuate the long, low lines of his Prairie style houses, such as the 1908 Robie House in Chicago. His compounds at Taliesin in Spring Green, Wisconsin, and Taliesin West in the Arizona desert were founded on principles deriving from the Arts and Crafts Movement.

Frank Lloyd Wright and Ellen Shipman, Graycliff Estate, Derby, New York

Wright was not known for collaborating with landscape architects, but at the request of his clients, Darwin and Isabelle Martin, Ellen Shipman was invited to provide additional design input for the couple's lakeside house near Buffalo, New York. Wright designed Graycliff in 1928–29, a volatile time for wealthy industrialists, many of whom lost their fortunes during the Great Depression. His initial designs for the grounds included sketches for the dramatic entrance water garden, which Shipman later modified, and other landscape features that she removed. The Martins' decision to hire Shipman was based on her renown as a landscape architect. Her design scheme specified groups of trees and shrubs around the forecourt, a naturalistic evergreen garden filled with swaths of lilies, an intricate flower garden, and other areas of the steep lakefront property that rose seventy feet (twenty-one meters) above Lake Erie. In the end, Wright's low, sweeping house in his later period Prairie-style architecture was beautifully complemented by Shipman's landscape. It is an excellent example of how American designers embraced the principles of the Arts and Crafts Movement while respecting regional aesthetics and traditions.

Other, less famous Chicago architects were also influenced by the Arts and Crafts Movement. Howard Van Doren Shaw (1869–1926), who designed country houses in Lake Forest and other fashionable suburbs ringing Chicago, was a devoted Anglophile and conversant with his British contemporaries. Ragdale, Shaw's summer house and country retreat for his growing family, is located in a once-rural farm property with an old apple orchard and views to acres of meadows. Today it is hailed as "one of the finest examples of Arts and Crafts architecture in America, because it has remained untouched and is well preserved."[12] The twin-gabled white stucco house, with low, sweeping roofs and wood shutters with heart motifs, bears a striking resemblance to Voysey's own house, The Orchard, built the following year. The interior is unpainted oak, with light and airy rooms, inglenooks, and fireplaces; the dining room was once papered with one of Voysey's patterns. Porches around the house link it with the gardens and the distant meadows.

In comparison with Shaw's more classically inspired gardens, Ragdale is more homespun and personal. Over the years, he and his family enhanced the grounds with kitchen and vegetable gardens, flower gardens, a bowling green, and an outdoor theatre, known as the Ragdale Ring, where audiences watched performances by his wife, Frances Wells Shaw.[13] The pleasant flower garden has cross-axial paths, a flourishing grape arbor, a wellhead, and an English-inspired dovecote at one end. At the center of the garden enclosure, a sundial, designed by Shaw, is inscribed "Hours Fly. Flowers Die. New Ways. New Days. Pass By. Love Stays." Shaw's garden planning at Ragdale fits within the parameters laid down by Morris and Robinson, with its essential combination of work and leisure and its harmonious link with nature, where informal lanes rambled through the woods to the meadows beyond.[14]

ABOVE
Dovecote in the flower
garden at Ragdale

PREVIOUS
Howard Van Doren
Shaw, Ragdale, Lake
Forest, Illinois

Bloomfield Hills, Michigan, is a design mecca that extends into the Modern Movement. The founding of the Cranbrook Academy of Art in the 1920s marked the beginning of an essential moment in American architecture and decorative arts. The campus was designed by Eliel Saarinen (1873–1950), who brought his extensive experience in the Arts and Crafts Movement in Finland to the United States. Saarinen House, which was completed in 1930 and now serves as the home for the academy's president, is furnished throughout with Saarinen's designs. The courtyard garden, designed by C. Deforest Platt, was filled with roses and other climbers as well as ornamental shrubs.[15] Cranbrook would never have been founded without the visionaries Ellen and George Booth, whose interest in landscape gardening and involvement with the American Arts and Crafts Movement made the project happen. Their residence, Cranbrook House, was built in 1908 by noted Detroit architect Albert Kahn. Built in an English Tudor style, the design was inspired by British Arts and Crafts architecture. The Booths commissioned the furnishings from American and European workshops. The extensive naturalistic gardens were laid out by Ossian Cole Simonds (1855–1931), a well-known regional landscape architect and the author of *Landscape Gardening* (1920). The landscape includes a number of features, but of interest are the Arts and Crafts–inspired herb garden and walled garden as well as rustic bridges and summerhouses.

In California, the American Arts and Crafts Movement found its greatest fulfillment. The land of golden opportunity, California is renowned for its delightful climate and the promise of healthful living. Wealthy industrialists looking for vacation homes and artists alike were attracted to the sweeping views of mountains, the sparkling sunshine, and fresh air that were in short supply in large cities such as Chicago, Boston, and New York. The climate varied considerably, from hot and desertlike in the south to cool and moist in the San Francisco Bay Area. In architecture, the Spanish influence prevailed, with its indigenous adobe Mission architecture, coupled with the outdoor lifestyle brought by Mexican settlers. Mission Revival houses and gardens were to California what the Colonial Revival was to the Northeast. Gardens are ideally suited to the West Coast, where the Mediterranean climate lends itself to outdoor living, with terraces and courtyards. Walled enclosures surrounding the house range from a simple courtyard to a series of garden rooms, each with a different theme. The English influence was not a strong consideration in California, where gardens tended to be informal. Californians also had a special bond with nature and a wonderful palette of plants both native and imported.

California also had its fair share of visionaries, such as Charles Fletcher Lummis (1859–1928), whose passion for California missions and Spanish culture in general led him to build an extraordinary house, El Alisal (The Place of Sycamores), in Pasadena in 1898. Constructed from round boulders collected from the Arroyo Seco, the house overlooked a true Robinsonian wildflower meadow. In that same year in Berkeley, the poet Charles Augustus Keeler formed the Hillside Club, an improvement society aimed at transforming the Berkeley hills into a lush, natural-istic landscape. Keeler teamed up with architect Bernard R. Maybeck (1862–1957) to build his own house, which he hoped his neighbors would emulate. Keeler's 1904 book, *The Simple Home*, became somewhat of a bible for his ideas regarding housing design. About gardens, he wrote, "My own preference for a garden for the simple home is a compromise between the natural and formal types—a compro-mise in which the carefully studied plan is concealed by a touch of careless grace that makes it appear as if nature had unconsciously made bowers and paths and sheltering hedges."[16] Maybeck was known for his highly original structures in the

Albert Kahn and O. C. Simonds, Cranbrook House and Garden, Bloomfield Hills, Michigan

Greene and Greene,
David B. Gamble
House, Pasadena,
California

San Francisco Bay Area, especially in Berkeley, which were built from local materials. His hallmark wisteria-covered trellises merge imperceptibly with the timber-framed buildings.

California's distinctive architecture was formulated around the California bungalow, which featured porches, terraces, and outdoor spaces. A number of architects left their marks on the California landscape, but none more so than Charles Sumner Greene (1868–1957) and his brother, Henry Mather Greene (1870–1954). In many ways, Greene and Greene were comparable to the Barnsley brothers in England, as they were both architects and woodworkers. Born in Ohio and educated in manual arts in St. Louis, they studied architecture at the Massachusetts Institute of Technology in Cambridge and later apprenticed with Boston architects. Upon opening their first office in Pasadena in 1894, they created some of the most brilliant examples of Arts and Crafts architecture in the country, demonstrating their exquisite workmanship, detailing, and planning. Rejecting the prevailing Beaux-Arts approach to design, they were particularly influenced by the simplicity of Japanese architecture and furniture.[17]

ABOVE
Charles Sumner Greene,
water garden at Green
Gables, Woodside,
California

OPPOSITE
Rustic stone grotto at
Green Gables

Charles Sumner Greene traveled to Britain in 1901, where he was exposed to the Arts and Crafts Movement, visiting, among other places, the Glasgow International Exhibition where Charles Rennie Mackintosh's work was displayed. Regular subscribers to *The Craftsman* magazine, the brothers began designing furnishings for their architectural commissions in 1904. After visiting Charles's workshops in 1909, C. R. Ashbee wrote, "I think C. Sumner Greene's work beautiful; among the best there is in this country . . . beautiful cabinets and chairs [executed with] a supreme feeling for the material, quite up to our best English craftsmanship."[18]

The David B. Gamble House in Pasadena, designed in 1908, features exquisite detailing both inside and out, sensitive grading, and Japanese-inspired landscaping. As Henry recalled, "we were able to do our best design when we could control a complete landscape and then decorate it, as well as the house. This is the only possible way to achieve integration of all three."[19] The terraces, which function as outdoor living spaces, hug the low, cantilevered house on three sides, under a canopy of California live oaks (*Quercus agrifolia*). Live oaks figure in Charles's magnificent teak-framed front door with its iridescent glass panels that were executed by local craftsmen. The interior is fully furnished with Greene and Greene furniture, paneling, and lighting fixtures. The Blacker House, designed in 1907 and also located in Pasadena, is noted for its Japanese-inspired garden that melds beautifully with the architecture. Charles commented, "fine gardens are like fine pictures, only it may take longer to paint them with nature's brush."[20]

Green Gables in Woodside is Charles Sumner Greene's masterpiece of landscape architecture. Designed for Mortimer Fleishhacker in 1911, the long, low house is sited in the midst of seventy-five acres of rolling meadow dotted with live oaks and views to the Santa Cruz Mountains. Charles, who envisioned the garden as a series of living rooms for the house, created terraces and reflecting pools to capitalize on the expansive views. In 1926 he designed a spectacular water garden in a problematic area where the site dropped off dramatically. His brilliant 300-foot-long (91 meters) pool terminates in a series of stone arches reminiscent of a Roman aqueduct. The garden, in fact, quotes many sites in Italy, England, and America. Looking back to the house from the lower garden, one sees a rustic stone grotto nestled between the massive horseshoe staircases ascending to the upper terrace. The lower garden is constructed in a warm-toned stone in a vernacular style of craftsmanship. The skillful planting of native and imported plants with strong architectural interest complements the rustic stonework in the staircases and paths. David C. Streatfield, the preeminent scholar of California gardens, believes that Green Gables is the largest garden in the country by an Arts and Crafts designer.[21] It is certainly one of the most significant and remains unchanged today.

BEAUTIFUL GARDENS IN AMERICA

IN HER 1915 BOOK, *BEAUTIFUL GARDENS IN AMERICA*, Louise Shelton asked, "Just as there are gardens peculiar to other nations . . . might we not give serious consideration to evolving someday a type particularly American [that embodies] the poetic and artistic sense of our country?"[1] For the same reasons that the American Arts and Crafts Movement was regional, the many differences in climate, plant palette, and heritage across the country could never develop into a national garden style. In the Northeast, the tradition of old-fashioned gardens, based to some extent on those of the early English settlers, was deeply entrenched. These gardens were companionable with eighteenth-century houses as well as new houses built along traditional lines. Sometimes called grandmother's gardens, they were captured on canvas by many well-known American Impressionist artists.[2] Historian and antiquarian Alice Morse Earle (1851–1911) was one of the first to recognize these uniquely American gardens. Her books, such as *Old Time Gardens Newly Set Forth* (1901) and *Sun-Dials and Roses of Yesterday* (1902), present nostalgic views of the colonial era embodied by the Colonial Revival. The Colonial Revival Movement, which focused on architecture and

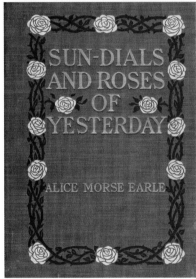

TOP
Louise Shelton, cover
of *Beautiful Gardens in
America*, 1915

ABOVE
Alice Morse Earle,
cover of *Sun-Dials
and Roses of Yesterday*,
1902

PREVIOUS
Florence Griswold
Museum, Old Lyme,
Connecticut

interior design, was a pervasive element in American cultural history, embracing an idealized view of the nation's past. In some respects, it was a reaction to nineteenth-century industrialization, the same force that galvanized Morris into action decades earlier in England.

Colonial Revival gardens are characterized by their straightforward geometric configuration, linear pathways, sundials and other traditional ornament, and features such as arbors and fences for enclosure. Billowing flower borders edged with boxwood, fragrant shrubs and vines, and fruit trees are memorable elements. The key to these gardens is their domestic scale and simplicity, which was the dominant aesthetic of gardens designed by homeowners in the Northeast. Landscape architects were more likely to respond to European Beaux-Arts and classical prototypes in grander estates.

The rediscovery of America's past in the Northeast came with an explosion of interest in gardening and a proliferation of popular books aimed at a largely female audience. Written mostly by New Englanders, books such as Helena Rutherfurd Ely's *A Woman's Hardy Garden* (1903) and Mabel Osgood Wright's *The Garden, You, and I* (1906) reached out to women who sought not only a pastime, but an outlet for their creative energy. These authors addressed the practical side along with the therapeutic rewards of gardening.[3] Most of the women who read these books managed households far smaller than the large Victorian estates of the mid-nineteenth century, where garden upkeep required teams of gardeners.

In 1893, the preeminent architectural critic Mariana Griswold Van Rensselaer (1851–1934) brought aristocratic recognition to gardening arts with her book *Art Out-of-Doors: Hints on Good Taste in Gardening*, which argued for consideration of gardening as an art. She defined the landscape gardener as "a gardener, an engineer, and an artist, who like an architect considers beauty and utility together."[4] This idea spurred a new field for women as garden designers and eventually landscape architects, a profession in which Beatrix Farrand, Ellen Shipman, and others excelled in the early 1900s. As opposed to the firms whose male designers specialized in parks and large estates, women designers found their own niche in creating small residential gardens that were distinguished by sophisticated plantings and architectural features inspired by the Arts and Crafts Movement.[5]

Around the same time, artists' colonies began springing up along the East Coast. One of the earliest and most significant was the Lyme Art Colony in Old Lyme, Connecticut. Today it is better known as the Florence Griswold Museum, named after the woman who established a boarding house there around 1900, which was frequented by visiting artists. Among the most famous residents was

Childe Hassam, known for his paintings of landscapes and gardens, most notably Celia Thaxter's island garden in Maine. Other visiting artists included Cecilia Beaux, the renowned Philadelphia portrait painter who was also affiliated with a smaller colony on Eastern Point in Gloucester, Massachusetts.[6] Griswold was an avid gardener who over the years created a classic grandmother's garden that many of the resident artists painted. Borders were filled with informal groupings of holly-hocks, irises, foxgloves, heliotropes, phlox, and daylilies. In the garden's heyday, two areas were devoted to summer flowers, another to roses, and a fourth to vegetables and herbs. These so-called old-fashioned gardens, once described as a veritable tangle of fragrant beauty, provided an enchanting setting for visiting artists.

The Cornish Colony in New Hampshire was also renowned for its gardens as well as its resident artists. Located in an area of exceptional natural beauty on the banks of the Connecticut River and overlooking Mount Ascutney in Vermont, the colony revolved around the American Renaissance sculptor Augustus Saint-Gaudens (1843–1907), who arrived in 1885, seeking relief from the summer heat of his New York City studio. His garden melded the Colonial Revival aesthetic in its configuration and plantings with pergolas, benches, and other

Augustus Saint-Gaudens, flower gardens at Saint-Gaudens National Historic Site, Cornish, New Hampshire

197

BELOW
Rose Standish Nichols,
Mastlands, Cornish,
New Hampshire, 1906

BOTTOM
Charles A. Platt, *Lark-spur [Garden at High Court]*, oil on canvas, 1895

classically inspired ornament. Saint-Gaudens in turn attracted other artists, such as Charles Platt, Thomas Dewing, and Stephen Parrish, who all created trendsetting gardens. In 1906, one critic declared that Cornish enjoyed the distinction of being "the most beautifully gardened village in all America."[7]

No one did more to mold the Cornish style of gardening than Charles Adams Platt (1861–1933), an etcher and landscape painter who later turned to garden design and architecture, building nearly a dozen significant houses in the colony.[8] Platt developed an architectural style that always ensured the intimate relationship of house and garden, with brick terraces and indoor-outdoor areas, such as loggias that framed the views out. His axial gardens, screened by masses of shrubbery to control these all-important views, were filled with luxurious flowers. Platt's protégées Ellen Shipman and Rose Nichols, both Cornish neighbors he tutored in design, carried on his work in a special style of gardening.

Rose Standish Nichols (1872–1960), a Boston landscape architect and the niece of Saint-Gaudens, specialized in flower gardens and often collaborated with architects, including Howard Van Doren Shaw and David Adler. As a young woman, Nichols toured England, where she studied briefly with F. Inigo Thomas as well as Platt in Cornish. Her 1902 book, *English Pleasure Gardens*, revealed the depth of her knowledge of English garden history and her unfailing critical eye as a designer. Writing about Gertrude Jekyll's garden, for example, she commented, "It is seldom that both wild and cultivated flowers have been grouped more successfully."[9] Pen-and-ink drawings that she created for her book are executed in the style of Thomas's illustrations for Reginald Blomfield's *The Formal Garden in England*. Nichols's reverence for the revival of the Elizabethan style, with its walled enclosures, green courts, pavilions, and wealth of flowers, surfaces in her own commissions.[10] In the 1890s, she designed a large walled garden at Mastlands, her family's summer home in Cornish. The low stone walls with seats notched into them enclosed a neatly ordered garden filled with dozens of beds filled with summer perennials. She chose an old

apple tree near the center of the garden as a focal point and designed a circular pool under its boughs. One writer dubbed it "one of the most delightful gardens in all artist-inhabited and garden-loving Cornish."[11]

The garden of Stephen Parrish (1846–1938) represents the pinnacle of Cornish gardening, from its overall conception to its skillful planting. Located on the side of an exposed hillside, where gardening was especially challenging, Parrish's Northcote exemplifies the true mingling of house and garden. A landscape painter and the father of Maxfield Parrish (who illustrated Edith Wharton's *Italian Villas and Their Gardens*), Parrish nestled his picturesque flower garden against the L-shaped house, designed by the Philadelphia architect Wilson Eyre. It was further sheltered by arbors festooned with wild grapes and Virginia creeper. In midsummer, the garden was filled with hollyhocks, lilies, hardy phlox, and poppies, all stalwarts of traditional New England gardens. Today, the tradition of Cornish gardening lives on in small residential gardens that capitalize on the historic tradition, the wealth of New England plants, and the breathtaking views of the countryside.

The English overlay in East Coast gardens was an equally strong factor in garden design. English-inspired knot gardens, geometrically hedged green gardens, and perennial borders went well with Tudor Revival houses that proliferated in 1920s America. The intricate Elizabethan-style knot garden at

ABOVE LEFT
Stephen Parrish, Anne Parrish in the garden at Northcote, Cornish, New Hampshire, 1898

ABOVE RIGHT
Stephen Parrish, *Garden Staircase [Northcote]*, oil on canvas, ca. 1907

Thornedale, in Millbrook, New York, designed by landscape architect Nellie B. Allen (1869–1960) in 1934 for Mrs. Oakleigh Thorne, reflects the designer's personal reverence for English gardens. A devotee of Jekyll, Allen was a frequent visitor to Munstead Wood and other English gardens such as the famed topiary gardens at Great Dixter.[12]

Agecroft Hall in Richmond, Virginia, boasts not only an Elizabethan-style knot garden, but also a sunken parterre that resembles the Privy Garden at Hampton Court. Unlike the Tudor-style mansions that were all the rage in the 1920s, Agecroft Hall is an actual fifteenth-century half-timbered manor house that was dismantled and transported from England to Virginia in 1925. The grounds were laid out by Charles Freeman Gillette (1886–1969), a landscape architect who had trained in the office of Warren Manning, to complement the house. Located in Windsor Farms, an elite subdivision in Richmond, the twenty-three-acre estate overlooks the James River, which Gillette capitalized on for his scheme for the grounds. The upper terrace has a boxwood-enclosed garden, while the lower terrace has a sunken parterre garden with a central fountain and lush flower borders. The knot garden is filled with fragrant herbs, harking back to the past. Gillette, who was an Anglophile, owed much of his design sensibilities to his admiration of Edwin Lutyens and the planting theories of Jekyll.[13]

In general, topiary and fanciful clipped hedges, which are often the backbone of any English-style garden, are somewhat unusual in American gardens, primarily because of the hot, dry summers and the necessary maintenance. One of the earlier and most famous is Horatio Hollis Hunnewell's lakeside topiary garden in Wellesley, Massachusetts, reputedly modeled after the garden at Elvaston Castle in Derbyshire, England. Hunnewell, a wealthy railroad financier, developed the extensive estate grounds, including an extensive pinetum, in the mid-nineteenth century. William Robinson, who visited the Hunnewell Estate in 1870 on an extended trip to America, undoubtedly was more interested in the pinetum and

champion trees than the topiary. Ladew Topiary Gardens, in Monkton, Maryland, and Green Animals in Rhode Island are equally famous. Ladew Gardens were created by Harvey Ladew in the late 1920s as an ode to fox hunting in the heart of Maryland hunt country. Hounds and birds, as well as garden rooms filled with billowing hedges trimmed as garlands or sculpted obelisks, continue to enchant visitors. Ladew, a devoted Anglophile who regularly visited England's great houses and gardens and attended hunts, enjoyed friendships with the Duke and Duchess of Windsor, among others.

Unquestionably, Jekyll's books left an indelible mark on American gardeners. As Louise Beebe Wilder, one of America's most important garden writers, wrote, "Miss Jekyll made us believe ourselves artists in embryo with a color box to our hands and a canvas ready stretched before us."[14] American gardeners, however, found the practical application of Jekyll's advice difficult to achieve in their widely variable climates, as Wilder explained in *Colour in My Garden* (1918).

ABOVE
Harvey Ladew, hunt scene topiary at Ladew Gardens, Monkton, Maryland

OPPOSITE TOP
Nellie B. Allen, knot garden at Thornedale, Millbrook, New York, 1934

OPPOSITE MIDDLE
Charles Gillette, sunken garden at Agecroft Hall, Richmond, Virginia

OPPOSITE BOTTOM
Horatio Hollis Hunnewell, topiary garden at the Hunnewell Estate, Wellesley, Massachusetts

Wilder recounts her own trials and occasional minor successes with Jekyll's recommendations in America's shorter, hotter, and drier summers. Flowers bloomed for days, rather than weeks, and the diffused bluish cast to the sky that enhances so many British gardens is more apt to be intensely bright sunlight in American gardens, thus changing the perception of color.

Jekyll's recommended plantings in her three American commissions, which she did not personally visit, were fraught with problems that resulted from her inexperience with the American climate and plant palette.[15] At the Old Glebe House in Woodbury, Connecticut, she designed a cottage-style garden (now restored), with a white picket fence and color-graded borders that were pleasant, but undistinguishable from any number of New England gardens.[16] The renowned horticulturist Henry Francis duPont, creator of the garden at Winterthur, Delaware, took Jekyll's recommendations to heart. Jottings in his notebooks after visits to Munstead Wood include suggestions for using clematis to create a "pulled-over Jekyll effect behind the Delphiniums" that has baffled gardeners for nearly a century.[17]

Of the many gardens in America that owe some of their inspiration to Robinson and Jekyll's books, Shelburne Farms blends many different themes. Overlooking Lake Champlain in Shelburne, Vermont, Shelburne Farms represents the

boundless energies and resources of Eliza Osgood (Lila) Vanderbilt Webb (her brother George Vanderbilt established the French-inspired Biltmore Estate in Asheville, North Carolina). She started with an elaborate Italianate garden, with long pergolas, reflecting pools, and beds of annuals. Later, she became smitten with the informal cottage-garden style as popularized by Robinson and Jekyll. Guided by Alice Martineau's 1923 book, *The Herbaceous Garden*, she filled her grand allée with herbaceous plants, separated by an English-style, wide turf walk. Masses of achilleas, aquilegias, campanulas, coreopsis, hollyhocks, lilies, and other perennials, arranged in clusters of hot and cool tones, replaced the Victorian-style potted dracaenas of earlier years.[18]

While Wilder's *Colour in the Flower Garden* inspired amateur gardeners about plantings, Jekyll and Weaver's *Gardens for Small Country Houses* opened many eyes to garden architecture and all the practical considerations of garden design. The book was especially influential on architects and landscape architects who replicated English-style garden buildings. Beatrix Farrand (1872–1959), one of America's foremost landscape architects, executed nearly 200 projects, from small cottage-style gardens, to large estate gardens with Beaux-Arts underpinnings, to campus planning.[19] Not exclusively a flower garden designer, as were

203

TOP
Beatrix Farrand, Peggy
Rockefeller Rose Garden,
New York Botanical
Garden, New York

ABOVE
Beatrix Farrand, Lovers
Lane Pool at Dumbarton
Oaks, Washington, D.C.

many of her female colleagues, Farrand painted her landscapes with a broader brush. At Bellefield in Hyde Park, New York, Farrand designed a small Arts and Crafts–inspired walled garden for her cousin, Thomas Newbold, in 1912. The simple, old-fashioned garden gracefully complements the colonial-era house. The view from the dining room looks out over the long, pastel-colored flower borders backed by stone walls and linear hedges. Outside the walled flower garden lies a wild garden inspired by William Robinson. In the early 1930s, the Newbolds' daughter, Julia Newbold Cross, began creating a remarkable walled garden in

New Jersey, designed by landscape architect Clarence Fowler, but definitely inspired by Farrand. In addition to the perennial garden, the Cross Estate Gardens include a wisteria-covered stone pergola, a garden of native plants, and a mountain laurel allée.

Farrand, who had studied horticulture with Charles Sprague Sargent at Boston's Arnold Arboretum, was an expert on roses, having learned about them as a child in her grandmother's garden in Newport, Rhode Island. In 1916, she was invited to design a large display garden for hundreds of varieties of heritage and modern

Beatrix Farrand, parterre garden at Garland Farm, Bar Harbor, Maine

TOP
Ellen Shipman, rose garden with Lutyens bench at the Mrs. Holden McGinley Garden, Milton, Massachusetts, 1925

ABOVE
Water rill at McGinley Garden, 1925

OPPOSITE
Ellen Shipman, Eugene duPont Garden, Greenville, Delaware

roses at the New York Botanical Garden. She designed an iron gazebo festooned with climbing roses to serve as a centerpiece for the elaborate garden filled with ornamental rose standards and hundreds of varieties of gallicas, damasks, centifolias, and China roses, among others. It is not a grandmother's garden for sure, and it serves as an everlasting display of one of America's favorite plants.

Dumbarton Oaks in Washington, D.C., is considered one of Farrand's greatest masterpieces. A large and complex estate with many Arts and Crafts features, it was laid out in the 1920s as a series of formal-style garden rooms hugging the house, with magnificent Robinson-inspired naturalistic areas on the hilly outer perimeter. It exemplifies Rose Nichols's opinion regarding Jekyll's ability to combine "both wild and cultivated flowers." An accomplished horticulturist, Farrand excelled at naturalistic groupings of native trees and shrubs, as well as intertwining architecture and plants. The year-round planting theme throughout the garden is green, with episodes of color in the spring and autumn. Farrand was also a master in designing garden gates, benches, planters, and small, rustic garden structures that reflect the Arts and Crafts approach to simplicity and individuality in design. Impeccably detailed, yet discrete, Dumbarton Oaks is the perfect example of Farrand's controlled approach to good design. At Garland Farm, Farrand's last home and garden in Maine, which she created at the end of her career in the 1950s, she skillfully combined hot and cool color schemes in her tiny parterre garden that harked back to gardens she had designed fifty years earlier.

Ellen Shipman (1869–1950) can be considered one of greatest proponents of the beautiful American flower garden and the equal of Jekyll in her knowledge of horticulture and artistic approach to the design of small gardens. After training in Cornish with Charles Platt, she went on to become one of the country's most sought-after designers, specializing in small residential gardens, with bountiful plantings and elegant furnishings, all done in a Colonial Revival or rusticated Arts and Crafts mode. Her library was filled with all the key volumes on English garden design, including many of Jekyll's books. Beginning in the mid-1910s, she was among the first American designers to use Lutyens's famous garden bench

206

in her commissions. She also lifted design elements directly from the pages of *Gardens for Small Country Houses*, including Triggs's water rill at Little Boarhunt, which resurfaces in her 1925 design for the McGinley Garden in Massachusetts. Her scheme was a simple but imaginative response to the gently sloping site. She divided the walled garden into a series of terraces, each with its own character: the upper terrace with the Triggs-inspired water rill, the middle terrace (just steps down from the upper terrace) dedicated to borders and a statue, and the lower terrace filled with beds of roses surrounding a small pool and fountain.

Architectural furnishings, such as dovecotes, pavilions, and other small structures modeled after English and American examples, are some of the trademarks of Shipman's style. Her elegant brick pavilion in a walled garden in Delaware is modeled after the house designed by the architect Harrie T. Lindeberg. From the sunroom of the house, the view includes boxwood-edged borders, a pavilion, and a small reflecting pool with an eye-catching period lotus fountain. Flowering fruit trees and masses of spring bulbs complete the garden picture.

ABOVE
Ellen Shipman, east
flower garden at
Chatham Manor,
Fredericksburg,
Virginia, 1927

OPPOSITE
Ellen Shipman, Crab
Tree Farm, Lake
Bluff, Illinois

An armchair traveler, Shipman was thoroughly American in her approach to design and planting, as opposed to many of her colleagues who embraced the Beaux-Arts aesthetic from travel abroad. Throughout her career, she relied on the axial Colonial Revival layout, with shaded walks overhung with wisteria and lilac and copious plantings of perennials, flowering shrubs, and ornamental trees. Using this basic vocabulary, she created some of the most elegant, domestically scaled gardens of the era that stand well in comparison with those of her best English counterparts.

As a planting designer, Shipman used bold blocks of color in a stained-glass-window effect rather than the impressionistic drifts that were Jekyll's specialty. This can be seen in vintage color photographs of her elaborate gardens at Chatham Manor, in Fredericksburg, Virginia, designed in the 1920s. Drifts of color-coordinated annuals filled geometric beds edged with low boxwood hedges. The secret to her success as a designer lay in limiting herself to six to eight main flowering plants, letting each in season "dominate the garden. For the time one flower is the guest of honor and is merely supplemented with other flowers," she wrote.[20] She cautioned, however, that "planting, however beautiful, is not a garden. A garden must be enclosed . . . or otherwise it would merely be a cultivated area."[21] For the essential enclosure, she used existing woodlands or she planted dense groups of hemlocks or other fast-growing trees to form a backdrop for

perennial borders. Her gardens were more three-dimensional than Jekyll's, with an overhead canopy of flowering trees color-coordinated to complement the borders below. Wisteria-clad pergolas and furnishings such as benches, statuary, and wooden gates completed her garden pictures.

Whereas Farrand tended to control all aspects of her design, Shipman gladly collaborated with many of the nation's foremost traditionalist architects, including Platt, with whom she had a decade-long partnership rivaling that of Lutyens and Jekyll. Other architects included the cream of American estate builders, such as David Adler, Delano and Aldrich, Mott B. Schmidt, John F. Staub, and Horace Trumbauer, as well as Warren Manning and a host of notable landscape architects. At Crab Tree Farm, located on a bluff north of Chicago overlooking Lake Michigan, Shipman designed a colonial-style garden as a perfect complement to Adler's summer house for the William McCormick Blair family in 1926. It was a small component of a larger estate, a former dairy farm, surrounded by acres of lush woodlands. Designed to provide axial views to the woodlands, this tiny formal garden is edged with low clipped boxwood hedges surrounding beds originally filled with peonies. Shipman's garden, with intersecting patterned brick paths and a tiny reflecting pool and bench in one corner, is in perfect harmony with the house, one of the basic tenets of the Arts and Crafts Movement.

12

COLOR IN THE FLOWER GARDEN

A HEIGHTENED SENSITIVITY TO PLANTING composition and the use of color were key components of Arts and Crafts gardens. In theory, the floral furnishings for outdoor rooms needed to be as carefully considered as the architectural elements. In place of carpets of annuals, designers sought soothing, more informal solutions by selecting plants for their compatibility with one another. This artistic approach to planting was adopted by artist-gardeners who were thoroughly versed in design and color theory, rather than by architects who delegated planting to nurserymen or horticultural advisers. Taking their cue from William Morris, William Robinson, and Gertrude Jekyll, all of whom advocated the use of perennials, this new breed of artist-gardeners looked to a more sensitive palette of plants and colors than that offered in traditional Victorian gardeners.

Jekyll's agility in combining form, texture, and color in her borders was legendary, but other artist-gardeners advocated a similar approach. Like Jekyll, Alfred Parsons (1847–1920) was an artist and an accomplished garden designer. A regular exhibitor at the Royal Academy and the New English Art Club, he was also president of the Royal Society

BELOW
Alfred Parsons, Luggers
Hall, Broadway,
Worcestershire

OPPOSITE
Parterre at Luggers Hall

PREVIOUS
Alfred Parsons, *China
Roses, Broadway*, water-
color, early 1900s

of Painters in Water Colours, an indication of the high regard in which he was held. Parsons's illustrations enhance many of Robinson's books and journals, including *The Wild Garden*, for which he illustrated a special edition. He lived in Broadway, a picture-book village in Worcestershire, where he was part of the Broadway Group of American illustrators for *Harper's Magazine* that centered on artists Edwin Austin Abbey (with whom he shared a home) and Frank Millet. Parsons once shared a studio with John Singer Sargent, who painted *Carnation, Lily, Lily, Rose* while based in Broadway in 1885.[1] Henry James, another Broadway habitué, commented that Parsons's work "forms the richest illustration of the English landscape that is offered us to-day. . . . One would like to retire to another planet with a box of Mr. Parsons's drawings, and be homesick there for the pleasant places they commemorate."[2]

Parsons's own garden at Luggershill (now Luggers Hall), near Broadway, was quintessential Arts and Crafts in both its planning and furnishing, with high green hedges shaped as battlements, topiary, beautifully composed flower and

COLOR IN THE FLOWER GARDEN

shrub borders, a picturesque summerhouse, a pergola, and a rose garden.[3] Parsons's paintings of Broadway gardens attest to his fine-tuned color sensitivity as well as a botanical accuracy that outdistances many less horticulturally inclined garden painters of the era. While based in Broadway, Parsons designed numerous gardens, such as Court Farm, for stage actress Mary Anderson de Navarro, which was as famous for its topiary peacocks and flower borders as it was for its famous visitors.[4] The timber-framed house, with thatched roof and dovecote, was covered in a "whirlwind of climbing roses," one of Parsons's signature effects.[5]

In 1907, Parsons advised on the gardens at Great Chalfield Manor, an exceptionally well-preserved fifteenth-century moated manor house in Wiltshire. He enhanced the old-fashioned pleasaunce with some of his standard design elements, such as climbing roses, topiary yews, and copious flower borders as well as a gazebo that was in architectural harmony with the house. At Wightwick Manor, Wolverhampton, West Midlands, designed by architect Edward Ould (1852–1909) in a picturesque half-timbered old English style derivative of Richard Norman Shaw,

Parsons and his partner, Walter Partridge, laid out the upper gardens near the
house, a formal rose garden surrounded by hedges and topiary yews, and a long
walk bordered with flowers. Clipped yew hedges, topiary peacocks, picture-perfect
borders, and cascades of roses typify Parsons's style.

Parsons's fame rests primarily on his artwork for Ellen Willmott's rare book,
The Genus Rosa (1910–14), containing 132 illustrations of rose species described
by the author. Although the book was a financial and artistic disaster, because
Willmott ignored Parsons's recommendations regarding papers and printers, the
resulting paintings are a legacy both to client and artist.[6] Ellen Ann Willmott
(1858–1934) was beautiful, intelligent, and wealthy, but she was not savvy when it
came to expenses. Financially independent from the age of eighteen, she overex-
tended her resources managing three gardens: Warley Place in Essex, where she

kept more than one hundred gardeners busy
for years; Tresserve in Aix-les-Bains, France;
and Boccanegra in Ventimiglia, Italy.[7]

Along with Robinson and Jekyll, Willmott
was one of the three most important gardeners
of the era. All three received the coveted Victoria Medal of Honour from the Royal Horticultural Society. Jekyll thought Willmott was
the greatest of living gardeners, and Robinson
had boundless respect for her accomplish-
ments as a hybridizer. Today, few gardens in
Britain do not include *Eryngium giganteum*, or
Miss Willmott's ghost, known for its intense
blue color. In its heyday, Warley Place was
fifty-five acres in extent, filled with rockeries,
roses, perennials, and naturalized sweeps of
snowdrops, crocuses, tulips, daffodils, and
other bulbs that Willmott hybridized. While
still a young woman, she commissioned an
extensive alpine garden from the Backhouse
firm in York, and from there her passion for
plants and gardens grew unabated until she
died, nearly destitute, at age seventy-six. Little
remains of her gardens, but her book *Warley
Garden in Spring and Summer* records that
garden in its most splendid state.

The Manor House, Sutton Courtenay,
Berkshire, is another vanished garden associated with a keen horticulturist and brilliant

designer. The home of Norah Lindsay (1876–1948), it exuded an air of spontaneity in its plantings, "as if the flowers and trees had chosen their own positions."[8] She laid out the gardens as a series of rooms to complement the low, half-timbered house. The Long Garden, punctuated with fastigiate yews and soft mounds of boxwood, was filled with bold groups of lupines, anchusas, and mulleins, followed by thalictrums, hollyhocks, campanulas, and other English flowers planted in big informal drifts. The color scheme, while appearing deceptively carefree, was carefully considered. The rich blues, deep purples, pinks, and yellows were kept separate from the "hot scarlet of the sizzling great poppies, the burning alstroemerias and all the metallic golds of the rudbeckias and sunflowers," noted Lindsay. An American visitor commented that Lindsay's colors were soft greens, gray, buff-violet, and softest salmon.[9]

Lindsay, a colorful, if not eccentric, woman, designed dozens of gardens for the cream of the aristocracy, including the Duke of Windsor at Fort Belvedere, Windsor, and Nancy Astor's garden at Cliveden, but her most famous association is that with Lawrence Johnston's Hidcote Manor, where she was a valued advisor, as was her daughter, Nancy Lindsay. Vestiges of her designs can be seen at Mottisfont Abbey, Devon, where she designed a small parterre near the house and advised on the plantings in the large walled garden. Her once-magnificent gardens at Blickling Hall, Norfolk, offer a glimpse into her rarified skills as a master garden-maker. Drifts of lavender along the garden enclosure walls, hundreds of roses, and color-themed borders in parterres accented with topiary are still visible today.

Jekyll's Munstead Wood, which has happily survived, was a proving ground for her nearly 400 garden commissions, the most famous of which were done in collaboration with Edwin Lutyens. Undoubtedly, Jekyll began designing gardens in response to many requests to supply the special plants she grew at Munstead Wood. Her notebooks detail shipments of plants to dozens of clients' gardens, ranging from small gardens owned by friends, to large, complex gardens she designed with

215

TOP
Alfred Parsons, *Warley Place, Lilies*, watercolor, 1898

ABOVE
Norah Lindsay, Long Garden at Manor House, Sutton Courtenay, Berkshire

Lutyens. Jekyll was omnivorous in her appreciation of plants, commenting that there were no "bad" plants, only plants badly used. In the 1920s, when she was in her eighties and nearly blind, she designed borders from her memory of hundreds of plants, their colors, textures, fragrances, and habits. Sometimes she adjusted her planting style to suit the needs of the architect or the client, as was the case at Hestercombe, which represents only one side of Jekyll's planting genius. In other cases, she was given a greater amount of freedom to indulge her passion for artistic planting combinations.

The Manor House at Upton Grey, Hampshire, is one of the best surviving private gardens demonstrating Jekyll's skills as a planting artist and garden designer. The gardens display Jekyll's versatility in planning both formal and wild gardens for a small property. For inspiration, it dips deeply into her planting schemes at

Munstead Wood, Hestercombe, and Millmead. The Manor House was the home of Charles Holme, founder of *The Studio*, who lived there for twenty years after moving from William Morris's Red House in 1902. He commissioned Ernest Newton to design a comfortable Edwardian family home around the core of an old Tudor farmhouse, and the design of the four-and-a-half acres of ground happily fell to Jekyll.

On the east side of the house, she designed a formal garden within the frame-work of yew hedges, converting the grass slopes into four descending terraces, each defined with low dry-stone walls filled with rock plants in soft pinks and grays. A small pergola that links the house to the steps leading to the lower garden is covered with roses, clematises, and other vines. The rose garden, divided into geometric beds with square stone pads, is simply planted with roses and peonies and softly edged with stachys. On the lower levels are a wide bowling green and a tennis lawn enclosed by ornamental trees and shrubs. Surrounding borders are planted with *Yucca filamentosa*, *Y. gloriosa*, *Bergenia cordifolia*, and other familiar Jekyll favorites. In contrast with the soft coloring of the rose and lily parterre, the main border's flowers are more dramatically colored, following the same ideas of color gradation used in the main border at Munstead Wood. A large wild garden at the west front of the house follows Robinsonian principles with its informal design and naturalistic plantings. Mown grass paths wind through taller grass, with rambling roses, walnut trees, and clumps of bamboo. The pond at the far end of the garden

nourishes water-loving plants, and in spring, the meadows are carpeted with daffodils, snowdrops, scillas, muscari, fritillarias, anemones, hellebores, and primroses.[10]

Jekyll's books were a profound influence on nearly everyone who was interested in the finer points of garden design and horticulture. Her *Colour in the Flower Garden* (1908) influenced writers and gardeners on both sides of the Atlantic because it is eminently readable, reflecting nearly thirty years' worth of experience in the subject, and Munstead Wood, which was used as illustrations for her ideas, was by then world famous. The book also includes planting plans for every conceivable type of border that could be used as a practical resource. There are few gardens in

CLOCKWISE FROM
BELOW
Simon Dorrell, *The
Manor House, Upton
Grey*, line drawing, 2003

Lawrence Johnston,
red borders at Hidcote
Manor, Gloucestershire

Summer borders at the
Manor House

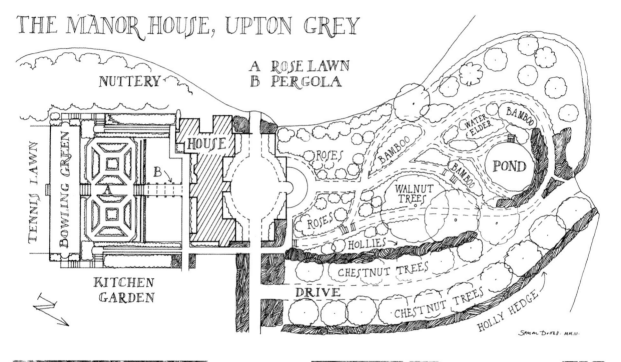

THE MANOR HOUSE, UPTON GREY

A ROSE LAWN
B PERGOLA

Crathes Castle, Banchory, Aberdeenshire

ABOVE
George S. Elgood,
Crathes (Elgood and
Jekyll, 1904)

OPPOSITE TOP
Red section of main
flower border at Mun-
stead Wood, auto-
chrome, ca. 1912

OPPOSITE MIDDLE
Penelope Hobhouse,
red border at Tintinhull
House, Somerset

OPPOSITE BOTTOM
Peter Healing, color
borders at The
Priory, Kemerton,
Worcestershire

Britain that do not owe something to Jekyll's ideas. At Hidcote Manor, Lawrence Johnston's striking red borders, composed of deep maroon foliage as well as red and orange flowers, continues to enchant visitors. At Crathes Castle, a picture-book Scottish tower house in Banchory, near Aberdeen, the Burnett family embellished the ancient gardens with a series of color gardens directly influenced by *Colour in the Flower Garden*, including blue, white, and red borders as well as a gold foliage garden, the last added by Lady Burnett in 1973. Though they do not replicate Jekyll's designs, the borders at Crathes drink of their spirit. Long before the color borders were added, Jekyll had admired the Edwardian gardens at Crathes in her book *Some English Gardens* (1904), noting the excellence of their color and diversity of texture and, no doubt, the ancient yew hedges.

The eminent plantsman and botanical artist Graham Stuart Thomas (1909–2003) remarked that *Colour in the Flower Garden* had piqued his interest enough to seek a visit to Munstead Wood in 1931, the year before Jekyll died. "I was spell-bound," he wrote. "The gradation of tints" in the main flower border with a hot red center "testified to the skill of her garden staff, and to her ideas, developed from the deep study of various arts. . . . any plant which would grow well in her sandy soil was a colour in a paint-box."[11] In his long career as gardens adviser to the National

Trust, Thomas had the opportunity to put some of Jekyll's lessons to work. At Cliveden in Berkshire, he designed two herbaceous borders facing each other on a wide lawn to the north of the house. One in cool colors, the other in hot, the borders successfully weave a complex tapestry of color and texture. He described these borders as providing maximum color in July and August, augmented with purple clematises and yellow roses on the "hot" wall, and lavender and pink clematises and pink roses on the east-facing "cool" wall. He also designed the rose garden at Mottisfont Abbey.

Penelope Hobhouse, a noted garden designer clearly influenced by Jekyll, praised Thomas for his understanding and execution of the subtleties of her art. Jekyll's genius lies in "the gradual build-up of related shades and tones of colour [and] in a sure sense of what ancillary plants should be used as links to unite the whole scheme."[12] Hobhouse proved an expert at this concept during her years at Tintinhull House, Somerset, where she was the gardening tenant for the National Trust property. Tintinhull's famous color borders, with cool tones on one side of the lawn and warmer tones on the other, were originally devised by Phyllis Reiss, who worked on the gardens for nearly thirty years before donating the property to the National Trust in 1954. Of Tintinhull, Hobhouse wrote that the "planting style is very much in the tradition of Hidcote Manor and Sissinghurst, where plants in tightly packed flower beds appear to grow in casual profusion."[13] To keep Reiss's intended effect, Hobhouse replaced many aging plants with better, more vigorous varieties. The original series of garden rooms is of great interest, including a white pool garden and a dramatic red shrub border, and owes much to Jekyll's planting theories.

In the 1940s, plantsman Peter Healing created a series of remarkable color borders in his four-acre garden, The Priory, near Tewkesbury. Though not replicating Jekyll's main border at Munstead Wood, which was filled with annuals and perennials, the borders at The Priory are

equally innovative in their discerning use of color. Subtle color combinations are interwoven imaginatively with the various textures of shrubs, annuals, and hardy perennials. One border is given over to gray, silver, and white, with warm yellows and reds. A red border, similar to the one at Tintinhull House, creatively combines bronze, purple, and red foliage and flowers. Tim Richardson credited Healing for having "created effervescent planting schemes of great complexity and originality."[14] Like the more famous color borders at Hidcote and the White Garden at Sissinghurst, ingenuity in planting often takes its inspiration from books, but the results are always individual.

Probably the most famous herbaceous borders in England today are at Newby Hall in North Yorkshire, created in the 1920s by Major Edward Compton, whose family had owned the eighteenth-century hall and surrounding twenty-five acres of land since 1948. Much influenced by the garden rooms at Hidcote Manor, Compton reorganized the grounds to include various color-themed gardens typical of the Edwardian era, including a naturalistic rock garden and laburnum-covered pergola

Double borders at
Newby Hall, Ripon,
North Yorkshire

attributed to Willmott. But the main attractions are the matching 600-foot-long double herbaceous borders leading from the Queen Anne house down a slight slope to the River Ure. The grand borders, backed by dark yew hedges and separated by a wide grass path, far outdistance Jekyll's single 200-foot-long border. Large clumps of well-established perennials, such as peonies, irises, and other hardy plants, add to the bold, dramatic effect.

Christopher Lloyd, Long Border at Great Dixter, Northiam, East Sussex

The late Christopher Lloyd's iconic garden at Great Dixter near Rye, in East Sussex, is a testament to the creative use of a period Arts and Crafts framework as a showcase for dynamic contemporary plantings. In 1910, Lloyd's father, Nathaniel Lloyd, commissioned Lutyens to remodel and enlarge an ancient manor house complex and devise a garden layout that melded together the ancillary buildings, some of which were dilapidated and tumbling to the ground. Nathaniel, an architectural historian and an expert in topiary, liked order, while his wife, Daisy, leaned more to William Robinson's ideas of informality. Lutyens's ingenious plan marrying formality and informality includes two topiary gardens, a sunken garden enclosed by ancient farm sheds, an intimate wall garden, and a network of paths that connected the formal gardens with an informal wildflower meadow and orchard. The diverse areas were tied together with Lutyens's signature architectural features, including archways, paved walks, and steps. Within this framework, Christopher Lloyd (1921–2006), who was a genius in nontraditional color and textural combinations, created an ever-changing testament to his horticultural prowess. "I take it as a challenge to combine every sort of colour effectively [and] if I think a yellow candelabrum or mullein will look good rising in the middle of a quilt of pink phlox, I'll put it there." [15] To his credit, Lloyd was never constricted by the layout but used it to great advantage. Today the garden enjoys a new chapter under the direction of Fergus Garrett, who has injected his own genius into revitalizing a period garden with innovative ideas and a new, bolder plant palette.

Of the many outstanding gardeners today, one stands out for her romantic sensibility to design and unusual combinations of plants. Helen Dillon's former garden in Dublin never ceased to inspire because of its small size and suburban location. Her 2016 decision to give it up after forty years in order to create a smaller garden confirms her wish to be known as a creator, not a curator. Dillon is passionate about plants, traveling far from home to acquire unusual specimens,

BELOW
Sunk Garden at
Great Dixter

OPPOSITE
Helen Dillon, color
borders at Dillon
Garden, Dublin

but the garden she created is not a collector's garden. In creating her garden, she wrestled with how "to reconcile the collector's instinct with the desire to make a garden that is pleasant to be in. This is a challenging task because a collector's garden is all too frequently a cabinet of curiosities, a glorious confection of plants," she wrote.[16] Jekyll opined that "the possession of a quantity of plants, however good the plants may be themselves and however ample their number, does not make a garden: it only makes a *collection*."[17] Dillon has observed that "visitors assume that one night, in a flash of creativity, I designed this garden. Not so. My method is to wait until some part of it annoys me and then take action. . . . Endless adjustments have taken place—in the paths, the shapes of the beds, and, above all, in the planting."[18]

In its heyday, the Dillon Garden was filled with surprises and many special effects, but the twin borders, best viewed from the window in the Georgian townhouse, literally took the viewer's breath away. The blue border, she wrote,

was a "glorious muddle of different blues . . . turquoise, sapphire, lapis lazuli." She was willing to break a few rules, even Jekyll's stern dictum that a garden with only blue flowers is senseless: "Surely the business of the blue garden is to be beautiful as well as to be blue . . . the blues will be more telling—more purely blue—by the juxtaposition of rightly placed complementary colour."[19] With the subtle shading from blue to mauve to violet, illuminated with mounds of artemisias, Dillon proved otherwise.

The challenge of arranging these borders is endlessly fascinating, "perhaps because there's no chance whatsoever of getting it right—the more I think about it the more complicated it becomes," she wrote.[20] Only those who are truly knowledgeable about plants, whether Jekyll, Lindsay, Lloyd, or Dillon, can even begin to compose artistic borders. The architects who provided such a firm foundation for Arts and Crafts garden design would have been nowhere had there not been dedicated horticulturists to create the plantings.

13

CONTEMPORARY GARDENS

MANY OF THE ESSENTIAL CHARACTERISTICS of Arts and Crafts gardens are even more relevant in contemporary garden design. A selection of new gardens reveals the individual ways in which the basic tenets of Arts and Crafts garden planning are still meaningful. Many gardens have been conceived by artist-gardeners (homeowners and professional designers alike) who have created personal statements. Among the many innovative designers in Britain today, Isabel and Julian Bannerman, Jinny Blom, Christopher Bradley-Hole, George Carter, Mary Keen, Arabella Lennox-Boyd, Dan Pearson, Tom Stuart-Smith, Xa Tollemache, and Kim Wilkie bring new heights to contemporary garden design based on the Arts and Crafts design philosophy. Older gardens created during the Arts and Crafts era, notably Christopher Lloyd's Great Dixter, William Robinson's Gravetye Manor, and several of Edwin Lutyens's private gardens (especially Folly Farm and Marsh Court), have been imaginatively recast with updated plantings by prominent designers and gardeners.

Veddw, Anne Wareham's imaginative garden in South Wales, presents an array of dazzling borders and contemporary architectural features within a spectacular framework of hedges clipped as undulating waves. Roger Last's Corpusty Mill and George Carter's Silverstone

BELOW
Anne Wareham,
Veddw, Devauden,
Monmouthshire

PREVIOUS
Roy Strong, The
Laskett, Much Birch,
Herefordshire

Farm in East Anglia are noteworthy for their whimsy and restraint as well as an impeccable sense of scale and craftsmanship. At Wyken Hall, Carla Carlisle's gardens surrounding her old manor house in Suffolk include a quincunx (five interlocking brick circles) inspired by a Gertrude Jekyll design and a period-inspired box parterre designed by Arabella Lennox-Boyd.[1] More ambitious undertakings, such as Prince Charles's Highgrove in the Cotswolds (created in part by the Bannermans) and Charles Jencks's Garden of Cosmic Speculation in Scotland, take the concept of garden rooms to new intellectual plateaus. In the end, none of these gardens replicates period Arts and Crafts gardens, but each one shows the value of their enduring lessons.

The Laskett, on the Welsh Borders in Herefordshire, is one of the most significant formal gardens created in recent years. It is the masterwork of Sir Roy Strong, who contributed his vast intellectual prowess in collaboration with his late wife, Dr. Julia Trevelyan Oman, the renowned stage designer. The garden,

set out in a series of traditional interlocking rooms defined by clipped hedges, is a showcase for personal monuments and artifacts, statue-lined walks, small buildings, fountains, statues, urns, and benches, but few flowers. The gardens envelop the picture-perfect Georgian house that holds Strong's incomparable art library and picture collection. The Laskett owes much to Hidcote, Levens Hall, and other Arts and Crafts models as well as classical gardens abroad, but the result is an entirely personal statement reflecting Strong's distinguished careers as art historian, scholar, and museum director.[2]

East Ruston Old Vicarage is an architectural and horticultural triumph and one of the most important private gardens created in the late twentieth century. Located on a flat and windy site a mile (one-and-a-half kilometers) or so from the Norfolk coast, it consists of themed garden rooms surrounding an partially tile-clad Art and Crafts house built around 1913.[3] "Horticultural extravaganza" does not entirely describe the gardens, begun in the 1970s by Graham Robeson and Alan Gray. "We try to be as original as possible with the planting combinations here, [some are] soothing [while others are] shocking, but that's the fun of gardening."[4] The high caliber of craftsmanship in the pavilions and other architectural components is outstanding and a great complement to the exquisite plantings. Among the many features are peepholes in the hedges that provide views to the Happisburgh lighthouse and church framed in the distance. Nearly twenty garden rooms are intertwined around the house, ranging from a formal Dutch garden to the desert wash designed to resemble parts of Arizona where rain is infrequent, but heavy. Christopher Lloyd commented that the garden contained "one of the most effective deliberate cornfield displays that I have seen."[5]

Bryan's Ground, near Presteigne in Herefordshire, is a magical garden surrounding a Tuscan-toned half-timbered Arts and Crafts house dating from 1913, poised on the banks of the River Lugg on the border between England and Wales. An existing kitchen garden with high brick walls and a thick yew hedge as well as a sunken garden with a circular waterlily pool to the south of the house provided the underpinnings for a new garden that continues to grow. Since 1993, Bryan's Ground has been the home of David Wheeler and Simon Dorrell, the editor and the art director of *Hortus*, a quarterly garden publication founded by Wheeler in 1987. The garden proper occupies two acres, the largest feature being the old kitchen garden that has been divided into

TOP
Carla Carlisle, Wyken Hall, Bury St Edmunds, Suffolk

ABOVE
Graham Robeson and Alan Gray, East Ruston Old Vicarage, Norfolk

quadrants, each with a different focus. A formal garden, serpentine-edged canal, topiary garden, and other areas have been developed, many of which have been named after a significant place or person: St. Anne's (for Anne Raver, a reporter at *The New York Times* who first wrote about the garden), Standen (Philip Webb's house), the George Walk (a beloved dog's constitutional run), St. Ives (a timber potting shed), and the Lighthouse (a garden folly that was originally a domestic gas plant). In addition to the formal gardens hugging the dwelling, Bryan's Ground also features informal areas on the outer edges of the grounds. The current orchard was replanted on the bones of an existing orchard with more than thirty different apple varieties set within ten-foot squares planted with carpets of *Anemone blanda*, followed in May by dense drifts of blue *Iris sibirica* 'Papillon'. Equally ambitious is Cricket Wood, a new arboretum with some original specimen trees, such as a fully mature *Sequoiadendron giganteum* (the giant sequoia, or Wellingtonia). Dense

plantations of new hydrangea cultivars add dazzling blue notes to the woods. Whimsical architectural features, such as the Belevedere, the Sulking House, and Simon's lych gate embellish this enchanting ground.

Traditional herbaceous borders, which are the mainstay of many English gardens, continue to draw from Jekyll's timeless harmonious color theories, but with new, more contemporary planting combinations. Coton Manor in Northamptonshire, which comprises ten acres of informal, yet atmospheric gardens originally laid out in the 1920s, is celebrated for its breathtaking borders: a red border, meadow border, and holly hedge border. Susie and Ian Pasley-Tyler have devoted decades to fine-tuning the gardens, which range from formal areas adjacent to the house to informal wildflower meadows and a stream garden with resident flamingos. The whole effect is one of a relaxed atmosphere, rather than architectural high drama and intensity. Maintaining and updating the borders originally

BELOW
Canal garden at
Bryan's Ground

OPPOSITE
Simon Dorrell and
David Wheeler, sunken
garden at Bryan's
Ground, Stapleton,
Herefordshire

BELOW
Ian and Susie
Pasley-Tyler, Coton
Manor, Guilsborough,
Northampton

OPPOSITE
John and Leslie
Jenkins, Wollerton
Old Hall, Market
Drayton, Shropshire

created by Susie's mother-in-law takes patience and experimentation, sometimes with surprising results. "It's true that adjacent colours on the colour wheel harmonise, while opposites are stimulating and exciting, but overdoing the first can be dull, and too much of the latter is overkill," Susie said.[6]

Wollerton Old Hall in Shropshire has been described as the quintessential English garden, but it is much more. The creation of Lesley Jenkins over a thirty-year period, the four-acre garden stands out for its luscious, contemporary plantings within a formal layout that was dictated to some extent by the old Tudor manor house. David Wheeler of Bryan's Ground called it "a tight but logical layout, slackening at its limits where the garden appears to dissolve into the countryside."[7] Each garden room is beautifully conceived and imaginatively planted, and

all interlock in such a way as to draw the visitor eagerly from one area to the next, similar to the experience at Hidcote and Sissinghurst. What makes the difference here is the high level of exquisite plantsmanship and color artistry. Walls and dense hedges (some rather whimsical) define each of the fourteen different areas. In the end, it's less about the specific plants and more about the drifts of intermingling colors and textures. Jenkins is not afraid of color, blending intense purples and oranges in one area and softer sweeps of lavenders, pinks, and grays in another.

Jinny Blom, an unconventional designer who originally trained as a psychotherapist, is an expert at contemporary garden planning. She claims, however, that she has no style; she just wants to make gardens "that work for the place and the person."[8] Temple Guiting, a private garden in the Cotswolds, is a fine example

ABOVE
Jinny Blom, The Manor,
Temple Guiting,
Gloucestershire

OPPOSITE
Robin Spencer, York
Gate, Yorkshire

236

of Blom's work. Here she transformed a dilapidated medieval-era farmstead (in more recent years, a llama farm) into a contemporary interpretation with nods to the past, including whimsical farmyard topiaries. Her framework, which progresses from formal to informal, as dictated by the challenging site, consists of a series of walled rooms. The unforgettable centerpiece of the scheme is a canal garden surrounded by a variety of small compartments, each with a different theme. In early summer, pale lavender irises flank the pool under the shade of a line of pleached hornbeams. The long, narrow Granary Walk, once the local village road, is informally planted with clumps of pale blue and white flowers between columns of yew. Old-fashioned roses abound throughout the garden. The enchanting composition glows with an artist's sense of romance and delight.

York Gate, in Adel, Yorkshire, is remarkable for its small scale, ingenious planning, and architectural detailing. Located in a quiet suburban community five miles (eight kilometers) from Leeds, the garden comprises less than an acre of ground. It was designed by the Spencer family, beginning in 1951: Frederick Spencer, a surveyor; his wife, Sybil, who oversaw the garden after his death; and their son, Robin, who was also a surveyor. The garden has an ordered geometry in its planting and detailing but is more informal in how the twelve or so compartments interlock imperceptibly with one another, creating both intimacy and the illusion of a far larger place. The planting scheme is architectural, with an emphasis on a diversity of foliage, texture, and form, mostly in shades of green, rather than a flowery confection. Linear waves of dark hedges, golden globes of yew, and spikes of evergreens balance water features and simple garden ornaments, such as a row of discarded lead cans, an obelisk, and a sundial. Most of the architectural elements, from paving stones to small buildings, were constructed from recycled materials.

Tony Ridler's minimalist half-acre garden, near Swansea, Wales, is conceived as a series of defined spaces with an emphasis on hedges of yew, Portuguese laurel, and box and tightly manipulated companion plantings of santolinas, hostas, hellebores, and other plants with strong foliage interest.[9] The tiny terrace house is nearly engulfed by the long, linear T-shaped garden (composed of several family allotments). Neatly clipped box spheres and spirals of yew are offset by the odd window in a hedge that provides a peek into the next area. Walls painted black and deep gray, plus other artful effects, reveal Ridler's profession as a graphic designer.

Beautifully executed and highly original, Ridler's garden owes little to the self-conscious replicas of iconic gardens that more conventional designers revel in.

One garden deserves mention for melding a contemporary design within an Arts and Crafts setting. Througham Court, tucked away in a small hamlet in Gloucestershire, consists of a seventeenth-century manor house renovated by the Cotswold architect Norman Jewson in the late 1920s, surrounded by a traditional garden with clipped hedges and topiaries. Dr. Christine Facer, a biologist turned landscape designer, created three acres of new gardens on the sloping hill behind the house that are a tribute to the cosmic laws of the universe. Her hero, of course, is Charles Jencks, but Facer's creation is more intimate by comparison and focuses sharply on mathematical and scientific theories, including a tribute to the Italian mathematician, Fibonacci. Serpentine walks, mounded landforms, and visual markers such as red flags fluttering in the wind signal an intellectual and highly individual garden-maker.

On the other side of the Atlantic, numerous gardens, in particular those under the umbrella of the Garden Conservancy, show the continuing relevance of lessons derived from Arts and Crafts gardens with many regional variations.[10] They range from country house gardens designed by local professionals, such as Craig Bergmann in Lake Forest, Illinois, to larger, contemporary landscapes by the Oehme van Sweden firm in Washington, D.C. Personal gardens, such as Ben and Cindy Lenhardt's immaculate parterre garden in Charleston, South Carolina, the late Tom Armstrong's coastal garden on the Long Island Sound, and Caesar and Dorothy Stair's Lutyens-inspired garden in Knoxville, Tennessee, designed by the late Ryan Gainey, are among the many outstanding gardens. In addition, there are numerous revitalized gardens and landscapes associated with Arts and Crafts houses designed by Frank Lloyd Wright and other period architects.

Perhaps the most ambitious garden of all is Les Quatre Vents, Frank Cabot's extensive creation near Québec, Canada, consisting of two-dozen themed garden rooms, not unlike Hidcote in scale and scope. Some of the areas were refurbished from existing gardens (such as the White Garden) in the family compound, while others are fanciful creations directly inspired by Cabot's extensive world travels. Its beautiful setting, near the St. Lawrence River in La Malbaie and remote from urban areas, is the equal of any English landscape. Naturalistic drifts of wildflowers and alpine plants complement more formal areas, such as the whimsical topiaries in the Guest Garden and Bread Garden. Several water gardens, such as Lac Libellule, the Watercourse (inspired by Geoffrey Jellicoe's garden at Shute House in Dorset), and the Stream Garden (inspired by Hidcote), offset formal notes, such as allées, both green and perennial. Architectural features, including the Moon Bridge, Pigeonnier, Music Pavilion, and the Arch (inspired by Lutyens), are numerous and diverse. At Les Quatre Vents, the magnitude of craftsmanship, horticultural expertise, ornament, and wide-ranging influences in general transcend the intimacy of an Arts and Crafts garden, but the heady blend of influences all helped create this majestic garden.[11]

BELOW
Christine Facer,
Througham Court,
Gloucestershire

OPPOSITE TOP
Tony Ridler, Ridler
Garden, Swansea

OPPOSITE BOTTOM
Ryan Gainey, Caesar
Stair Garden, Knoxville,
Tennessee

BELOW
Bill Noble, Bragg Hill,
Norwich, Vermont

PREVIOUS LEFT
Frank Cabot, Les Qua-
tre Vents, La Malbaie,
Québec

PREVIOUS RIGHT
Robert Dash, archway
at Madoo, Sagaponack,
New York

Some of the most interesting smaller scale gardens are those designed by artists, such as the late Robert Dash and his spectacular garden, Madoo, in Sagaponack, Long Island. Brilliant color hues, including a bright yellow door, a lilac-colored summerhouse, and a blue entry gate, reflect the personality of this important American Expressionist painter and poet. Nearly forty years in the making, Madoo (which means My Dove in Welsh) is highly personal and devoid of all the much-imitated quotations that bedevil many other new gardens. Garden hats hang on posts, box spheres lounge beneath fastigiate gingko trees like bowling balls, and ladderlike fences enclose the gardens. Dash was also a well-versed plantsman, propagating many of the plants himself and using them with an artist's eye. In his book, *Notes From Madoo*, Dash wrote, "Foliant umbrage is silvery and cottony below and lanced, blunted, toothed, or indented; strap, ovate, and round; margined with white and yellow or speckled silver."[12]

Bill Noble's private garden at Bragg Hill, near Norwich, Vermont, is a proving ground for a noted horticulturist, preservationist, and lover of gardens of the

242

nearby Cornish Art Colony. A sweep of towering Lombardy poplars encloses the outer boundaries of this superb plantsman's garden, which has been twenty-five years in the making. Reusing a former owner's vegetable garden, Noble created a series of garden rooms, where his knowledge of foliage, texture, and color come together. Purple-leaved barberries add structural notes to a color display from early summer through autumn. An eclectic collection of alliums, roses, peonies, Joe-pye weed, delphiniums, monkshood, rodgersias, rhubarb, and agastache offer their brilliant colors and varying forms through the seasons. As a dedicated plant collector, Noble seeks out new plants each year. His borders rival those at Hidcote and Great Dixter, where he has spent some time studying.

George Schoellkopf, Hollister House, Washington, Connecticut

243

One of the most important garden undertakings in America is Hollister House Garden in a quiet corner of New England. The six-acre garden skillfully combines a spectacular setting, an ingenious layout, and storied plantings, as conceived by art historian and garden aficionado George Schoellkopf. Located in rural northwestern Connecticut, Hollister House is a connoisseur's garden set within an eighteenth-century New England farmstead that includes an antiques-filled saltbox house. Schoellkopf's love of antique American furniture and decorative arts complements his garden confection. Judiciously selecting snippets from his garden travels in England, such as Hidcote, Sissinghurst, and Great Dixter, he has created an American interpretation of an English garden, and more. As Schoellkopf says, "the garden unfolds in successive layers of space and color with delightful informal vistas from one section to the next."[13]

This jewel of a garden is nestled in a hollow that overlooks the rolling Litchfield hills in the distance. Dramatic level changes provided the challenge in creating an architectural framework for the garden. Boxwood-edged stone paths, clipped yew hedges (some eight feet, or two-and-a-half meters, high), and rows of ornamental trees provide the framework for the abundant plantings. Like Alice in Wonderland, visitors step from one garden room to the next, not knowing what treats awaits them. Although the garden is English in inspiration, it is decidedly American in spirit. It is not a replica of an eighteenth-century garden, but a contemporary garden that perfectly complements the historic site and its antique farm buildings. Hollister House is certainly one of America's best gardens and owes a great debt to the principles of the Arts and Crafts Movement.

14

DESIGN INSPIRATION

ALTHOUGH FEW PEOPLE TODAY would replicate a period Arts and Crafts house and garden, the movement's basic concepts continue to inspire homeowners and garden designers. Whether the house is an Edwardian manor, a modest suburban dwelling, a small cottage, or a contemporary family home, the companion garden can easily reflect Arts and Crafts design principles. Although many books have been written about garden design, few can surpass the timeless advice offered by Gertrude Jekyll, Lawrence Weaver, and Thomas Mawson. Published more than one hundred years ago, Jekyll and Weaver's *Gardens for Small Country Houses* (1912) provides homeowners and designers essential guidelines for garden design and the use of simple but well-crafted ornamental features. Jekyll's lavishly illustrated tome, *Garden Ornament* (1908), offers countless historic and modern examples of architectural features suitable for gardens both large and small. Mawson's classic, *The Art and Craft of Garden Making* (1900), was the first book to provide practical design advice from a professional viewpoint. Examples ranging from garden structures, water features, and construction details to planting suggestions are still relevant today.

BELOW
Walter Brierley and
George Dillistone,
Goddards, York

PREVIOUS
Gertrude Jekyll, Grey
Walk at Hestercombe,
Cheddon Fitzpaine,
Somerset

GENERAL LAYOUT IDEAS
FOR SMALL SITES

"It is upon the right relation of the garden to the house that its value and the enjoyment that is to be derived from it will largely depend," Jekyll and Weaver wrote in
the introduction to *Gardens for Small Country Houses.* "The connection must be
intimate, and access not only convenient, but inviting."[1] Detailed discussions of
several projects designed or admired by Jekyll, such as Millmead, Deanery Garden, and Munstead Wood (all involving architect Edwin Lutyens), outline how
garden-makers can achieve the essential connection between house and garden.
Mawson offered more practical advice, starting with site selection and treatment:
"To produce a successful scheme, art and several crafts must be brought into line
[in order to produce] a design which shall shew [*sic*] unity of feeling and good
fellowship."[2] As a young designer, Mawson sometimes had trouble convincing
his clients as well as the architect that his role as a garden designer was essential.

On the other hand, he had much to say about the placement of the house and ancillary buildings. In his view, "a garden has to serve the double purpose of foreground to the landscape when seen from the house, and as a base or setting to the house when viewed from the surrounding country."[3] The garden should be treated in the simplest and most direct manner, with the different areas arranged in levels to suit the ground. The outer areas should not have "shaven lawns," but wild gardens, "where snowdrops and daffodils, primroses and violets, wood hyacinths and anemones, and a host of other hardy plants may be naturalized."[4]

George Schoellkopf, Hollister House, Washington, Connecticut

Goddards, on the outskirts of York, is a perfect period example of a harmonious Arts and Crafts house and garden that closely follows the advice of Jekyll and Mawson. Designed in the mid-1920s by Yorkshire Arts and Crafts architect Walter Brierley (1862–1926), Goddards is a modest country house near the city of York, where Brierley carried out several commissions, including his own house, Bishopsbarns (with gardens designed by Jekyll).[5] After Brierley's garden scheme for Goddards was rejected by the client, chocolatier Noel Terry, George Dillistone (1877–1957), who famously worked with Lutyens at Castle Drogo in Devon, was engaged. The most memorable feature at Goddards is the water garden below the broad paved terrace on the south side of the house. The gently sloping ground was ideally suited for a formal treatment near the house and for informality where the ground slopes away from the house and merges with the countryside. Dillistone's scheme is exemplar for its discretion rather than excesses of features. Gentle steps and simple paving enhance rather than compete with the elegant house. A long green walk flanked by double borders is featured on one side of the house, with a series of other linked areas, including a bowling green, screened by hedges. Dillistone's book *The Planning and Planting of Little Gardens* (1920) is filled with excellent advice, ranging from misplaced garden seats and forced symmetry to the proper use of ornament and appreciation of fragrance and color in planting schemes.

Hollister House, in Connecticut, is an excellent example of the treatment of a steep site suited to the development of modestly scaled interlocking terraces. Each terrace has a different theme, yet is related to the others with hedging or paving. On the upper levels, the individual rooms are defined by formal English-style hedged

BELOW, CLOCKWISE
FROM LEFT
Edwin Lutyens, archway
at Great Dixter, Nor-
thiam, East Sussex

Beatrix Farrand, rustic
stone wall and gate
at Eolia, Waterbury,
Connecticut

George Schoellkopf,
double borders and
hedges at Hollister
House

OPPOSITE
High Garden at Great
Dixter

enclosures with traditional borders, while on the lower levels, the scheme becomes more naturalistic, with large clumps of vigorous perennials that melt into the surrounding fields and woods.

ENCLOSURE

After outlining the overall scheme, the garden-maker's next essential step entails creating a sense of enclosure with walls, hedging, belts of trees and shrubs, or other means of defining the space. In general, a small-scale house requires a simple solution, such as dry-stone walls, while a larger, more formal house merits a grander solution that might include terracing and balustrades. As Jekyll wrote in *Gardens for Small Country Houses*, "Very often the designer of a small garden is faced by the difficulty of giving it privacy, and shrinks from the uninteresting solution of building a plain high wall," which she did at Munstead Wood.[6] Jekyll

advocated that rough stone walls should allow space (and drainage) for growing rock plants. At Hestercombe, the substantial stone walls require bold plantings, while at Eolia, the Harkness family estate in Connecticut designed by Beatrix Farrand, the rustic stone walls and modest plantings are perfect for the seaside setting. Brick walls and arched openings, such as those at Great Dixter, are ideally suited to enclosing more formal garden areas.

In areas with accommodating climates, green hedges provide a soothing visual means of defining boundaries and delineating individual garden areas. Clipped yew hedges, such as those at Hollister House, offer a perfect background for flower borders, while informal groupings of trees and shrubs provide an easy transition from formal to informal areas of the garden. Whimsical topiaries, hedges, and other clipped forms were essential to many Arts and Crafts gardens, although their maintenance and upkeep may present problems for today's busy gardeners. The High Garden at Great Dixter still remains one of the most captivating topiary gardens, as part of a suite of diverse garden rooms.

Hedged enclosure
at Stobshiel House,
Humbie, East Lothian

PATHS AND PAVING

The progression from one area of the garden to another offers endless challenges for designers. Paths and walkways, whether gravel, stone, brick, or grass, help define spaces and keep visitors from wandering into the planting beds. In general, grass paths are used for more informal parts of the garden, while stone and brick work well in more formal areas. Farrand's beautifully detailed brick paths at Dumbarton Oaks complement the formal, linear hedging, while the bold, geometrical paved paths at York Gate are more suited to a small modern garden. Farrand's fanciful horseshoe steps at Dumbarton Oaks gracefully lead up to the upper terrace. Lutyens's endless ingenuity at Great Dixter, such as the half-moon steps transitioning from the formal terraces to the informal wildflower meadow, is unsurpassed. Ideally, the garden-maker would use local stone for paving rather than importing stone from another region or using a material that is unsuited to the informality of the site. "Some of the most interesting methods of paving [for example] are those that are peculiar to a district," Jekyll wrote. "In the case of places near the sea, pretty pavings can be made by collecting stones of different colours from among banks of shingle."[7] Unfortunately, the use of local materials and construction methods has largely vanished today in garden design, only to be replaced by the universal use of bluestone and similar paving, for example. Ever practical, Dillistone, who often judged amateur design competitions, eschewed paving just for the sake of paving.

ARCHITECTURAL FEATURES

Appealing architectural features are one of the hallmarks of an Arts and Crafts garden. Whatever the size of the site, consider small structures ranging from utilitarian garden sheds to gazebos, pavilions, and follies. Jekyll, of course, who looked to historical examples for inspiration rather than line-by-line replication, advised, "The quality to be aimed at in all garden architecture is coherence in the relationship

BELOW
Robin Spencer, stone path at York Gate, Yorkshire

OPPOSITE. CLOCKWISE FROM TOP LEFT
Beatrix Farrand, brick path at Dumbarton Oaks, Washington, D.C.

Beatrix Farrand, horseshoe steps at Dumbarton Oaks

Edwin Lutyens, half-moon steps to the meadow at Great Dixter

253

CLOCKWISE FROM LEFT
Ernest Barnsley, garden
house at Rodmarton
Manor, Gloucestershire

Alfred Parsons, garden
pavilion built from
local materials at
Luggers Hall, Broadway,
Worcestershire

Simon Dorrell and
David Wheeler, dove-
cote at Bryan's Ground

of the parts. A pavilion [for example] should not stand alone, but be tied to the rest of the scheme by orderly design."[8] Mawson advised, "Nothing imparts character to a garden and gives more interest than well-designed and carefully executed architectural details."[9] He eschewed a rustic-style garden house near a classical house, for example. A well-executed pavilion (whether brick, stone, or wood) gives finish to a formal terrace and provides a focal point along a path in a wild garden.

The attractive gazebo in the walled garden at Luggers Hall, which is built from local materials, provides a comfortable shelter and serves as a focal point. The steep roofline of Ernest Barnsley's picture-perfect stone garden house at Rodmarton Manor, which is echoed in the clipped hedges, is an important focal point for the traditional English-style double borders. Simon Dorrell's whimsical half-timbered dovecote at Bryan's Ground opens on three sides for garden viewing. On one side, small beds of bright yellow and orange perennials complement the ochre color of the building.

Ellen Shipman excelled in designs for small structures and pavilions that were sympathetic in style and scale to the architecture of the house. These buildings served a dual purpose: an interesting focal point for her axial gardens and a practical place for storing pool or garden equipment. Shipman often used English-inspired dovecotes, which were not only eye-catchers, but practical buildings for storing equipment or providing a pleasant place for tea. She modeled the whimsical brick dovecote (or pigeonnier) in the wild garden at Longue Vue House and Gardens in New Orleans after one at a nearby plantation.

Pergolas and arbors can lend charm and beauty to a garden. Whether constructed of brick piers, rough stone, or masonry, and covered with climbing roses, wisteria, or fragrant vines, they afford a shady retreat in hot weather. Lutyens, who routinely used pergolas to great effect for reinforcing the geometry of the garden, often used alternating round and square piers to create visual interest, such as those at Hestercombe. Pergolas are versatile, because when densely covered with vines, they can enclose the garden entirely, but when sparsely planted or discontinuous, they draw the eye to the greater landscape in the distance. In kitchen gardens, rustic pergolas constructed of larch poles are perfect supports on which to grow gourds or small fruit. In smaller gardens, a simple arbor can become the essential design element that completes the garden picture.

257

TOP
Rustic arbor at the Florence Griswold Museum, Old Lyme, Connecticut

ABOVE
L. Rome Guthrie, stone wall and wisteria-clad pergola at Townhill Park, Southampton, Hampshire

OPPOSITE TOP
Ellen Shipman, brick pigeonnier at Longue Vue House and Gardens, New Orleans

OPPOSITE BOTTOM
Edwin Lutyens, tile-built pergola with alternating round and square piers, at Hestercombe

In Lutyens's and Jekyll's day, pergolas were all the rage in gardens both large and small. The Edwardian architect and garden designer Harold Peto, whom Jekyll greatly admired, was a master designer of elaborate pergolas in grander gardens in England and the South of France. Most were far too large and elaborate for intimate Arts and Crafts gardens that were based on simplicity and practicality. For Jekyll, pergolas were a means of displaying climbing vines rather than design features, while Lutyens took pergolas to another level as important architectural components. Jekyll favored rough larch poles for constructing a pergola rather than solid piers of marble or rubble as was common in Europe. For many Arts and Crafts gardens, both British and American, architects used the pergola as an important means of connecting the house to the garden.

At Townhill Park, Hampshire, where Jekyll collaborated with architect L. Rome Guthrie, elevated pergolas on stone walls enclose the formal sunken garden. Jekyll planted *Wisteria sinensis*, Virginia creeper, and several varieties of clematis to create a stunning visual effect. Inside the enclosure, long flower beds were dedicated to

Arbor and bench at Wollerton Old Hall, Market Drayton, Shropshire

labor-intensive annuals and perennials.[10] Despite the complexity of the original scheme, the basic concept of ringing the enclosure, or even parts of it, with pergolas creates a dynamic framework for a larger garden. In smaller gardens or individual compartments within a larger garden, arbors can be effectively used in place of pergolas. The attractive arbor at Wollerton Old Hall provides the main interest for one of the compartments in a formal garden. Whether festooned with climbers or left bare, arbors provide a simple architectural touch to any garden.

GARDEN ORNAMENT

Including garden ornament is a simple way to embellish any garden, but the pieces should best be suited to the specific site. Simple ornament, such as containers, work best; statuary and garden figures can be difficult to include, because they must be chosen to reflect the scale and individuality of the garden. Jekyll

BELOW, CLOCKWISE FROM LEFT
Obelisk and bench at York Gate

Lunaform pot at Thuya Garden, Northeast Harbor, Maine

Antique urn at Coton Manor, Guilsborough, Northampton

259

ABOVE
Poolside arrangement
of planters at the Dillon
Garden, Dublin

PREVIOUS LEFT
Charles Sumner Greene,
rustic planter at Green
Gables, Woodside,
California

PREVIOUS RIGHT
Planters lining Lutyens's
steps at Great Dixter

advised that ornament be used sparingly in a small garden; otherwise, it would look like a vision from a contractor's yard. An obelisk used at York Gate has no place in an informal country garden; in a traditional English garden, such as Coton Manor, an antique urn fits comfortably in the setting. A rustic planter sits comfortably in a California garden; a locally make Lunaform pot works well in an informal woodland garden in coastal Maine.

Small containers offer endless possibilities for staging effects around steps, pools, and other important garden features. Jekyll's small courtyard garden on the shady north side of her house was filled with a precise arrangement of containers featuring hostas, lilies, and cannas, while the edge of the nearby tank was lined with better planters filled with *Francoa ramosa*. At Great Dixter, the steps are softened with seasonal planters that help lead the visitor down to the lower gardens, while in Helen Dillon's garden, the color and textural statements in her dazzling borders extend to a staging of individual containers along the edges of the pool.

SMALL FURNISHINGS

A well-placed garden bench, either a stone bench built into the wall with plenty of paving in front or a wooden one of special design, adds to the enjoyment of a garden of any size. "Good design in garden furniture is just as necessary to the success of a garden as the furniture is to the house itself," advised Mawson.[11] Lutyens's famous wooden bench, which made its first appearance at Munstead Wood in the late 1890s and now proliferates in gardens around the world, has somewhat overshadowed other thoughtfully designed benches.

Mawson recommended oak as the best choice for a bench because it lasted the longest, but for a painted bench, he advised using green painted pine. Jekyll thought the best material was untreated oak that eventually takes on silvery hues, and she also observed that regularly painted benches stood up well. As to the appropriate color, she said, green is doubtful, "as it is likely to quarrel with varied natural greens which are near it [and] white is safe, but looks rather staring

ABOVE, CLOCKWISE FROM TOP LEFT
Edwin Lutyens, wooden bench at Holker Hall, Cark-in-Cartmel, Cumbria

Beatrix Farrand, sheltered bench at Dumbarton Oaks

Painted bench at Saint-Gaudens National Historic Site, Cornish, New Hampshire

during the seasons when there is no brilliant colour in the flower garden to relieve it."[12] Farrand's various custom-designed benches and outdoor furnishings for Dumbarton Oaks were purposely left unpainted. Artists, such as the sculptor Augustus Saint-Gaudens, also took pride in designing their own furnishings for exact placement in the garden.

Garden gates, trellises, and fencing should also be in the proper scale and harmonious with other features in the garden. Metal gates often overshadow a small garden, while painted wooden ones that harmonize with seats and benches are more relevant to an Arts and Crafts aesthetic. A charming wooden gate with a squirrel motif is part of a suite of furnishings, including benches and a birdhouse, custom designed by Farrand for a small garden in coastal Maine. Shipman frequently used Chippendale-style gates in some of her gardens, including one in a North Carolina garden.

WATER FEATURES

Both Mawson and Jekyll thought that water features, preferably with bubbling fountains or water jets, were essential to any garden. In fact, Mawson questioned whether a garden was complete without water. Jekyll loved the sound of water, which she put to good use at Hestercombe, with its numerous water features, including rills, tanks, and spouting masques. For a smaller garden based on Arts and Crafts design principles, however, only the simplest solutions are appropriate, whether a small reflecting pool or a tank filled with waterlilies. "Although very simple forms are the safest for pools, there is room for an occasional burst of gaiety in outline, especially when the rest of the garden plan is of necessity treated in a severe fashion," Jekyll wrote.[13] Whether surrounded by brickwork or paving, a simple pool can easily become a focal point for the entire scheme.

At Hollister House, a rectangular tank in one of the hedged enclosures not only reflects the clouds above but also the dazzling borders surrounding the pool. Even in a small garden such as York Gate, a small water feature is nothing more than an elevated waterlily trough with a dolphin fountain. On the other hand, a naturalistic pond garden is an attractive, but high-maintenance addition to a large country garden, such as Jekyll's wild garden at the Manor House at Upton Grey. The pond is filled with water-loving plants, while the edges surrounding the pond merge quietly into the meadow plantings and apple orchard.

ABOVE
Beatrix Farrand, wooden gate and arch at the McCormick Garden, Bar Harbor, Maine

OPPOSITE
Ellen Shipman, Chippendale-style gate at the Hanes Garden, Winston-Salem, North Carolina

BELOW
Arabella Lennox-Boyd,
mixed borders at Gresgarth
Hall, Caton, Lancaster

PREVIOUS, CLOCKWISE
FROM LEFT
Robin Spencer, waterlily
trough at York Gate

Edwin Lutyens, recessed
pool with spouting masque
at Hestercombe

Gertrude Jekyll, naturalistic
pond at Manor House at
Upton Grey, Hampshire

George Schoellkopf, pool at
Hollister House

FLOWER BORDERS

Much has been said by Jekyll and her followers about flower borders, including how to design, plant, and maintain them. Mawson, who was more of an expert on ornamental trees and shrubs, deferred to William Robinson's 1883 book, *The English Flower Garden*, for advice. As Jekyll famously wrote in *Colour in the Flower Garden*, "To plant and maintain a flower-border, *with a good scheme for colour*, is by no means the easy thing that is commonly supposed. I believe that the only way in which it can be made successful is to devote certain borders to certain times of year; each border or garden region to be bright for from one to three months." [14] Bill Noble's country garden in Vermont does exactly that, with formal borders near the house and bolder, more vigorous plantings where the garden merges into the landscape. Jekyll's overall advice is still timely today, but garden-makers should use plants that perform well in their own climates.

Slavishly replicating a plant palette meant for a specific Jekyll design is questionable, but adapting one of her designs, while challenging, is a possibility. Susanne Clark, in searching for a suitable layout for a new terraced garden in Massachusetts, was intrigued by a scheme Jekyll created for a terraced garden in Surrey in the 1920s. For the actual planting, she studied the plants specified in Jekyll's plans and notes from the standpoint of color, texture, and bloom time, and then substituted plants that worked in her climate. The resulting garden is astonishing.[15] Through trial and error over the course of many years, she was able to achieve the all-important hot and cool elements essential to the design.

Both American and British gardens can feature beautiful borders of every size and configuration. Whether in a single border flanking a grass path or in double borders meant to be admired from a terrace above, an appealing presentation of color and texture is the objective in an Arts and Crafts garden. Although there are no hard and fast rules for creating a border suited for an Arts and Crafts garden,

BELOW, CLOCKWISE FROM TOP LEFT
Bill Noble, boldly colored borders at Bragg Hill, Norwich, Vermont

Susanne Clark, terrace garden in Chilmark, Massachusetts

Long double borders at Parcevall Hall, Skyreholme, Yorkshire

Traditional herbaceous borders at Bourton House, Gloucestershire

269

informality rather than rigidity best reflects the aesthetic. At Gresgarth Hall, Arabella Lennox-Boyd's home garden in Lancashire, newer borders reflect an interest in ornamental grasses, while earlier borders are more traditionally themed.

BELOW
Roses covering courtyard wall at Cothay Manor, Wellington, Somerset

BOTTOM
W. H. Romaine-Walker, roses in archery at Great Fosters, Egham, Surrey

OPPOSITE
Gertrude Jekyll, rose arch at Manor House at Upton Grey

CLIMBERS AND ROSES

No Arts and Crafts garden is complete without the addition of some climbers, especially roses, on arbors, pergolas, or walls. Jekyll cautioned, however, that "the appearance of many a house is made or marred by the wise or injudicious use of climbing plants. A house of no special character may become a thing of beauty [while] one of architectural value may have that whole value obliterated and the structure greatly damaged."[16] Beautiful houses strangled by rampant ivy and untamed wisteria left to uproot stonework were among her pet peeves. Her favorite climbers were rambling roses and *Clematis montana*, which she used at Munstead Wood and in many of her garden commissions, including the Manor House at Upton Grey. At Cothay Manor, an historic manor house in Somerset, the entrance courtyards are covered with old-fashioned climbing roses, which provide a hint to the beauty of the gardens beyond. Jekyll often used nonclimbing shrubs trained to walls for an attractive architectural look. Among her favorites were figs, *Pieris japonica*, *Chimonanthus* species, *Abutilon vitifolium*, and ceanothus.

Mawson also extolled the judicious use of climbers, noting that "even architects, who . . . advised the banishment of all vegetable life from the walls which their ingenuity had contrived, are now . . . recognizing that they are indispensable, not only for the decoration of plain wall surfaces, but also for beautifying portions of buildings [which] otherwise might have been unsightly."[17] *The Art and Craft of Garden Making* provides a detailed list of hardy climbers, their habits, and their uses. High among his favorites is *Clematis montana*, which is well suited for small cottages or for covering a pergola.

271

NATURALISTIC GARDENS

For informal country gardens of several acres, less formal elements can be included along the edges where the property melts into the landscape, such as naturalistic groupings of trees and shrubs or more naturalistically planted borders. Mawson tried to steer his readers from creating "a tangled mess of thorn and briar" and specimen trees engulfed by rampant vines. Instead, he encouraged the landscape gardener to create a picture, much like an artist does on canvas.[18] A judicious selection

of trees and ornamental shrubs on the edges of the garden can help meld formality and informality. At Bragg Hill, the plantings are bolder along the edges, with informal clusters of shrubs and small trees. At Gresgarth Hall, the character of the individual garden rooms progress from formal to informal. No matter the size of the garden, whether it is in a backyard in a suburban setting or in large estate such as Dumbarton Oaks, masses of wildflowers and spring bulbs help connect the garden to nature.

BELOW
Beatrix Farrand,
Mélisande's Allée,
Dumbarton Oaks

OPPOSITE
Bill Noble, perimeter
plantings at Bragg Hill

273

HOUSES AND GARDENS TO VISIT

GREAT BRITAIN

Consult the National Garden Scheme of the United Kingdom (ngs.org.uk) and Scotland (ngs.org.uk/scottish-gardens/), The National Trust (nationaltrust.org.uk), The National Trust for Scotland (nts.org.uk), and The Royal Horticultural Society (rhs.org.uk), for information.

ATHELHAMPTON
HOUSE GARDENS
Dorchester
Dorset DT2 7LG
athelhampton.co.uk

BARRINGTON COURT
(G. JEKYLL)
Ilminster
Somerset TA19 0NQ
nationaltrust.org.uk/
barrington-court

BERKELEY CASTLE
Gloucestershire GL13 9BQ
berkeley-castle.com

BLACKWELL, THE ARTS
& CRAFTS HOUSE
(M. H. BAILLIE SCOTT)
Bowness-on-Windermere
Cumbria LA23 3JT
blackwell.org.uk

BLICKLING HALL
(N. LINDSAY)
Aylsham
Norfolk NR11 6NF
nationaltrust.org.uk/
blickling-estate

BOURTON HOUSE GARDEN
Bourton-on-the-Hill
Gloucestershire GL56 9AE
bourtonhouse.com

BRICKWALL
(Frewen College)
Northiam
East Sussex TN31 6NL
ngs.org.uk

BROAD LEYS
(C. F. A. VOYSEY)
(Windermere Motor Boat
and Racing Club)
Windermere
Cumbria LA23 3LJ
wmbrc.co.uk

BROCKHOLE ON
WINDERMERE
(T. MAWSON)
(Lake District Visitor Centre)
Windermere
Cumbria LA23 1LJ
brockhole.co.uk

BRYAN'S GROUND (S. DOR-
RELL AND D. WHEELER)
Stapleton
Herefordshire LD8 2LP
bryansground.co.uk

CLIVEDEN HOUSE HOTEL
Taplow
Berkshire SL6 0JF
clivedenhouse.co.uk

COLETON FISHACRE
(O. MILNE)
Kingswear
Devon TQ6 0EQ
nationaltrust.org.uk/
coleton-fishacre

COTHAY MANOR (A. ROBB)
Wellington
Somerset TA21 0JR
cothaymanor.co.uk

COTON MANOR GARDEN
(I. AND S. PASLEY-TYLER)
Guilsborough
Northampton NN6 8RQ
cotonmanor.co.uk

COTSWOLD FARM
(N. JEWSON)
Duntisbourne Abbots
Gloucestershire GL7 7JS
ngs.org.uk

THE COURTS GARDEN
Holt
Wiltshire BA14 6RR
nationaltrust.org.uk/
the-courts-garden

CRATHES CASTLE
Banchory
Aberdeenshire AB31 5QJ
nts.org.uk

DYFFRYN GARDENS
(T. MAWSON)
St. Nicholas
Vale of Glamorgan CF5 6SU
Nationaltrust.org.uk

EARLSHALL (R. LORIMER)
Leuchars
Fife KY16 0DP
scotlandsgardens.org

EAST RUSTON OLD
VICARAGE (A. GRAY
AND G. ROBESON)
East Ruston
Norfolk NR12 9HN
eastrustonoldvicarage.co.uk

EDZELL CASTLE
Brechin
Angus DD9 7UE
historicenvironment.
scot/visit-a-place/places/
edzell-castle-and-garden/

FOLLY FARM (E. LUTYENS
AND G. JEKYLL)
Sulhamstead
Berkshire RG7 4DR
lutyenstrust.org.uk

GODDARDS (E. LUTYENS
AND G. JEKYLL)
Abinger Common
Surrey RH5 6JL
lutyenstrust.org.uk

GODDARDS HOUSE AND
GARDEN (W. BRIERLEY
AND G. DILLISTONE)
Dringhouses
York YO24 1GG
nationaltrust.org.uk/
goddards-house-and-garden

GODINTON HOUSE
(R. BLOMFIELD)
Ashford
Kent TN23 3BP
godinton-house-gardens.co.uk

GRAVETYE MANOR HOTEL
(W. ROBINSON)
East Grinstead
West Sussex RH19 4LJ
gravetyemanor.co.uk

GRAYTHWAITE HALL AND
ESTATE (T. MAWSON)
Ulverston
Cumbria LA12 8BA
graythwaite.com

GREAT CHALFIELD
MANOR AND GARDEN
(A. PARSONS)
Melksham
Wiltshire SN12 8NH
nationaltrust.org.uk/
great-chalfield-manor-and-garden

GREAT DIXTER
(E. LUTYENS
AND LLOYD FAMILY)
Northiam
East Sussex TN31 6PH
greatdixter.co.uk

GREAT FOSTERS HOTEL
(W. H. ROMAINE-WALKER)
Egham
Surrey TW20 9UR
greatfosters.co.uk

GRESGARTH HALL GARDENS
(A. LENNOX-BOYD)
Caton
Lancaster LA2 9NB
arabellalennoxboyd.com/gres-
garth/-public.html

GREYWALLS HOTEL
(E. LUTYENS)
Gullane
East Lothian EH31 2EG
greywalls.co.uk

HEALE GARDEN
(D. BLOW AND H. PETO)
Middle Woodford
Wiltshire SP4 6NT
healegarden.co.uk

HESTERCOMBE
GARDENS (E. LUTYENS
AND G. JEKYLL)
Cheddon Fitzpaine
Taunton
Somerset TA2 8LG
hestercombe.com

HIDCOTE MANOR
(L. JOHNSTON)
Hidcote Bartrim
Gloucestershire GL55 6LR
nationaltrust.org.uk/hidcote

HIGH GLANAU MANOR
(H. A. TIPPING)
Lydart
Monmouth
Gwent NP25 4AD
ngs.org.uk

HIGH MOSS
(W. H. WARD)
Portinscale
Keswick
Cumbria CA12 5TX
ngs.org.uk

THE HILL (T. MAWSON)
Inverforth Close
London NW3 7EX
hampsteadheath.net

HILL HOUSE
(C. R. MACKINTOSH)
Helensburgh
Strathclyde G84 9AJ
nts.org.uk

HILL OF TARVIT
(R. LORIMER)
Cupar
Fife KY15 2BA
nts.org.uk

HOLKER HALL AND
GARDENS
Cark-in-Cartmel
Lancaster
Cumbria LA11 7PL
holker.co.uk

IFORD MANOR
(H. PETO)
Bradford-on-Avon
Wiltshire BA15 2BA
ifordmanor.co.uk

KELLIE CASTLE
(R. LORIMER)
Pittenweem
Fife KY10 2 RF
nts.org.uk

KELMSCOTT MANOR
(W. MORRIS)
Lechlade
Gloucestershire GL7 3HJ
sal.org.uk/kelmscott-manor

LANGDALE CHASE HOTEL
(T. MAWSON)
Windermere
Cumbria LA23 1LW
langdalechase.co.uk

THE LASKETT GARDENS
(R. STRONG)
Much Birch
Herefordshire HR2 8HZ
thelaskettgardens.co.uk

LEVENS HALL
Kendal
Cumbria LA8 0PD
levenshall.co.uk

LINDISFARNE CASTLE
(E. LUTYENS AND G. JEKYLL)
Holy Island
Berwick-upon-Tweed
Northumberland TD12 2SH
nationaltrust.org.uk/
lindisfarne-castle

LLANGOED HALL
(C. WILLIAMS-ELLIS)
Llyswen
Powys LD3 0YP
llangoedhall.co.uk

THE MANOR (J. BLOM)
Temple Guiting
Stow-on-the-Wold
Gloucestershire GL54 5RP
ngs.org.uk

THE MANOR HOUSE
(G. JEKYLL)
Upton Grey
Basingstoke
Hampshire RG25 2RD
gertrudejekyllgarden.co.uk

MONTACUTE HOUSE
Montacute
Somerset TA15 6XP
nationaltrust.org.uk/
montacute-house

MOUNT STEWART
(G. JEKYLL)
Newtonards
County Down BT22 2AD
nationaltrust.org.uk/
mount-stewart

MUNSTEAD WOOD
(E. LUTYENS AND
G. JEKYLL)
Heath Lane
Busbridge
Surrey GU7 1UN
munsteadwood.org.uk

NEWBY HALL AND GARDENS
Ripon
North Yorkshire HG4 5AE
newbyhall.com

OARE HOUSE
(C. WILLIAMS-ELLIS)
Pewsey
Wiltshire SN8 4JQ
ngs.org.uk

OWLPEN MANOR
(N. JEWSON)
Uley
Gloucestershire GL11 5BZ
owlpen.com

PARCEVALL HALL
GARDENS (W. MILNER)
Skyreholme
Skipton
North Yorkshire BD23 6DE
parcevallhallgardens.co.uk

PENSHURST PLACE
Tonbridge
Kent TN11 8DG
penshurstplace.com

PLAS BRONDANW
(C. WILLIAMS-ELLIS)
Llanfrothen
Penrhyndeudraeth
Gwynedd LL48 6SW
brondanw.org

PORTMEIRION
(C. WILLIAMS-ELLIS)
Penrhyndeudraeth
Gwynedd LL48 6ET
portmeirion.com

THE PRIORY
(P. HEALING)
Kemerton
Tewkesbury
Worcestershire GL 20 7JN

RED HOUSE
(W. MORRIS)
Bexleyheath
Kent DA6 8JF
nationaltrust.org.uk/red-house

RODMARTON MANOR
(E. BARNSLEY)
Rodmarton
Gloucestershire GL7 6PF
rodmarton-manor.co.uk

RYDAL HALL (T. MAWSON)
(Christian Conference Centre)
Ambleside
Cumbria LA22 9LX
rydalhall.org

SNOWSHILL MANOR
(M. H. BAILLIE SCOTT)
Snowshill
Worcestershire WR12 7JR
nationaltrust.org.uk/
snowshill-manor-and-garden

STANDEN (P. WEBB)
East Grinstead
West Sussex RH19 4NE
nationaltrust.org.uk/
standen-house-and-garden

STOBHALL
By Perth
Perthshire PH2 6DR
stobhall.co.uk

STOBSHIEL HOUSE
Humbie
East Lothian EH36 5PD

STONEYWELL COTTAGE
(E. GIMSON)
Ulverscroft
Leicestershire LE67 9QE
nationaltrust.org.uk/stoneywell

THROUGHAM COURT
(C. FACER)
Througham
Gloucestershire GL6 7HG
christinefacer.com/througham-
court-garden-gloucestershire

TINTINHULL HOUSE
(P. REISS AND
P. HOBHOUSE)
Tintinhull
Yeovil
Somerset BA22 8PZ
nationaltrust.org.uk/
tintinhull-garden

TIRLEY GARTH (C. E. MAL-
LOWS AND T. MAWSON)
Tarporley
Cheshire CW6 0LZ
ngs.org.uk

TOWNHILL PARK HOUSE
(L. ROME GUTHRIE AND
G. JEKYLL)
(The Gregg School)
Southampton
Hampshire SO18 3RR
gregg-school-trust.co.uk/greggs/
gardens/townhill-park.asp

TYLNEY HALL HOTEL
(R. W. SCHULTZ AND
G. JEKYLL)
Rotherwick
Hampshire RG27 9AZ
tylneyhall.co.uk

VANN (G. JEKYLL)
Hambledon
Surrey GU8 4EF
vanngarden.co.uk

VEDDW HOUSE AND
GARDEN (A. WAREHAM)
Devauden
Monmouthshire NP16 6PH
veddw.com

VOEWOOD (E. S. PRIOR)
High Kelling
Norfolk NR25 6QS
voewood.com

WIGHTWICK MANOR
(A. PARSONS AND
T. MAWSON)
Wolverhampton
West Midlands WV6 8EE
nationaltrust.org.uk/
wightwick-manor-and-gardens

WOLLERTON OLD HALL
GARDEN (J. AND L. JENKINS)
Market Drayton
Shropshire TF9 3NA
wollertonoldhallgarden.com

WYKEN HALL GARDENS
(C. CARLISLE)
Bury St Edmunds
Suffolk IP31 2DW
wykenvineyards.co.uk/gardens/

WYNDCLIFFE COURT
SCULPTURE GARDENS
(H. A. TIPPING)
St. Arvans
Monmouthshire NP16 6EY
wyndcliffecourt.co.uk

YORK GATE (R. SPENCER)
Back Church Lane
Adel
West Yorkshire LS16 8DW
perennial.org.uk/garden/york-
gate-garden/

UNITED STATES

For more information about visiting private and public gardens, consult The Garden Conservancy's Open Days Program (gardenconservancy.org), The National Trust for Historic Preservation (savingplaces.org), The Cultural Landscape Foundation's What's Out There (tclf.org), the National Park Service (nps.gov), and local organizations and historical societies.

AGECROFT HALL
(C. GILLETTE)
4305 Sulgrave Raod
Richmond, Virginia 23211
agecrofthall.org

BEAUPORT
(H. D. SLEEPER)
SleeperMcCann House
75 Eastern Point Boulevard
Gloucester, Massachusetts 01930
historicnewengland.org/property/
beauport-sleeper-mccann-house

BELLEFIELD (B. FARRAND)
4097 Albany Post Road
Hyde Park, New York 12538
beatrixfarrandgardenhydepark.org

BRAGG HILL (B. NOBLE)
Norwich, Vermont 05055
billnoblegardens.com

CHATHAM MANOR
(E. SHIPMAN)
Fredericksburg and
Spotsylvania Military Park
120 Chatham Lane
Fredericksburg, Virginia 22405
nps.gov/frsp

CRANBROOK ACADEMY
(E. SAARINEN)
1221 North Woodward Avenue
Bloomfield Hills, Michigan 48303
cranbrook.edu

CRANBROOK HOUSE
AND GARDENS
(A. KAHN AND
O. C. SIMONDS)
380 Lone Pine Road
Bloomfield Hills, Michigan 48303
cranbrook.edu

CROSS ESTATE GARDENS
61 Jockey Hollow Road
Bernardsville, New Jersey 07924
crossestategardens.org

DUMBARTON OAKS
(B. FARRAND)
1703 32nd Street NW
Washington, D.C. 20007
doaks.org

EOLIA (B. FARRAND)
Harkness Memorial State Park
275 Great Neck Road
Waterford, Connecticut 06385
ct.gov/deep/harkness

FAIRSTED
Frederick Law Olmsted
National Historic Site
99 Warren Street
Brookline, Massachusetts 02146
nps.gov/frla/index.htm

FLORENCE
GRISWOLD MUSEUM
96 Lyme Street
Old Lyme, Connecticut 06371
florencegriswoldmuseum.org

FRANK LLOYD WRIGHT
HOME AND STUDIO
951 Chicago Avenue
Oak Park, Illinois 60302
cal.flwright.org/tours/
homeandstudio

DAVID B. GAMBLE HOUSE
(GREENE AND GREENE)
4 Westmoreland Place
Pasadena, California 91103
gamblehouse.org

GARLAND FARM
(B. FARRAND)
Beatrix Farrand Society
475 Bay View Road
Bar Harbor, Maine 04660
beatrixfarrandsociety.org/
garland-farm

THE GLEBE HOUSE
MUSEUM AND GERTRUDE
JEKYLL GARDEN
49 Hollow Road
Woodbury, Connecticut 06798
theglebehousemuseum.org

GRAYCLIFF
CONSERVANCY
(F. L. WRIGHT AND
E. SHIPMAN)
6472 Lake Shore Drive
Derby, New York 14047
experiencegraycliffestate.org

GREEN ANIMALS
TOPIARY GARDENS
380 Corys Lane
Portsmouth, Rhode Island 02871
newportmansions.org/explore/
green-animals-topiary-garden

GREENWOOD GARDENS
(W. W. RENWICK)
274 Old Short Hills Road
Short Hills, New Jersey 07078
greenwoodgardens.org

HOLLISTER HOUSE
(G. SCHOELLKOPF)
300 Nettleton Hollow Road
Washington, Connecticut 06793
hollisterhousegarden.org

HUNNEWELL GARDEN
Wellesley, Massachusetts 02481
gardenconservancy.org

LADEW TOPIARY GARDENS
3535 Jarrettsville Pike
Monkton, Maryland 21111
ladewgardens.com

LONGUE VUE HOUSE
AND GARDENS
(G. AND W. PLATT
AND E. SHIPMAN)
7 Bamboo Road
New Orleans, Louisiana 70124
longuevue.com

MADOO CONSERVANCY
(R. DASH)
618 Main Street
Sagaponack, New York 11962
madoo.org

PEGGY ROCKEFELLER ROSE
GARDEN (B. FARRAND)
New York Botanical Garden
2900 Southern Boulevard
Bronx NY 10458-5126
Nybg.org

RAGDALE (H. V. D. SHAW)
1260 North Green Bay Road
Lake Forest, Illinois 60045
ragdale.org

ROBIE HOUSE (F. L. WRIGHT)
5757 South Woodlawn Avenue
Chicago, Illinois 60637
flwright.org/visit/robiehouse

ROYCROFT CAMPUS
AND INN (G. STICKLEY)
31 South Grove Street
East Aurora, New York 14052
roycroftcampuscorporation.com
roycroftinn.com

SAINT-GAUDENS NATURAL
HISTORIC SITE
Cornish, New Hampshire 03745
sgnhs.org

SHELBURNE FARMS
Harbor Road
Shelburne, Vermont 05481
shelburnefarms.org

STAN HYWET HALL AND
GARDENS (W. MANNING
AND E. SHIPMAN)
714 North Portage Path
Akron, Ohio 44303
stanhywet.org

STICKLEY MUSEUM AT
CRAFTSMAN FARMS
2352 Route 10 West
Parsippany, New Jersey 07950
stickleymuseum.org

TALIESIN
(F. L. WRIGHT)
Highway 23
Spring Green, Wisconsin 53588
taliesinpreservation.org

TALIESIN WEST
(F. L. WRIGHT)
126 North Frank Lloyd Wright
Boulevard
Scottsdale, Arizona 85259
franklloydwright.org/taliesin-west

THUYA GARDEN
AND LODGE
15 Thuya Drive
Northeast Harbor, Maine 04662
gardenpreserve.org/thuya-garden

WINTERTHUR
MUSEUM AND GARDEN
(H. F. DUPONT)
Winterthur, Delaware 19735
winterthur.org

YEW DELL
BOTANICAL GARDENS
6220 Old Lagrange Road
Crestwood, Kentucky 40014
yewdellgardens.org

CANADA

LES QUATRE VENTS
(F. CABOT)
La Malbaie
Québec G5A 1A2
cepas.qc.ca/
jardins-de-quatre-vents/

278

NOTES

INTRODUCTION

1. See Charlotte Gere and Lesley Hoskins, *The House Beautiful: Oscar Wilde and the Aesthetic Interior* (London: Lund Humphries, 2000).
2. Mark Girouard, *Sweetness and Light: The Queen Anne Movement, 1860–1900* (New Haven: Yale University Press, 1984), explores the ramifications of the style in architecture, interiors, and garden design.
3. Ernest Newton, "Domestic Architecture of To-Day," in Lawrence Weaver, ed., *The House and Its Equipment* (London: Country Life, 1911), 1.
4. Margaret Richardson, *The Craft Architects* (New York: Rizzoli, 1983), 11.
5. Judith B. Tankard and Martin A. Wood, *Gertrude Jekyll at Munstead Wood* (London: Pimpernel Press, 2015), 77–79.
6. For more on these offices, see Richardson, *The Craft Architects*.
7. Hermann Muthesius, *Das Englische Haus* (Berlin: Wasmuth, 1908–1910), Vol. 2, 168. Muthesius's three-volume work, originally published in 1904–05, was translated into English in an abridged volume in 1979.
8. Helen Allingham and Marcus B. Huish, *Happy England* (London: Adam and Charles Black, 1903).
9. Mary Greensted, *The Arts and Crafts Movement in the Cotswolds* (Stroud: Alan Sutton, 1993), 1–2.
10. The founders were Gerald Horsley, William Lethaby, Mervyn Macartney, Ernest Newton, and Edward Prior.
11. Muthesius, *Das Englische Haus*, Vol. 1, 218.

CHAPTER 1: GARDENS OLD AND NEW

1. For a detailed discussion of Edwardian garden design and the principal architects, see David Ottewill's *The Edwardian Garden* (New Haven: Yale University Press, 1989).
2. Reginald Blomfield, *The Formal Garden in England* (London: Macmillan, 1892), x.
3. Muthesius, *Das Englische Haus*, Vol. 1, 218.
4. Ernest Newton, "Domestic Architecture of To-Day," in Lawrence Weaver, ed., *The House and Its Equipment* (London: Country Life, 1911), 1.
5. The other partners in Kenton and Company (1890–92) were Sidney Barnsley, Ernest Gimson, William Lethaby, and Mervyn Macartney, all from Shaw's office.

6. George S. Elgood and Gertrude Jekyll, *Some English Gardens* (London: Longmans, Green, 1904), 56.
7. For the career of F. Inigo Thomas, see Ottewill, *The Edwardian Garden*, 13–21.
8. Robert Nathan Cram, "Athelhampton Hall," *House Beautiful*, June 1926, 789. In the 1920s, Thomas Mawson made further improvements to Athelhampton.
9. John Sedding, *Garden-Craft Old and New* (London: John Lane, 1890), vi–vii.
10. Walter Crane, *A Floral Fantasy in an Old English Garden Set Forth in Verses of Coloured Designs* (London: Harper and Brothers, 1899).
11. "A Garden in Westmoreland," *Gardening Illustrated*, 22 November 1884, 459.
12. Elgood and Jekyll, *Some English Gardens*, 63.
13. In 1914, Walter Hindes Godfrey (1881–1961), a former pupil of Devey's architectural partner, wrote a modest book that served to reintroduce Devey nearly thirty years after his death. Ignoring the great strides in garden design that had transpired since the publication of Sedding's and Blomfield's books, *Gardens in the Making* continued to champion their basic tenets.
14. Elgood and Jekyll, *Some English Gardens*, 87–89.
15. *Some English Gardens*, 24.
16. Muthesius, *Das Englische Haus*, Vol. 1, 217.
17. William Robinson, *Garden Design and Architects' Gardens* (London: John Murray, 1892), ix–xi.
18. Robinson, *Garden Design and Architects' Gardens*, 66.
19. Muthesius, *Das Englische Haus*, Vol. 1, 218.

CHAPTER 2: WILLIAM MORRIS'S EARTHLY PARADISE

1. J. W. Mackail, *The Life of William Morris* (1899, reprinted in 1968 by Benjamin Blom), Vol. 1, 143.
2. For an excellent discussion of Morris's flowers and gardening interests, see Derek Baker, *The Flowers of William Morris* (London: Barn Elms, 1996), and Jill Hamilton, Penny Hart, and John Simmons, *The Gardens of William Morris* (New York: Stewart, Tabori & Chang, 1998).
3. The founders were William Morris, Edward Burne-Jones, Philip Webb, Dante

Gabriel Rossetti, Ford Madox Brown, Charles Faulkner, and Peter Paul Marshall. In 1875, Morris reorganized the firm, naming it Morris and Company, and in 1881 he moved it from London to Merton Abbey.
4. May Morris, ed., *The Collected Works of William Morris* (London: Longmans, Green, 1910–15), Vol. 22, 77.
5. Examples of the firm's furnishings can be seen at Standen, Wightwick Manor, and Red House, all National Trust properties. Additionally, the William Morris Gallery, Kelmscott Manor, and Victoria and Albert Museum have collections of the firm's work.
6. William Morris, letter to Emma Lazarus, 21 April 1884, in "A Day in Surrey with William Morris," *Century* 32 (July 1886), 397. Emma Lazarus (1849–87) was a social reformer and poet whose poem, "The New Colossus," is mounted on a plaque at the base of the Statue of Liberty in New York Harbor. Lazarus visited Merton Abbey in 1886.
7. William Morris, "Making the Best of It," *Hopes and Fears for Art* (London: Longmans, Green, 1908), 124–25. This was originally presented as a paper for the Birmingham Society of Artists in 1879.
8. Morris, *Hopes and Fears for Art*, 126–27.
9. *Hopes and Fears for Art*, 128.
10. Mackail, *The Life of William Morris*, 143–44.
11. Fiona MacCarthy, *William Morris: A Life for Our Time* (New York: Alfred A. Knopf, 1995), 164.
12. May Morris and George Bernard Shaw, *William Morris: Artist, Writer, Socialist* (1936, reprinted by Russell and Russell in 1966), Vol. 1, 12.
13. The account, possibly by Georgiana Burne-Jones, appears in Aymer Vallance, *William Morris: His Art, His Writings, and His Public Life* (London: George Bell and Sons, 1897), 49.
14. Hermann Muthesius, *The English House* (abridged version of *Das Englische Haus*, 1904–05; New York: Rizzoli, 1979), 17–18; MacCarthy, *William Morris: A Life for Our Time*, 144.
15. Mackail, *The Life of William Morris*, 144.
16. Jill Hamilton, in "Morris's Garden of Inspiration," *Country Life* 196 (19 September 2002), 166–69, suggests that the lavish plantings were at variance with the austerity

of the interior and the symmetry of the garden contrasts with the irregularity of the house.

17. Some of Webb's drawings for Red House (now housed at the Victoria and Albert Museum) are reproduced in Edward Hollamby, *Red House, Bexleyheath, 1859: Phillip Webb* (New York: Van Nostrand Reinhold, 1991).

18. For a detailed history of the house, see Corona More, "Kelmscott Manor, Oxfordshire: The Home of William Morris," *Country Life* 50 (20 August 1921), 224–29; 27 August 1921, 256–62.

19. After Morris's death in 1896, his widow, Jane, bought the lease in 1913 and lived there until her death in 1938. After May Morris's death, the house was acquired by the Society of Antiquaries in 1962.

20. William Morris, "Gossip About an Old House on the Upper Thames," *The Quest* (Birmingham Guild of Handicraft), November 1895.

21. Morris, "Gossip About an Old House."

22. Rossetti, letter to his mother, 1871, cited in Vallance, *William Morris*, 191.

23. William Morris, *News from Nowhere* (1891, reprinted by Longmans, Green, 1910), 264–65.

24. Morris, "Gossip About an Old House."

25. Lazarus, "A Day in Surrey," 394.

CHAPTER 3: THE LURE OF THE COTSWOLDS

1. Norman Jewson, *By Chance I Did Rove* (1951, reprinted privately in 1973), 26.

2. W. R. Lethaby, Alfred H. Powell, and F. L. M. Griggs, *Ernest Gimson: His Life and Work* (Stratford-upon-Avon: Shakespeare Head Press, 1924), 7.

3. Robert Weir Schultz (1860–1951), who worked in the offices of Norman Shaw and later George and Peto, where he overlapped Edwin Lutyens, designed in the vernacular style, but he was also fascinated with Byzantine architecture.

4. Liberty and Company, the popular shop on Regent's Street, London, was founded in 1895 by Arthur Lasenby Liberty, who commissioned decorative arts (especially metalwork and textiles) from all the leading designers of the day. See Martin Wood, *Liberty Style* (London: Frances Lincoln, 2014).

5. The Cheltenham Museum has an extensive collection of their work, including drawings for executed and unexecuted architectural projects.

6. H. Avray Tipping, "Daneway House, Gloucestershire," *Country Life* 25 (6 March 1909), 347.

7. Tipping, "Pinbury, Gloucestershire," *Country Life* 27 (30 April 1910), 634–36.

8. Tipping, "A House at Sapperton by Mr. A. Ernest Barnsley," *Country Life* 25 (10 April 1909), 522–27. The house, gardens, and stable cost £1,700 (about $250,000 in 2018), proof that careful architectural alterations can cost more than building from scratch.

9. Lethaby et al., *Ernest Gimson: His Life and Work*, 9.

10. Tipping, "A House at Sapperton Designed by Mr. Ernest Gimson," *Country Life* 25 (6 March 1909), 348–54. The thatch roof burned in 1941.

11. Gertrude Jekyll and Lawrence Weaver, *Gardens for Small Country Houses* (London: Country Life, 1912), 165–66. Stoneywell Cottage, which Gimson built as a rural retreat for his brother Sydney in 1898, was nestled in among the rough boulders on the site. Gimson's superb placement of the cottage in the natural landscape is an excellent example of the "organic" approach to architecture that many other architects failed miserably at. See Mary Comino, *Gimson and the Barnsleys* (New York: Van Nostrand Reinhold, 1982), 138–39.

12. Judith B. Tankard and Martin A. Wood, *Gertrude Jekyll at Munstead Wood*, 145–46.

13. Planting plans and correspondence for Combend Manor are included in the Jekyll Collection, Environmental Design Archives, University of California, Berkeley.

14. For a detailed discussion of the plantings, see David Wheeler and Simon Dorrell, *Over the Hills from Broadway: Images of Cotswold Gardens* (Stroud: Alan Sutton, 1991), 111–16.

15. Jewson, *By Chance I Did Rove*, 13–14.

16. Today, Owlpen Manor is a small hotel and is furnished with many pieces designed and created in the Sapperton workshops.

17. James Lees-Milne, *Some Cotswold Country Houses* (Stanbridge, Dorset: Dovecote Press, 1987), 119.

18. Jekyll and Weaver, *Gardens for Small Country Houses*, 2nd ed. (1913), xix.

19. Harold D. Eberlein, "Owlpen Manor House, Gloucestershire," *Architectural Forum*, August 1927, 192.

20. An enigmatic figure, Milne went on to great acclaim for his artful house and garden at Coleton Fishacre, in Devon, for Rupert D'Oyly Carte in 1925. See Christopher Hussey, "A Modern Country House, Coleton Fishacre, Devonshire," *Country Life* 67 (31 May 1930), 782–89.

21. Lawrence Weaver, *Small Country Houses of To-Day*, Vol. 2 (London: Country Life, 1919), 76.

22. Christopher Hussey, "A Modern Country House," 784.

23. C. R. Ashbee, journal entry, 1914, as cited in Simon Biddulph, *Rodmarton Manor* (Gloucestershire, privately printed, 2001), 5.

24. Ernest Barnsley worked on Rodmarton from 1909 until his death in January 1926 (with a suspension between 1914 and 1917 during the First World War), when the project was taken over by his brother Sidney until his death later that year. Rodmarton was completed by Norman Jewson in 1929.

25. Illustrations from 1931 show the Portuguese laurels and other developed parts of the garden. See Arthur Oswald, "Rodmarton, Gloucestershire," *Country Life* 69 (4 April 1931), 422–27.

26. Tipping, "Hidcote Manor, Gloucestershire," *Country Life* 67 (22 February 1930), 286.

CHAPTER 4: ARCHITECTURAL GARDENING

1. Charles Holme (1848–1923) lived at Red House from 1876 until 1902, when he purchased the Manor House at Upton Grey in Hampshire.

2. Its content was "tailored to the preferences and tastes of the middle-class art lover and amateur [who avoided] the stale academicism of the Royal Academy and its aging mentors," according to Clive Ashwin, in *High Art and Low Life: The Studio and the Fin de Siècle*, London: Victoria and Albert Museum, 1993, 7.

3. Holme's editorial team included editor Gleeson White (who wrote many of the early articles) and art editor C. Lewis Hind (the author of numerous monographs on artists). When Holme retired in 1919, he was succeeded by his son Geoffrey Holme, a brilliant businessman to whom credit should be given for the longevity of the magazine. See *The Studio: A Bibliography, the First Fifty Years, 1893–1943* (London: Sims and Reed, 1978) for a detailed history of the magazine.

4. Bryan Holme, "Introduction," *The Studio*, 1.

5. William Henry Ward was a protégé of architect Arthur Blomfield (the uncle of Reginald Blomfield) and the author of two books on French architecture of the Renaissance period. He worked for the firms of George and Peto, Dan Gibson, and Edwin Lutyens.

6. Lawrence Weaver, in *Small Country Houses of To-Day*, 71–75, praised High Moss as a success, but he failed to mention the garden. The house still exists, but the gardens are not as shown in the rendering.

7. Hermann Muthesius, *The English House* (abridged version of *Das Englische Haus*, 1904–05; New York: Rizzoli, 1979), 51.

8. Gleeson White, "Some Glasgow Designers," *The Studio* 11 (July 1897), 86–100.

9. Muthesius suggests that their work was initially ridiculed in England, but modern scholarship has begun to dispute this notion.

10. Mackintosh's watercolors are held at the Hunterian Art Gallery, University of Glasgow. See Roger Billcliffe, ed., *Mackintosh Watercolours* (London: John Murray, 1978) and *Architectural Sketches and Flower Drawings by Charles Rennie Mackintosh* (New York: Rizzoli, 1977).

11. James Macaulay, *Hill House: Charles Rennie Mackintosh* (London: Phaidon, 1994), 15.

12. For the site plan, see Wendy Kaplan, ed., *Charles Rennie Mackintosh* (New York: Abbeville Press, 1996), 179.

13. J. J. Joass, "On Gardening: With Descriptions of Some Formal Gardens in Scotland," *The Studio* 11 (August 1897), 167–68.

14. Robert Lorimer, cited in Sir Herbert Maxwell, *Scottish Gardens* (London: Edward Arnold, 1908), 188.

15. Margaret Richardson, *The Craft Architects* (New York: Rizzoli, 1983), 45.

16. See Gertrude Jekyll and Lawrence Weaver, *Gardens for Small Country Houses*, 89–91, for a critique of Home Place.

17. Edward S. Prior, "Garden-Making," *The Studio* 21 (October 1900), 28, 31.

18. Prior, "Garden-Making III: The Conditions of Material," *The Studio* 21 (December 1900), 176.

19. Prior, "Garden-Making II: The Conditions of Practice," *The Studio* 21 (November 1900), 95.

20. A partial list of Mallows's commissions includes Joyce Grove, Nettlebed, Oxon (1911); Dalham Hall, Suffolk; Canons Park, Edgware, Middlesex; Crocombe, Happisburgh, Norfolk (1909); Brackenston, Pembury, Kent (1904); Tirley Garth, Taporley, Cheshire (1912); and Craig-y-Parc, Pentyrch, Wales (1913).

21. Jekyll and Weaver, *Gardens for Small Country Houses*, xvii.

22. For the life and work of Griggs, see Jerrold Northrop Moore, *F. L. Griggs: The Architecture of Dreams* (Oxford: Clarendon Press, 1999).

23. Griggs illustrated E. V. Boyle's *Seven Gardens and a Palace* (1900), Harry Roberts's *The Chronicle of a Cornish Garden* (1901), and Mary Pamela Milne-Home's *Stray Leaves from a Gorder Garden* (1901) as well as more than a dozen volumes of Macmillan's popular *Highways and Byways* series.

24. C. E. Mallows, "Architectural Gardening," *The Studio* 44 (August 1908), 181–82.

25. Mallows, "Architectural Gardening IV," *The Studio* 46 (March 1909), 120–21.

26. Jekyll and Weaver, *Gardens for Small Country Houses*, 64.

27. Clive Aslet, "Tirley Garth," *Country Life* 171 (18 March 1982), 702.

28. Janet Waymark, "Mallows, Charles Edward (1864–1915)," *Oxford Dictionary of National Biography* (Oxford: Oxford University Press, 2008).

CHAPTER 5: INDIVIDUALITY AND IMAGINATION

1. *Studio Year Book of Decorative Art 1909* (London: The Studio, 1909), 28; C. F. A. Voysey, *Individuality* (London: Chapman and Hall, 1915).

2. John Betjeman, "Charles Francis Annesley Voysey, the Architect of Individualism," *The Architectural Review*, October 1931, 93.

3. For more on Voysey's life and career, consult Wendy Hitchmough, *C. F. A. Voysey* (New York: Phaidon, 1995). There is a large archive of Voysey's architectural work in the Drawings Collection at the Royal Institute of British Architects, London, and an archive of his textiles and wallpapers at the Victoria and Albert Museum, London.

4. M. H. Baillie Scott, "On the Characteristics of Mr. C. F. A. Voysey's Architecture," *The Studio* 42 (October 1907), 19.

5. Sir Edwin Lutyens, "Foreword," *The Architectural Review*, October 1931, 91.

6. T. Raffles Davison, *Modern Homes: Selected Examples of Dwelling Houses* (London: George Bell, 1909), 119.

7. Betjeman coined the term "Metro-land" for the bedroom communities ringing London where Voysey built many of his houses.

8. "An Interview with Mr. C. F. A. Voysey, *The Studio* 1 (September 1893), 232.

9. Gertrude Jekyll and Lawrence Weaver, *Gardens for Small Country Houses*, 162, fig. 220.

10. Examples of his garden architecture can be seen at Greyfriars, Lowicks, Norney Grange, Littleholme, Priors Garth, and New Place. A discussion of Littleholme is included in Jekyll and Weaver, *Gardens for Small Country Houses*, 76–80.

11. W. Duggan, "The Gardens at New Place, Haslemere," *The Garden* 85 (6 August 1921), 388.

12. "Some Recent Work of C. F. A. Voysey, an English Architect," *House and Garden* 3 (May 1903), 256.

13. See Hermann Muthesius, *Das Englische Haus*, Vol. 2, 113, 114, for photographs of these garden houses. Voysey designed summerhouses for Lowicks, which also sports a similar weathercock, and Norney Grange.

14. See planting plan in Jane Brown, "The Garden of New Place," *The Garden* 108 (June 1983), 232, based on files in the Gertrude Jekyll Collection, Environmental Design Archives, University of California, Berkeley.

15. See Alan Powers, "Blackwell, Cumbria," *Country Life* 195 (12 July 2001), 86–91.

16. Betjeman, "Mackay Hugh Baillie Scott," *Journal of the Manx Museum*, 1968, cited in Diane Haigh, *Baillie Scott: The Artistic House* (London: Academy, 1995), 116.

17. "An Ideal Suburban House," *The Studio* 4 (January 1895), 127–32; "The Decoration of the Suburban House," *The Studio* 5 (April 1895), 15–21.

18. Baillie Scott, *Houses and Gardens* (London: George Newnes, 1906), 1.

19. Baillie Scott and A. Edgar Beresford, *Houses and Gardens* (London: Architecture Illustrated, 1933), 32.

20. *Houses and Gardens* (1906), 81, 84.

21. *Houses and Gardens* (1906), 82.

22. *Houses and Gardens* (1906), 3, 85.

23. The three projects were Greenways, Sunningdale (1907); Runton Old Hall, Norfolk (1908); and Garden Corner, Guildford (1915).

24. Letter, M. H. Baillie Scott to Gertrude Jekyll, 12 August 1907, Gertrude Jekyll Collection, Environmental Design Archives, University of California, Berkeley.

25. "Recent Designs in Domestic Architecture," *The Studio* 51 (December 1910), 222.

26. Judith B. Tankard and Martin A. Wood, *Gertrude Jekyll at Munstead Wood*, 146.

27. "The Studio Prize Competitions," *The Studio* 41 (June 1907), 86.

28. Gervase Jackson-Stops, *An English Arcadia 1600–1990* (Washington, D.C.: AIA Press/The National Trust, 1990), 147; A. E. Richardson, in "Snowshill Manor, Gloucestershire," *Country Life* 62 (1 October 1927), 470–77, attributes the design of the garden to Wade.

29. Haigh, *Baillie Scott: The Artistic House*, 69.

CHAPTER 6: THE ART AND CRAFT OF GARDEN MAKING

1. In *The Art and Craft of Garden Making*, Mawson designated himself "garden architect"; his autobiography is entitled *The Life & Work of an English Landscape Gardener* in Britain, while the American edition is entitled *The Life & Work of an English Landscape Architect*.

2. Ken Lemmon, "Landscaper of the World: Thomas H. Mawson, a Self-Help Victorian," *Country Life* 175 (10 May 1984), 1318.

3. Thomas H. Mawson, *The Life & Work of an English Landscape Architect* (New York: Scribner's, 1927), 41–42.

4. Geoffrey Beard, *Thomas H. Mawson: A Northern Landscape Architect* (University of Lancaster, 1978), 11.

5. His four most significant gardens are Thornton Manor, Cheshire (1905); Rivington Pike, Bolton (1906); Roynton Cottage, Bolton (1906); and The Hill, Hampstead, London (1906).

6. "Since the appearance of *The Formal Garden* by Reginald Blomfield, we have seen no work on the fascinating subject of artistic gardens to be compared in interest with the one under review" (*The Studio* 20 [July 1900], 135.)

7. Mawson, *Life & Work*, 164.

8. Mawson, *The Art and Craft of Garden Making* (London: Batsford, 1901), xi. Unless otherwise noted, all citations are taken from this edition.

9. Mawson worked with Voysey at Moor Crag (1898) and Baillie Scott at Blackwell (1902), both in Windermere.

10. Mawson, *The Art and Craft of Garden Making*, 222.

11. *The Art and Craft of Garden Making*, 224.

12. Dyffryn Gardens, with its magnificent collection of specimen trees, is currently undergoing a full-scale restoration by the National Trust. The layout of the grounds is basically unaltered.

13. Reginald Cory (1871–1934), a longtime benefactor to the Royal Horticultural Society, where he bequeathed his extensive horticultural library, was renowned for his work in hybridizing plants. His collection of dahlias, for example, numbered 600 varieties. Cory was also interested in town planning and had Mawson design a projected model village, Glyn Cory, near Dyffryn.

14. Thomas H. Mawson and E. Prentice Mawson, *The Art and Craft of Garden Making*, 5th ed. (London: Batsford, 1926), 386–89.

15. Within three months of the book's initial publication in October 1912, a second, revised edition, was printed, with an expanded introduction that included measured drawings that were not completed in time for the first edition. All citations are taken from this edition.

16. Gertrude Jekyll and Lawrence Weaver, *Gardens for Small Country Houses*, xxxiii.

17. *Gardens for Small Country Houses*, 55–59.

18. Mawson, *The Art and Craft of Garden Making*, 69.

19. *Gardens for Small Country Houses*, 99.

20. *The Art and Craft of Garden Making*, 118–19.

21. *Gardens for Small Country Houses*, 147, 158.

CHAPTER 7: AT HOME WITH TWO MASTER GARDENERS

1. Among William Robinson's books, the most important are *The Parks, Promenades, and Gardens of Paris* (1869), *Alpine Flowers for English Gardens* (1870), *The Wild Garden* (1870), *The Subtropical Garden* (1871), *The English Flower Garden* (1883), *Garden Design and Architects' Gardens* (1892), *The Garden Beautiful* (1907), *Gravetye Manor* (1911), *The Virgin's Bower* (1912), and *Home Landscapes* (1914), all published in London by John Murray.

2. For the history of some of Robinson's books, see Judith B. Tankard, "A Perennial Favourite: 'The English Flower Garden'," *Hortus* 17 (Spring 1991), 74–85, and "William Robinson and the Art of the Book," *Hortus* 27 (Autumn 1993), 21–30.

3. Tankard, "A Perennial Favourite," 74–85.

4. Like Robinson, Wilhelm Miller (1869–1938) founded or wrote for several magazines, including *Country Life in America*. His book, *What England Can Teach Us about Gardening* (Garden City: Doubleday, Page, 1911), reflects his travels in England in 1908.

5. *The Studio* 32 (15 July 1904), 174.

6. Robinson's original "Tree and Garden Books," containing plant lists and other information omitted from *Gravetye Manor*, are held in the Lindley Library, London.

7. Robinson thought that Devey's remodeling of Gravetye Manor, undertaken between August 1885 and September 1886 and one of his last commissions, was carelessly done. See Jill Allibone, *George Devey Architect, 1820–1886* (Cambridge: Lutterworth Press, 1991).

8. Letter, Edwin Lutyens to Emily Lutyens, 24 August 1903, cited in Clayre Percy and Jane Ridley, eds., *The Letters of Edwin Lutyens to His Wife Lady Emily* (London: Collins, 1985), 106.

9. Robinson, "In the Garden," *Country Life* 34 (4 October 1913), 452.

10. Robinson, *Gravetye Manor*, 96.

11. Robinson, "The Flower Garden at Gravetye Manor," *Country Life* 32 (28 September 1912), 409.

12. Henry James, *Pictures and Text* (New York: Harper and Brothers, 1893), 88–89.

13. Robinson, "The Flower Garden at Gravetye Manor," 411.

14. Robinson, *Gravetye Manor*, 95.

15. Tankard, "Moonscape," *Country Life* 190 (9 May 1996), 72–73.

16. Last Will and Testament of William Robinson, 17 January 1928, 7, H. M. Probate Registry, London.

17. Peter Herbert, "Foreword," *The Wild Garden*, new ed. (New York: Sagapress, 1994), and in conversation with the author.

18. Peter Savage, *Lorimer and the Edinburgh Craft Designers* (Edinburgh: Paul Harris, 1980), 25.

19. See Tankard, "The Garden Before Munstead Wood," *Hortus* 20 (Winter 1991), 17–26, for a description. See also Tankard and Wood, *Gertrude Jekyll at Munstead Wood* (London: Pimpernel Press, 2015), for a detailed discussion of Munstead Wood.

20. William Goldring, "Munstead, Godalming," *The Garden* 22 (26 August 1882), 191–92.

21. Gertrude Jekyll and Lawrence Weaver, *Gardens for Small Country Houses*, 36.

22. Jekyll, *Colour in the Flower Garden* (London: Country Life, 1908), 55.

23. See Tankard, "Miss Jekyll's True Colours," *Country Life* 191 (15 May 1997), 140–43, for period views of these gardens in color.

24. Herbert Baker, *Architecture and Personalities* (London: Country Life, 1944), 16.

25. Jekyll, *Home and Garden* (London: Longmans, Green, 1900), 1.

26. Despite the simplicity of Jekyll's house, it cost her almost £4,000 (about $600,000 in 2018), a considerable sum in 1897.

CHAPTER 8: A PERFECT HOUSE AND GARDEN

1. Judith B. Tankard, "Gardening with *Country Life*," *Hortus* 30 (Summer 1994), 72–86. See also Tankard, *Gertrude Jekyll and the Country House Garden: From the Archives of Country Life* (London: Aurum Press; New York: Rizzoli, 2011).

2. See Fenja Gunn, "Jekyll's Country Life Style," *Country Life* 187 (26 August 1993), 46–49, for a discussion of Lutyens's commissions for Hudson.

3. Christopher Hussey, *The Life of Sir Edwin Lutyens* (London: Country Life; New York: Charles Scribner's, 1950), 95.

4. Hussey, *The Life of Lutyens*, 96.

5. [H. Avray Tipping], "A House and a Garden," *Country Life* 13 (9 May 1903), 602–11. In his discussion of Deanery Garden, T. Raffles Davidson, in *Modern Homes* (London: George Bell, 1909), gives credit to Jekyll's role: "It is a signal tribute to the ability of its architect, Mr. E. L. Lutyens, to create a house, and to Miss

Gertrude Jekyll to create a garden which are so entirely in sympathy with each other."

6. Lawrence Weaver, *Houses and Gardens of E. L. Lutyens* (London: Country Life, 1913), 58.

7. Gertrude Jekyll and Lawrence Weaver, *Gardens for Small Country Houses*, 26.

8. After being in continuous private ownership, Goddards became the headquarters of the Lutyens Trust in 1991 and is now under the management of the Landmark Trust.

9. Weaver, *Houses and Gardens of E. L. Lutyens*, 39.

10. Weaver, "Marshcourt, Hampshire," *Country Life* 33 (19 April 1913), 562.

11. Jekyll and Weaver, *Gardens for Small Country Houses*, 158.

12. Tipping, "Millmead, Bramley," *Country Life* 21 (11 May 1907), 677.

13. Jekyll and Weaver, *Gardens for Small Country Houses*, 1–2. The property had experienced an unglamorous history, with pigs being kept there at one time. The Jacobean cottages were demolished in 1898.

14. Tipping, "Millmead, Bramley," 676.

15. Jekyll and Weaver, *Gardens for Small Country Houses*, 2–3.

16. *Gardens for Small Country Houses*, 2–3.

17. Unlike many of the earlier Lutyens and Jekyll projects, there are ample working drawings and notes pertaining to the gardens at Folly Farm in the Gertrude Jekyll Collection at the University of California, Berkeley. Curiously, most of the plans relate to the 1906 scheme and little information exists for the later, more important, scheme of 1912. Handwritten notes on the drawings, such as "Steps up to the Croquet Court?," confirm Jekyll's involvement in design decisions as well as the planting.

18. The one at Westbury Court, Gloucestershire, is one of the few remaining examples of this type of water feature. Most were destroyed by "Capability" Brown in the eighteenth century, when the landscape style replaced formality in garden design.

19. Hussey, "Folly Farm," *Country Life* 51 (28 January 1922), 114.

20. In the 1970s, American landscape architect Lanning Roper simplified the plantings, replacing high-maintenance flowers with perennials, giving Folly Farm an updated look. See Lanning Roper, "A Garden of Vistas," *Country Life* 157 (15 May 1975), 1230–32.

21. Tipping, "Hestercombe, Somerset II," *Country Life* 14 (17 October 1908), 528.

CHAPTER 9:
BEYOND THE BORDERS

1. Lawrence Weaver, "Ardkinglas," *Country Life* 29 (27 May 1911), 746.

2. The 27 September 1912 issue of *Country Life* contains a special supplement devoted to Lorimer's work.

3. Gertrude Jekyll designed Whinfold, Hascombe, Surrey (1898); High Barn, Hascombe, Surrey (1901); Brackenburgh, Penrith, Cumberland (1901); and Barton Hartshorn, Buckingham, Oxfordshire (1902).

4. Jekyll and Weaver, *Gardens for Small Country Houses*, xliii; see also Weaver, "The Walled Garden at Edzell Castle," *Country Life* 32 (14 December 1914), 859–62.

5. Christopher Hussey, *The Work of Sir Robert Lorimer* (London: Country Life, 1931), 7, 17, 18.

6. Robert Lorimer, "On Scottish Gardens," *The Architectural Review*, November 1899, 194–205, as cited in Peter Savage, "Lorimer and the Garden Heritage of Scotland," *Garden History, Journal of the Garden History Society* 5 (Summer 1977), 30.

7. Hussey, *The Work of Robert Lorimer*, 24.

8. Hew Lorimer, *Kellie Castle and Garden* (National Trust for Scotland, 1985), 4.

9. Hussey, *The Work of Robert Lorimer*, 15.

10. George Elgood and Gertrude Jekyll, *Some English Gardens*, 48, 50.

11. Kathleen Sayer, "Kellie Castle Garden in Spring," *Hortus* 29 (Spring 1994), 46–52.

12. "Earlshall, Fifeshire, the Seat of Mr. R. W. Mackenzie," *Country Life* 17 (1 July 1905), 942–50.

13. Hussey, *The Work of Robert Lorimer*, 24; Peter Verney, *The Gardens of Scotland* (London: B. T. Batsford, 1976), 77.

14. Peter Savage, *Lorimer and the Edinburgh Craft Designers* (Edinburgh: Paul Harris, 1980), 11.

15. All four properties are owned by The National Trust.

16. Hussey, "Gardener and Antiquary," *Country Life* 74 (25 November 1933), 567.

17. Lady Congreve, "The Late H. Avray Tipping, a Personal Recollection," *Country Life* 74 (25 November 1933), 566–67.

18. [H. A. Tipping], "Mathern Palace, Monmouthshire," *Country Life* 28 (19 November 1910), 725.

19. Tipping, *English Gardens* (London: Country Life, 1925), 219.

20. Tipping, *The Garden of To-Day* (London: Martin Hopkinson, 1933), 44.

21. See Tipping, *English Gardens*, 225–38, for garden plan and photographs of Mounton House.

22. Tipping, "High Glanau, Monmouthshire" *Country Life* 65 (8 June 1929), 829.

23. Tipping, "High Glanau II, Monmouthshire," *Country Life* 65 (15 June 1929), 856.

24. David Wheeler, "A Corner of Wales That Is Forever England," *Country Life* 192 (16 July 1998), 61.

25. C. H. Reilly, *Representative British Architects of the Present Day* (London: Batsford, 1931), 93.

26. In 1919, Williams-Ellis published a book on *Cottage Building in Cob, Pisé, Chalk and Clay*.

27. See Richard Haslam, *Clough Williams-Ellis: RIBA Drawings Collection Monographs* (London: Academy, 1996) for examples of his work.

28. *England and the Octopus* (London: Geoffrey Bles, 1928). Williams-Ellis also wrote (with his wife, Amabel) *The Pleasures of Architecture* (London: Jonathan Cape, 1924), and his autobiography, *Architect Errant* (London: Constable, 1971).

29. Jekyll and Hussey, *Garden Ornament* (London: Country Life, 1927), 365.

30. Hussey, "Plas Brondanw, Merionethshire," *Country Life* 69 (31 January 1931), 136.

31. Gertrude Knoblock, whose studio was located in London, designed fountain figures with cherubs and small children that were popular in American as well as British gardens in the 1930s.

CHAPTER 10: CRAFTSMAN STYLE

1. See Jens Jensen, *Siftings* (1939, reprinted by Johns Hopkins Press, 1990), and O. C. Simonds, *Landscape Gardening* (1920, reprinted by University of Massachusetts Press, 2000).

2. Mabel Tuke Priestman, "History of the Arts and Crafts Movement in America," *House Beautiful*, October and November 1906, as reprinted in *History of the Arts and Crafts Movement in America* (Berkeley: The Arts and Crafts Press, 1996), 21.

3. Mark Alan Hewitt, *Gustav Stickley's Craftsman Farms: The Quest for an Arts and Crafts Utopia* (Syracuse: Syracuse University Press, 2001), 1.

4. Natalie Curtis, "The New Log House at Craftsman Farms: An Architectural Development of the Log Cabin," *The Craftsman* 21 (November 1911), 201.

5. "Craftsman Farms: Its Development and Future," *The Craftsman* 25 (October 1913), 8–15.

6. "The Growing Individuality of the American Garden," *The Craftsman* 20 (April 1911), 54–62.

283

7. As Baillie Scott explained in *Houses and Gardens* (1933), "The house in America is one of those for which we merely supplied the drawings." It was built by an architect associated with the firm of McKim, Mead and White.

8. See David Cathers, "The Close: Old England in New Jersey," *American Bungalow* 29 (Spring 2001), 9–14.

9. Judith B. Tankard, "Pleasant Days: A Millionaire's Dream Castle," *The Magazine Antiques*, June 2005, 58–64.

10. Alan Crawford, *C. R. Ashbee: Architect, Designer and Romantic Socialist* (New Haven: Yale University Press, 1985), 407.

11. Frank Lloyd Wright, "Concerning Landscape Architecture," *Frank Lloyd Wright Collected Writings, 1894–1939.* Courtesy of John Arthur, who provided this reference.

12. Virginia A. Green, *The Architecture of Howard Van Doren Shaw* (Chicago: Chicago Review Press, 1998), 13.

13. See Suzanne Turner, *The Landscape of Ragdale, Home of the Howard Van Doren Shaw Family and the Ragdale Foundation* (Cultural Landscape Report, privately printed, 2002) and Alice Hayes and Susan Moon, *Ragdale, A History and Guide* (Berkeley: Open Books/Ragdale Foundation, 1990).

14. Ragdale has always been the home of artists, first with members of Shaw's family, and now it is an artists' retreat. One of his daughters, Sylvia Shaw Judson, was a renowned sculptor, whose sculptural pieces enhance the site today.

15. See Diana Balmori, "Saarinen House Garden," in *Saarinen House and Garden: A Total Work of Art* (New York: Harry N. Abrams, 1995).

16. Charles Keeler, *The Simple Home* (1904, reprinted by Peregrine Smith, 1979), 15.

17. They may have visited the Japanese pavilion at the World's Columbian Exposition in Chicago in 1893. See Edward R. Bosley, "Greene and Greene: The British Connection," *The Tabby: A Chronicle of the Arts and Crafts Movement* 3 (July–August 1997), 7.

18. Bosley, "Greene and Greene," 16–17.

19. David C. Streatfield, "Echoes of England and Italy 'On the Edge of the World': Green Gables and Charles Greene," *Journal of Garden History* 2 (October–December 1982), 380.

20. Thaisa Way, *Arts and Crafts Gardens in California* (master's thesis, University of Virginia, 1991), 1.

21. Streatfield, *California Gardens: Creating a New Eden* (New York: Abbeville Press, 1994), 83.

CHAPTER 11: BEAUTIFUL GARDENS IN AMERICA

1. Louise Shelton, *Beautiful Gardens in America* (New York: Scribners, 1915), 7.

2. For a comprehensive history, see May Brawley Hill, *Grandmother's Garden: The Old-Fashioned American Garden, 1865–1915* (New York: Harry N. Abrams, 1995).

3. See Virginia Lopez Begg, "Mabel Osgood Wright: The Friendship of Nature and the Commuter's Wife," *Journal of the New England Garden History Society* 5 (1997), 35–41, for the role of women in garden literature.

4. Mariana Griswold Van Rensselaer, *Art Out-of-Doors* (New York: Scribners, 1893), 8.

5. Judith B. Tankard, "Defining Their Turf: Pioneer Women Landscape Designers," *Bard Studies in Decorative Arts* 8 (Fall–Winter 2000–2001), 31–53.

6. Tankard, "Henry Davis Sleeper's Gardens at Beauport," *Journal of the New England Garden History Society* 10 (2002), 30–43.

7. Frances Duncan, "The Gardens of Cornish," *The Century Magazine*, May 1906, 3–19.

8. Alma Gilbert and Judith Tankard, *A Place of Beauty: The Artists and Gardens of the Cornish Colony* (Berkeley: Ten Speed Press, 2000), 69–75.

9. Rose Standish Nichols, *English Pleasure Gardens* (Boston: David R. Godine, 2003), 255.

10. Nichols designed approximately seventy gardens, but little is known about most of her commissions because her office records were discarded after her death.

11. Duncan, "A Cornish Garden," *Country Life in America*, March 1908, 507.

12. Tankard, "Nellie B. Allen," in Birnbaum and Karson, eds., *Pioneers of American Landscape Design* (New York: McGraw-Hill, 2000).

13. Reuben Rainey, "Biography of Charles Freeman Gillette," The Culural Landscape Foundation, tclf.org.

14. Louise Beebe Wilder, *Adventures in a Suburban Garden* (Garden City: Doubleday, 1931), 53.

15. The other commissions were for a woodland garden in Greenwich, Connecticut, and an elaborate terraced garden (unbuilt) near Cincinnati, Ohio.

16. In the 1920s, Jekyll received the Old Glebe House commission from Standard Oil heiress Annie Burr Jennings, in much the same spirit as Americans today who mistakenly look to English designers for their inspiration.

17. Notebooks, 1909–1912, Henry Francis duPont Winterthur Museum Archives, Delaware. See also Denise Magnani, *The Winterthur Garden* (New York: Harry N. Abrams, 1995).

18. Tankard, "Shelburne Farms, the Family Gardens," *Old-House Interiors*, Fall 1998, 66–73.

19. See Tankard, *Beatrix Farrand: Private Gardens, Public Landscapes* (New York: Monacelli Press, 2009) for an overview of Farrand's life and career.

20. Lamar Sparks, "A Landscape Architect Discusses Gardens," *Better Homes and Gardens*, November 1930, 20.

21. Ellen Shipman, "Garden Notebook," unpublished manuscript, author's collection, 38. See also Tankard, *Ellen Shipman and the American Garden* (Athens: University of Georgia Press/LALH, 2018).

CHAPTER 12: COLOR IN THE FLOWER GARDEN

1. The famous painting, featuring two young girls at twilight holding lighted paper lanterns among the lilies and carnations, is at the Tate Gallery in London.

2. Henry James, "Our Artists in Europe," *Harper's New Monthly Magazine* 79 (June 1889), 58.

3. Luggers Hall, now a private home, has fully restored gardens.

4. Even though Parsons's career as a garden designer is elusive, he is known to have designed gardens for Percy's Wyndham at Philip Webb's Clouds, Wiltshire (now demolished); Great Chalfield Manor, Wiltshire; Hartpury House, Gloucestershire (with Thomas Mawson); and others. See Diana Baskervyle-Glegg, "Bulbs Shine Bright in Broadway," *Country Life* 192 (29 January 1998), 40–43; Nicole Milette, *Parsons, Partridge, Tudway: An Unsuspected Garden Design Partnership, 1884–1914* (York: Institute of Advanced Architectural Studies, 1995); and Marian Mako, "Painting with Nature in Broadway, Worcestershire," *Garden History*, 34 (Summer 2006).

5. Giles Edgerton, "Mary Anderson 'At Home' in the Cotswolds," *Arts & Decoration*, March 1937, 12–15.

6. See Bryan N. Brooke, "Willmott, Parsons, and *Genus Rosa*," *The Garden* 112 (October 1987), 455–58. Parsons's original watercolors were presented to the Royal Horticultural Society's Lindley Library through the Reginald Cory Bequest.

7. Willmott shared her bounty with her younger sister, Rose, who married Robert Berkeley of Berkeley Castle, Gloucestershire, U.K., and was also an accomplished gardener. For biographical details, see Audrey Le Lièvre,

Miss Willmott of Warley Place: Her Life and Her Gardens (London: Faber and Faber, 1980).

8. Norah Lindsay, "The Manor House, Sutton Courtenay, Berks.," *Country Life* 69 (16 May 1931), 610.

9. Nellie B. Allen, an American garden designer, noted these colors on the back of her framed photograph of Lindsay's Long Garden, in the author's collection.

10. To learn more about the recent restoration, see Rosamund Wallinger, *Gertrude Jekyll's Lost Garden: The Restoration of an Edwardian Masterpiece* (Woodbridge, Suffolk. U.K.: Garden Art Press, 2000).

11. Graham Stuart Thomas, "Foreword," Tankard and Wood, *Gertrude Jekyll at Munstead Wood*, 6–9.

12. Penelope Hobhouse, ed., *Gertrude Jekyll on Gardening* (Boston: David R. Godine, 1984), 281.

13. Hobhouse, "My Tenure at Tintinhull," *Horticulture*, October 1988, 42.

14. Tim Richardson, "Lost Heroes of Gardening," *The Telegraph*, 24 June 2011.

15. Christopher Lloyd and Charles Hind, *A Guide to Great Dixter* (Angel Design, 1995).

16. Helen Dillon, *Garden Artistry* (New York: Macmillan, 1995), 9.

17. Gertrude Jekyll, *Colour in the Flower Garden*, (London: Country Life, 1908), vi.

18. Dillon, *Garden Artistry*, 13.

19. Jekyll, *Colour in the Flower Garden*, 90.

20. Dillon, *Garden Artistry*, 65.

CHAPTER 13:
CONTEMPORARY GARDENS

1. Barbara Segall, "A Family Affair: Wyken Hall," *The English Garden*, July 2017, 45–50.

2. Sir Roy Strong is the former director of the Victoria and Albert Museum and the National Portrait Gallery, London. He has written more than two dozen books on art, historic gardens, and other subjects, including several memoirs.

3. Patsy Dallas, Roger Last, and Tom Williamson, *Norfolk Gardens and Designed Landscapes* (Oxford: Windgather Press, 2013), 146–49.

4. Graham Robeson and Alan Gray, *A Guide to East Ruston Old Vicarage* (East Ruston, privately printed, n.d.), 6.

5. *A Guide to East Ruston Old Vicarage*, 17.

6. "Coton Manor," *The English Garden*, June/July 2017, 41.

7. David Wheeler, "High Summer: A Trip to Wollerton Old Hall," *Gardens Illustrated*, July 2010, 36.

8. Jodie Jones, "Jinny Blom," *Gardens Illustrated*, December 2012, 64. See also Anna Pavord, "Golden Touch," *Gardens Illustrated*, June 2010, 44–47, and Jinny Blom, *The Thoughtful Gardener* (London: Jacqui Small, 2017).

9. As of 2017, the garden is closed because of an invasive boxwood blight that necessitated the removal of all the plantings. No doubt Ridler will welcome this as an opportunity to redevelop the garden and unleash even more creative ingenuity.

10. Page Dickey, ed., *Outstanding American Gardens: A Celebration: 25 Years of the Garden Conservancy* (New York: Stewart, Tabori & Chang, 2015).

11. Francis H. Cabot, *The Greater Perfection: The Story of the Gardens at Les Quatre Vents* (New York: W. W. Norton, 2001).

12. Robert Dash, *Notes from Madoo: Making a Garden in the Hamptons* (Boston: Houghton Mifflin, 2000).

13. George Schoellkopf, "Our Story: History," *Hollister House Garden* (hollisterhousegarden.org).

CHAPTER 14: DESIGN INSPIRATION

1. Gertrude Jekyll and Lawrence Weaver, *Gardens for Small Country Houses* (London: Country Life, 1912), i.

2. Thomas Mawson, *The Art and Craft of Garden Making* (London: Batsford, 1901). 16.

3. *The Art and Craft of Garden Making*, 17.

4. *The Art and Craft of Garden Making*, 18.

5. Judith B. Tankard, "Bishopsbarns, York," *Gertrude Jekyll and the Country House Garden* (London: Aurum Press; New York: Rizzoli, 2011), 150–51; Martin Wood, "One Vision," *The Garden*, June 1996, 328–31.

6. Jekyll and Weaver, *Gardens for Small Country Houses*, 105.

7. *Gardens for Small Country Houses*, 171, 176,

8. *Gardens for Small Country Houses*, 209.

9. Mawson, *The Art and Craft of Garden Making*, 69.

10. Tankard, *Gertrude Jekyll and the Country House Garden*, 158–61.

11. Mawson, *Art and Craft of Garden Making*, 77.

12. Jekyll and Weaver, *Gardens for Small Country Houses*, 238.

13. *Gardens for Small Country Houses*, 157.

14. Jekyll, *Colour in the Flower Garden* (London: Country Life, 1908), v.

15. See Fenja Gunn's watercolor depiction of Walsham House, Surrey, in *Lost Gardens of Gertrude Jekyll* (New York: Macmillan, 1991), 93–98.

16. Jekyll and Weaver, *Gardens for Small Country Houses*, 111.

17. Mawson, *The Art and Craft of Garden Making*, 167.

18. *The Art and Craft of Garden Making*, 125.

Allan, Mea. *William Robinson, 1838–1935: Father of the English Flower Garden.* London: Faber and Faber, 1982.

Alexander, Rosemary, and Fergus Garrett, eds. *The View from Great Dixter: Christopher Lloyd's Garden Legacy.* Portland, Oregon: Timber Press, 2010.

Anscombe, Isabelle. *Arts and Crafts Style.* New York: Rizzoli, 1991.

Anscombe, Isabelle, and Charlotte Gere. *Arts and Crafts in Britain and America.* New York: Rizzoli, 1978.

Aslet, Clive. *The Last Country Houses.* New Haven: Yale University Press, 1982.

———. *The Arts and Crafts Country House: From the Archives of Country Life.* London: Aurum Press, 2011.

———. *The Edwardian Country House: A Social and Architectural History.* London: Frances Lincoln, 2012.

Attlee, Helena. *The Gardens of Wales.* London: Frances Lincoln, 2009.

Ayers, Dianne, Timothey Hansen, et al. *American Arts and Crafts Textiles.* New York: Harry N. Abrams, 2002.

Baker, Derek. *The Flowers of William Morris.* London: Barn Elms, 1996.

Balmori, Diana, Diane Kostial McGuire, and Eleanor M. McPeck. *Beatrix Farrand's American Landscapes: Her Gardens and Campuses.* New York: Sagapress, 1985.

Bannerman, Isabel, and Julian Bannerman. *Landscape of Dreams: The Gardens of Isabel and Julian Bannerman.* London: Pimpernel Press, 2016.

Bartlett, Michael V., and Rose L. Bartlett. *The Bartlett Book of Garden Elements.* Boston: David R. Godine, 2014.

Birnbaum, Charles A., and Stephanie S. Foell, eds. *Shaping the American Landscape: New Profiles from the Pioneers of American Landscape Design Project.* Charlottesville: University of Virginia Press, 2009.

Birnbaum, Charles A., and Robin Karson, eds. *Pioneers of American Landscape Design.* New York: McGraw-Hill, 2000.

Bisgrove, Richard. *The Gardens of Gertrude Jekyll.* Frances Lincoln, 1992.

———. *William Robinson: The Wild Gardener.* London: Frances Lincoln, 2008.

Blom, Jinny. *The Thoughtful Gardener: An Intelligent Approach to Garden Design.* London: Jacqui Small, 2017.

Blomfield, Reginald. *The Formal Garden in England.* London: Macmillan, 1892.

Bosley, Edward R. *Gamble House: Greene and Greene.* London: Phaidon, 1992.

———. *Greene & Greene.* London: Phaidon, 2000.

Bowman, Leslie Greene. *American Arts and Crafts: Virtue in Design.* Boston: Bulfinch Press, 1990.

Brandon-Jones, John, et al. *C. F. A. Voysey: Architect and Designer, 1857–1941.* London: Lund Humphries, 1978.

Brown, Jane. *The Art and Architecture of English Gardens.* New York: Rizzoli, 1989.

———. *Gardens of a Golden Afternoon: The Story of a Partnership: Edwin Lutyens and Gertrude Jekyll.* New York: Penguin, 1995.

———. *The English Garden: Through the Twentieth Century.* Woodbridge, Suffolk: Garden Art Press, 1999.

Butler, A. S. G. *The Architecture of Sir Edwin Lutyens.* The Lutyens Memorial Series, 3 vols. London: Country Life, 1950.

Cabot, Francis H. *The Greater Perfection: The Story of the Gardens at Les Quatre Vents.* New York: W. W. Norton, 2001.

Callen, Anthea. *Women Artists of the Arts and Crafts Movement.* New York: Pantheon, 1979.

Cane, Percy S. *Modern Gardens: British and Foreign.* London: The Studio, 1926.

Carter, George. *Garden Magic: Making the Ordinary Extraordinary.* London: Double-Barrelled Books, 2015.

Clark, Robert Judson, ed. *The Arts and Crafts Movement in America: 1876–1916.* Princeton: Princeton University Press, 1972.

Clark, Robert Judson, Andrea P. A. Belloli, eds. *Design in America: The Cranbrook Vision 1925–1950.* New York: Harry N. Abrams, 1983.

Cole, David. *The Art and Architecture of C. F. A. Voysey: English Pioneer, Modern Architect and Designer.* London: Images Publishing Distribution, 2015.

Coleman, Brian D. *Historic Arts and Crafts Homes of Great Britain.* Salt Lake City: Gibbs Smith, 2005.

Comino, Mary. *Gimson and the Barnsleys: "Wonderful Furniture of a Commonplace Kind".* New York: Van Nostrand Reinhold, 1982.

Compton, Tania. *Private Gardens of England.* London: Constable and Robinson, 2015.

Cornforth, John. *The Inspiration of the Past: Country House Taste in the Twentieth Century.* New York: Viking, 1985.

Crane, Walter. *A Floral Fantasy in an Old English Garden Set Forth in Verses of Coloured Designs.* London and New York: Harper and Brothers, 1899.

Cumming, Elizabeth, and Wendy Kaplan. *The Arts and Crafts Movement.* New York: Thames & Hudson, 1991.

Darke, Rick. *In Harmony with Nature: Lessons from the Arts and Crafts Garden.* New York: Friedman/Fairfax, 2001.

Dash, Robert. *Notes from Madoo: Making a Garden in the Hamptons.* Boston: Houghton Mifflin, 2000.

Davey, Peter. *Arts and Crafts Architecture.* New York: Phaidon, 1995.

Davison, T. Raffles. *Modern Homes: Selected Examples of Dwelling Houses.* London: George Bell, 1909.

Dickey, Page, ed. *Outstanding American Gardens: A Celebration: 25 Years of the Garden Conservancy.* New York: Stewart, Tabori & Chang, 2015.

Dillistone, George. *The Planning and Planting of Little Gardens.* London: Country Life, 1920.

Dillon, Helen. *Garden Artistry: Secrets of Designing and Planting a Small Garden.* New York: Macmillan, 1995.

Dobyns, Winifred Starr. *California Gardens.* New York: Macmillan, 1931.

Drury, Michael. *Wandering Architects: In Pursuit of an Arts and Crafts Ideal.* Stamford, Linconshire: Shaun Tyas, 2000.

Earle, Alice Morse. *Old Time Gardens Newly Set Forth.* New York: Macmillan, 1901.

Eckstein, Eve. *George Samuel Elgood: His Life and Work, 1851–1943.* London: Alpine Fine Arts Collection, 1995.

Edward, Brian. *Goddards: Sir Edwin Lutyens.* London: Phaidon, 1996.

Edwards, Paul, and Katherine Swift. *Pergolas, Arbours, and Arches: Their History and How To make Them.* London: Barn Elms, 2001.

Elgood, George S., and Gertrude Jekyll. *Some English Gardens.* London: Longmans, Green, 1904.

Elliott, Brent. *Victorian Gardens.* London: Batsford, 1986.

———. *The Country House Garden from the Archives of Country Life, 1897–1939.* London: Mitchell Beazley, 1995.

Gere, Charlotte, and Lesley Hoskins. *The House Beautiful: Oscar Wilde and the Aesthetic Interior.* London: Lund Humphries/Geffrye Museum, 2000.

Gerrish, Helena. *Edwardian Country Life: The Story of H. Avray Tipping.* London: Frances Lincoln, 2011.

Gilbert, Alma M., and Judith B. Tankard. *A Place of Beauty: The Artists and Gardens of the Cornish Colony.* Berkeley, California: Ten Speed Press, 2000.

Girouard, Mark. *Sweetness and Light: The Queen Anne Movement, 1860–1900.* New Haven: Yale University Press, 1984.

Godfrey, Walter H. *Gardens in the Making.* London: Batsford, 1914.

Gow, Ian. *Scottish Houses and Gardens: From the Archives of Country Life.* London: Aurum Press, 1997.

Gradidge, Roderick. *Dream Houses: The Edwardian Ideal.* London: Constable, 1980.

Greene, Virginia A. *The Architecture of Howard Van Doren Shaw.* Chicago: Chicago Review Press, 1998.

Greensted, Mary. *The Arts and Crafts Movement in the Cotswolds.* Stroud: Alan Sutton, 1993.

Griggs, F. L., W. R. Lethaby, and Alfred H. Powell. *Ernest Gimson: His Life & Work.* Stratford-upon-Avon: Shakespeare Head Press, 1924.

Griswold, Mac, and Eleanor Weller. *The Golden Age of American Gardens: Proud Owners, Private Estates, 1890–1940.* New York: Harry N. Abrams, 1992.

Gunn, Fenja. *The Lost Gardens of Gertrude Jekyll.* New York: Macmillan, 1991.

Haigh, Diane. *Baillie Scott: The Artistic House.* London: Academy, 1995.

Hamilton, Jill, Penny Hart, and John Simmons. *The Gardens of William Morris.* New York: Stewart, Tabori & Chang, 1998.

Haslam, Richard. *Clough Williams-Ellis.* London: Academy, 1996.

Hayward, Allyson. *Norah Lindsay: The Life and Art of a Garden Designer.* London: Frances Lincoln, 2007.

Hewitt, Mark Alan. *The Architect & the American Country House.* New Haven: Yale University Press, 1990.

———. *Gustav Stickley's Craftsman Farms: The Quest for an Arts and Crafts Utopia.* Syracuse, New York: Syracuse University Press, 2001.

Hill, May Brawley. *Grandmother's Garden: The Old-Fashioned American Garden, 1865–1915.* New York: Harry N. Abrams, 1995.

———. *Furnishing the Old-Fashioned Garden: Three Centuries of American Summerhouses, Dovecotes, Pergolas, Privies, Fences, & Birdhouses.* New York: Harry N. Abrams, 1998.

Hitchmough, Wendy. *C. F. A. Voysey.* New York: Phaidon, 1995.

———. *Arts and Crafts Gardens.* New York: Rizzoli, 1997.

———. *The Arts and Crafts Lifestyle and Design.* New York: Watson-Guptill, 2000.

Hobhouse, Penelope. *Penelope Hobhouse's Natural Planting.* New York: Henry Holt, 1997.

———. *Colour in Your Garden: A Practical Source Book.* London: Collins, 1985.

Hobhouse, Penelope, and Christopher Wood. *Painted Gardens: English Watercolours, 1850–1914.* London: Michael Joseph, 1988.

Hollamby, Edward. *Red House, Bexleyheath, 1859: Philip Webb.* New York: Van Nostrand Reinhold, 1991.

Holme, Charles, ed. *The Gardens of England in the Southern and Western Counties.* London: The Studio, 1907–1908.

———. *The Gardens of England in the Midland and Eastern Counties.* London: The Studio, 1908–1909.

———. *The Gardens of England in the Northern Counties.* London: The Studio, 1911.

Hulse, Lynn, Jan Morris, et al. *May Morris: Arts & Crafts Designer.* London: Thames & Hudson/Victoria and Albert Museum Publications, 2017.

Hussey, Christopher. *The Work of Sir Robert Lorimer.* London: Country Life, 1931.

Hyde, Matthew. *Broad Leys: The Creation, Life and Times of an Arts and Crafts House.* Sittingbourne, U.K.: Compass Publishing, 2013.

Hyde, Matthew, and Esme Whittaker. *Arts and Crafts Houses in the Lake District.* London: Frances Lincoln, 2014.

Israel, Barbara. *Antique Garden Ornament: Two Centuries of American Taste.* New

York: Harry N. Abrams, 1999.

Jekyll, Gertrude. *Home and Garden: Notes and Thoughts, Practical and Critical, of a Worker in Both.* London: Longmans, Green, 1900.

———. *Colour in the Flower Garden.* London: Country Life, 1908.

———. *Garden Ornament.* London: Country Life, 1908.

Jekyll, Gertrude, and Lawrence Weaver. *Gardens for Small Country Houses.* London: Country Life, 1912

Jencks, Charles. *The Garden of Cosmic Speculation.* London: Frances Lincoln, 2003.

Jewson, Norman. *By Chance I Did Rove.* 1951. Reprint. Warwick: privately published, 1973.

Kaplan, Wendy. *Art That Is Life: The Arts and Crafts Movement in America, 1875–1920.* Boston: Museum of Fine Arts, 1987.

———. *The Arts and Crafts Movement in Europe and America: Design for the Modern World.* London: Thames & Hudson/Los Angeles County Museum, 2004.

Kaplan, Wendy, ed. *Charles Rennie Mackintosh.* New York: Abbeville Press and Glasgow Museums, 1996.

Keen, Mary. *The Garden Border Book.* Deer Park, Wisconsin: Capability's Books, 1987.

———. *Gardening with Color.* New York: Random House, 1991.

Kreisman, Lawrence, and Glenn Mason. *The Arts and Crafts Movement in the Pacific Northwest.* Portland: Timber Press, 2007.

Lambourne, Lionel. *Utopian Craftsmen: The Arts and Crafts Movement from the Cotswolds to Chicago.* Salt Lake City: Peregrine Smith, 1980.

Le Lièvre, Audrey. *Miss Willmott of Warley Place: Her Life and Her Gardens.* London: Faber and Faber, 1980.

Lees-Milne, James. *Some Cotswold Country Houses: A Personal Selection.* Stanbridge, Dorset: Dovecote Press, 1987.

Lennox-Boyd, Arabella. *Designing Gardens.* London: Frances Lincoln, 2012.

Lennox-Boyd, Arabella, and Selina Hastings. *Garden at Gresgarth.* London: Frances Lincoln, 2014.

Lethaby, William R. *Philip Webb and His Work.* Oxford: Oxford University Press, 1935.

Leyland, John, and H. Avray Tipping, eds. *Gardens Old and New: The Country House* and Its Garden Environment. 3 vols. London: Country Life, 1901–1907.

Livingstone, Karen. C. F. A. Voysey: Arts and Crafts Designer. London: Victoria and Albert Museum Publications, 2016.

Livingstone, Karen, and Linda Parry, eds. International Arts and Crafts. London: Victoria and Albert Museum Publications, 2005.

Lloyd, Nathaniel. Garden Craftsmanship in Yew and Box. London: Ernest Benn, 1925.

Longest, George C. Genius in the Garden: Charles F. Gillette & Landscape Architecture in Virginia. Richmond: Virginia State Library and Archives, 1992.

Lowell, Guy. American Gardens. Boston: Bates and Guild, 1902.

Macaulay, James. Hill House: Charles Rennie Mackintosh. London: Phaidon, 1994.

MacCarthy, Fiona. William Morris: A Life for Our Time. New York: Alfred A. Knopf, 1995.

———. Anarchy & Beauty: William Morris and His Legacy. London: National Portrait Gallery Publications, 2014.

Macdonald-Smith, Ian. Arts and Crafts Master: The Houses and Gardens of M. H. Baillie Scott. New York: Rizzoli, 2010.

Mackail, J. W. The Life of William Morris. 1899. Reprint. New York: Benjamin Blom, 1968.

Mander, Nicholas. Country Houses of the Cotswolds: From the Archives of Country Life. London: Aurum Press, 2008.

Marley, Anna O., ed. The Artist's Garden: American Impressionism and the Garden Movement. Philadelphia: University of Pennsylvania Press, 2014.

Marsh, Jan. William Morris & Red House. London: National Trust, 2005.

Mawson, Thomas H. The Art and Craft of Garden Making. London: Batsford, 1901.

———. The Life & Work of an English Landscape Architect. New York: Scribner's, 1927.

Meister, Maureen. Arts and Crafts Architecture: History and Heritage in New England. Boston: University Press of New England, 2014.

Meyer, Marilee Boyd. Inspiring Reform: Boston's Arts and Crafts Movement. New York: Davis Museum and Cultural Center/Harry N. Abrams, 1997.

Miller, Wilhelm. What England Can Teach Us about Gardening. Garden City, New York: Doubleday, Page, 1911.

Morgan, Keith N. Shaping an American Landscape: The Art and Architecture of Charles

A. Platt. Hanover: University Press of New England, 1995.

Morris, May, ed. The Collected Works of William Morris. 24 vols. London: Longmans, Green, 1910–15.

Morris, William. Hopes and Fears for Art. London: Longmans, Green, 1908.

———. News from Nowhere. 1891. Reprint. London: Longmans, Green, 1910.

Mowl, Timothy, and Marion Mako. The Historic Gardens of England: Cheshire. Bristol: Redcliffe Press, 2008.

———. The Historic Gardens of England: Somerset. Bristol: Redcliffe Press, 2010.

Mowl, Timothy, and Jane Whitaker. The Historic Gardens of England: Hampshire. Bristol: Stephen Morris, 2016.

Murmann, Eugene O. California Gardens. Los Angeles: Murmann, 1914.

Musson, Jeremy. The English Manor House: From the Archives of Country Life. London: Aurum Press, 1999.

Muthesius, Hermann. The English House (abridged version of Das Englische Haus. 3 vols., Berlin: Wasmuth, 1904–05), Janet Seligman, trans. New York: Rizzoli, 1979.

Naylor, Gillian. The Arts and Crafts Movement: A Study of Its Sources, Ideals and Influences on Design Theory. London: Studio Vista, 1971.

Newton, William Godfrey. The Work of Ernest Newton, R. A. London: Architectural Press, 1925.

Nichols, Rose Standish. English Pleasure Gardens. 1902. Reprint. Boston: David R. Godine, 2003.

Nuttgens, Patrick. Brierley in Yorkshire: The Architecture of the Turn of the Century. York: York Georgian Society, 1984.

O'Donnell, Anne Stewart. C. F. A. Voysey: Architect, Designer, Individualist. San Francisco: Pomegranate, 2011.

Oehme, Wolfgang, and James van Sweden. Bold Romantic Gardens: The New World Landscape of Oehme and van Sweden. New York: Acropolis Books, 1991.

Otis, Denise. Grounds for Pleasure: Four Centuries of the American Garden. New York: Harry N. Abrams, 2002.

Ottewill, David. The Edwardian Garden. New Haven: Yale University Press, 1989.

Parry, Linda. Textiles of the Arts and Crafts Movement. London: Thames & Hudson, 1988.

———. William Morris and the Arts and Crafts Movement: A Sourcebook. London: Studio Editions, 1989.

Parry, Linda, ed. William Morris. London: Victoria and Albert Museum, 1996.

Pearson, Dan. Natural Selection: A Year in the Garden. London: Guardian Faber, 2017.

Pearson, Graham S. Hidcote: The Garden and Lawrence Johnston. London: National Trust, 2007.

Pevsner, Nikolaus. Pioneers of Modern Design: From William Morris to Walter Gropius. New York: Museum of Modern Art, 1949.

Phillips, R. Randal. Small Country Houses of To-Day. Vol. 3. London: Country Life, 1925.

Richardson, Margaret. The Craft Architects. New York: Rizzoli, 1983.

Richardson, Tim. English Gardens in the Twentieth Century: From the Archives of Country Life. London: Aurum Press, 2005.

———. Great Gardens of America. London: Frances Lincoln, 2009.

———. The New English Garden. London: Frances Lincoln, 2013.

Robinson, William. The English Flower Garden. London: John Murray, 1883.

———. Garden Design and Architects' Gardens. London: John Murray, 1892.

———. Gravetye Manor, or Twenty Years' Work Round an Old Manor House. 1911. Reprint. New York: Sagapress, 1984.

———. The Wild Garden. 1870. Reprint. New York: Sagapress, 1994.

Robinson, William, and Rick Darke. The Wild Garden: Expanded Edition. Portland, Oregon: Timber Press, 2009.

Robinson, William, and Charles Nelson. The Wild Garden. Cork, Ireland: The Collins Press, 2010.

Rutherford, Sarah. The Arts and Crafts Garden. Botley, U.K.: Shire Books, 2013.

Savage, Peter. Lorimer and the Edinburgh Craft Designers. Edinburgh: Paul Harris, 1980.

Saville, Diana. Gardens for Small Country Houses. New York: Viking, 1988.

Scott, M. H. Baillie. Houses and Gardens. London: George Newnes, 1906.

Scott, M. H. Baillie, and E. Edgar Beresford. Houses and Gardens. London: Architecture Illustrated, 1933.

Scott-James, Anne. The Cottage Garden. London: Penguin Books, 1982.

Sedding, John. Garden-Craft Old and New. 1890. Reprint. London: John Lane: The Bodley Head, 1901.

Seebohm, Carolyn, and Curtice Taylor. Rescuing Eden: Preserving America's Historic Gardens. New York: Monacelli Press, 2015.

Shelton, Louise. Beautiful Gardens in America. New York: Scribners, 1915.

Smith, Bruce, and Alexander Vertikoff. *Greene & Greene Masterworks*. San Francisco: Chronicle Books, 1998.

Sparrow, Walter Shaw. *Our Homes and How To Make the Best of Them*. London: Hodder and Stoughton, 1909.

Sparrow, Walter Shaw, ed. *The British Home of To-Day: A Book of Modern Domestic Architecture and the Applied Arts*. New York: A. C. Armstrong, 1904.

———. *The Modern Home: A Book of British Domestic Architecture for Moderate Incomes*. London: Hodder and Stoughton, n.d.

Spens, Michael, ed. *High Art and Low Life: The Studio and the Fin de Siècle*. London: Victoria and Albert Museum, 1993.

Stamp, Gavin. *Edwin Lutyens Country Houses: From the Archives of Country Life*. London: Aurum Press, 2001.

Stickley, Gustav. *Craftsman Homes*. New York: Craftsman Publishing, 1909

Streatfield, David C. *California Gardens: Creating a New Eden*. New York: Abbeville Press, 1994.

Strong, Roy. *Country Life 1897–1997: The English Arcadia*. London: C. L. Bates, 1996.

———. *The Laskett: The Story of a Garden*. London and New York: Bantam Press, 2003.

———. *Remaking a Garden: The Laskett Transformed*. London: Frances Lincoln, 2014.

Studio Yearbook of Decorative Art. London: The Studio, 1906–60

Symonds, Joanna. *Catalogue of the Drawings Collection of the Royal Institute of British Architects: C. F. A. Voysey*. London: D. C. Heath, 1978.

Tamulevich, Susan. *Dumbarton Oaks: Garden Into Art*. New York: Monacelli Press, 2001.

Tankard, Judith B. *Beatrix Farrand: Private Gardens, Public Landscapes*. New York: Monacelli Press, 2009.

———. *Gertrude Jekyll and the Country House Garden: From the Archives of Country Life*. London: Aurum Press; New York: Rizzoli, 2011.

———. *Ellen Shipman and the American Garden*. Athens: University of Georgia Press/Library of American Landscape History, 2018.

Tankard, Judith B., and Michael R. Van Valkenburgh. *Gertrude Jekyll: A Vision of Garden and Wood*. New York: Harry N. Abrams, 1989.

Tankard, Judith B., and Martin A. Wood. *Gertrude Jekyll at Munstead Wood*. London: Pimpernel Press, 2015.

Thorne, Martha, ed. *David Adler, Architect: The Elements of Style*. New Haven: Yale University Press, 2002.

Tinniswood, Adrian. *The Arts and Crafts House*. New York: Watson-Guptill, 1999.

Tipping, H. Avray. *English Gardens*. London: Country Life, 1925.

———. *The Garden of To-Day*. London: Martin Hopkinson, 1933.

Tooley, Michael, and Primrose Arnander, eds. *Gertrude Jekyll: Essays on the Life of a Working Amateur*. London: Michaelmas Books, 1996.

Trapp, Kenneth R., ed. *The Arts and Crafts Movement in California: Living the Good Life*. New York: Abbeville Press, 1993.

Triggs, H. Inigo. *Formal Gardens in England and Scotland*. London: Batsford, 1902.

Triggs, Oscar Lovell. *Chapters in the History of the Arts and Crafts Movement*. 1902. Reprint. New York: Benjamin Blom, 1971.

Truscott, James. *Private Gardens of Scotland*. New York: Harmony Books, 1988.

Vallance, Aymer. *William Morris: His Art, His Writings, and His Public Life*. London: George Bell and Sons, 1897.

van Sweden, James. *Architecture in the Garden*. New York: Random House, 2003.

Via, Maria, and Marjorie R. Searl, eds. *Head, Heart and Hand: Elbert Hubbard and the Roycrofters*. Rochester, New York: University of Rochester Press, 1994.

Voysey, Charles Francis Annesley. *Individuality*. 1915. Reprint. Shaftesbury: Element Books, 1986.

Wallinger, Rosamund. *Gertrude Jekyll's Lost Garden: The Restoration of an Edwardian Masterpiece*. Woodbridge, Suffolk, U.K.: Garden Art Press, 2000

———. *Gertrude Jekyll: Her Art Restored at Upton Grey*. Woodbridge, Suffolk, U.K.: Garden Art Press, 2013.

Watters, Sam. *Gardens for a Beautiful America, 1895–1935*. New York: Acanthus Press, 2012.

Watters, Sam, ed. *American Gardens, 1890–1930: Northeast, Mid-Atlantic, and Midwest Regions*. New York: Acanthus Press, 2006.

Way, Twigs. *The Cottage Garden*. Botley, U.K.: Shire Books, 2011.

———. *Topiary*. Botley, U.K: Shire Books, 2010.

Waymark, Janet. *Thomas Mawson: Life, Gardens, and Landscapes*. London: Frances Lincoln, 2009.

Weaver, Lawrence. *Houses and Gardens by E. L. Lutyens*. London: Country Life, 1913.

———. *Small Country Houses: Their Repair and Enlargement*. London: Country Life, 1914.

———. *Small Country Houses of To-Day*. Second Series. London: Country Life, 1919.

Weaver, Lawrence, ed. *The House and Its Equipment*. London: Country Life, 1911.

———. *Small Country Houses of To-Day*. London: Country Life, 1910.

Whalley, Robin. *The Great Edwardian Gardens of Harold Peto: From the Archives of Country Life*. London: Aurum Press, 2007.

Whalley, Robin, and Anne Jennings. *Knot Gardens and Parterres*. London: Barn Elms, 1998.

Wheeler, David, and Simon Dorrell. *Over the Hills from Broadway: Images of Cotswold Gardens*. Stroud: Alan Sutton, 1991.

Whitsey, Fred. *The Garden at Hidcote*. London: Frances Lincoln, 2007.

Whittle, Elizabeth. *The Historic Gardens of Wales: An Introduction to Parks and Gardens in the History of Wales*. London: HMSO, 1992.

Wilder, Louise Beebe. *Colour in My Garden*. 1918. Reprint. Boston: Atlantic Monthy Press, 1990.

Wilhide, Elizabeth. *William Morris: Decor and Design*. New York: Harry N. Abrams, 1991.

Williams-Ellis, Clough. *Architect Errant*. London: Constable, 1971.

Wilson, Richard Guy, and Shaun Eyring, eds. *Re-Creating the American Past: Essays on the Colonial Revival*. Charlottesville: University of Virginia Press, 2006.

Winter, Robert, ed. *Toward a Simpler Way of Life: The Arts and Crafts Architects of California*. Berkeley: University of California Press, 1997.

Wittkopp, Gregory, and Diana Balmori, eds. *Saarinen House and Garden: A Total Work of Art*. New York: Harry N. Abrams, 1994.

Wood, Christopher. *Paradise Lost: Paintings of English Country Life and Landscape, 1850–1914*. New York: Crescent Books, 1993.

Wood, Martin, ed. *The Unknown Gertrude Jekyll*. London: Frances Lincoln, 2006.

Woodbridge, Sally B. *Bernard Maybeck: Visionary Architect*. New York: Abbeville Press, 1992.

Wright, Frank Lloyd. *An Autobiography*. New York: Longmans, Green, 1932.

———. *The Natural House*. New York: Horizon Press, 1954.

ACKNOWLEDGMENTS

THIS BOOK COULD NOT HAVE BEEN written without benefit of the knowledge of numerous experts who, over the years, have enlightened me about Arts and Crafts architecture, decorative arts, and gardens. Among them are Jane Balfour, David Berman, the late John Brandon-Jones, John Burrows, Rick Darke, Michael Edwards, Margaret Richardson, Bruce Smith, David Streatfield, Janet Waymark, Robin Whalley, and Martin Wood. I would like to thank all the homeowners and custodians who allowed me to tarry in their gardens. These include Mr. and Mrs. Simon Biddulph, Mrs. John Birchall, John and Neville Bryan, Ben and Susanne Clark, the late Sir Robert and Lady Clark, Helen Dillon, Simon Dorrell and David Wheeler, Hilary and Helena Gerrish, Noel Gibbs, the late Sir Samuel Goldman, Kay Haslam, Arabella Lennox-Boyd, Sir Nicholas and Lady Mander, Jean-Paul Marix-Evans, Mr. and Mrs. St. John-Mildmay, Gail Naughton, Charles and Joan Platt, Tony Ridler, George Schoellkopf, the late Sibyl Spencer, John and Rosamund Wallinger, and many others. In addition, William Brogden, Jane Brown, Rick Darke, Simon Dorrell, Art Miller, Bill Noble, Jeff Sainsbury, David Streatfield, Ann Uppington, Martin Wood, and others generously introduced me to some of the private gardens in this book. The late Peter Herbert deserves special mention for his unfailing hospitality that led me to imagine Gravetye Manor as my home.

I would also like to thank the following organizations, institutions, and individuals who have generously provided illustrations or information: Agecroft Hall (Katie Reynolds), Primrose Arnander, Blackwell Museum, Ed Bosley, Leslie Bottaro, John R. Burrows, Richard Cheek, Susanne Clark, Country Life Archives (Melanie Bryan, Justin Hobson, and Paula Fahey), Cultural Landscape Foundation (Charles Birnbaum, Barrett Doherty, Matthew Traucht), Simon Dorrell, Lee C. Dunn, Michael Edwards, Florence Griswold Museum (Tammi Flynn), The Garden Conservancy (George Shakespear), Garden History Society, Garden Museum, Gravetye Manor (Celine Leslie), Graycliff Conservancy (Reine Hauser, Patrick Mahoney), Graythwaite Estate (Edward Sandys), Greene and Greene Archives (Ann Scheid), Greenwood Gardens (Peter Blanchard, Matt Gundy, Vicki Johnson), Jonathan Hession, Mark Alan Hewitt, Hestercombe Gardens Trust (Philip White), Stephanie Holley, Hollister House (George Schoellkopf), Jason Ingram, Ladew Topiary Garden (Sheryl Pedrick and Julie Gilbert), The Lutyens Trust, The Madoo Conservancy (Alejandro Saralegui), Marianne Majerus, Marion Mako, Art Miller, Tim Mowl, Jonathan Myles-Lea, Bill Noble, Dan Pearson, Katie Reynolds, Royal Horticultural Society Lindley Library, Jeff Sainsbury, Christine Salwitz/The Personal Garden Coach, The Society of Antiquities of London, Stickley Museum at Craftsman Farm (Bernadette Rubbo), Surrey History Centre, John R. Tankard, Philip Tankard, Trustworth Studios (David Berman), Ann Uppington, Alex Vertikoff, Sam Watters, Janet Waymark, Dr. Lawrence Trevelyan Weaver, William Morris Society, the late Christopher Wood, and Martin Wood.

I also owe a debt to the booksellers who found special editions, periodicals, letters, or other treasured additions for my library: Robin Bledsoe, Anna Buxton, Jim Hinck and Ann Marie Wall, Daniel Lloyd, the late Timothy Mawson, Harvey Mendelsohn (who translated essential passages from Muthesius's *Das Englische Haus*), Janette Ray, Jane Robie, David Wheeler (who found a near complete run of *Country Life* magazine in a bookshop in Hay-on-Wye and allowed me to write about my collections in *Hortus*), Charles B. Wood, the late Elisabeth Woodburn, and many others.

Many thanks to Ruth Peltason, former editor at Harry N. Abrams, who commissioned the first edition of this book, and acquisitions editor Tom Fischer, manuscript editor Lisa Theobald, and the staff at Timber Press for assistance in preparing a revised and updated edition of the book. Especial thanks to Simon Dorrell, art editor of *Hortus*, who provided the pen-and-ink drawings of garden plans commissioned especially for this book.

And last, but not least, a special acknowledgment to my husband, John R. Tankard, my intrepid house-and-garden-visiting companion, who frequently offered pithy comments about things I otherwise would have overlooked, bailed me out when my camera failed, and regularly procured items for our library, including a twenty-year run of *The Studio* magazine that he spotted in a bookshop in Surrey.

PHOTO AND ILLUSTRATION CREDITS

Agecroft Hall, page 200 (middle)

Author's collection, pages 10, 12, 17, 18, 20, 24, 25 top, 27, 28, 29 top, 30, 32 top, 33, 35, 46 bottom, 50, 51 right, 58, 64, 72, 75, 77, 79, 82, 83, 86, 90, 91, 100, 101, 102, 109, 110, 111, 112, 113, 135, 139 left, 148, 162, 165, 178 bottom, 179, 182 top, 196, 198 top, 199 left, 200 top, 222, 274

© Leslie Bottaro, page 207

© John Burrows, page 46 top

Christopher Wood Gallery, pages 15 bottom, 16, 21, 36, 122, 128, 136, 215 top

© Richard Cheek, pages 203, 204 top left and bottom left, 252 top left and top right, 263 right, 273

© Susanne Clark, page 269 top right

Cornell University Library, page 206

© Country Life Picture Library, pages 78 (June Buck), 118, 119, 120, 121, 140, 142, 145 (Arthur Gill), 147, 149, 151 top (F. Sleigh), 154 (F. Sleigh), 166, 167, 215 bottom (A. L. Henson), 218 (Paul Barker), 219 bottom left (Paul Barker), 223 top, 270 (Paul Barker)

Cultural Landscape Foundation, page 189 (Charles Birnbaum)

© Simon Dorrell, pages 63, 66, 87, 97, 103 top, 127, 137, 143, 150, 161, 174, 219 top, 232, 233, 255 bottom right

© Lee C. Dunn, pages 25, 34, 103 bottom, 168, 217, 224, 237, 253

© Michael Edwards, page 144

Florence Griswold Museum, pages 194, 257 top

Garden Conservancy, pages 192, 260 (Anne Welles)

Gravetye Manor, pages 126 (Taylor Young), 129 (Paul Johnson)

Graycliff Conservancy, page 184

The Gamble House, USC, page 190 (Alex Vertikoff)

Greenwood Gardens, pages 176 (Vicki Johnson), 178 (Vicki Johnson), 182 bottom, 183 (Vicki Johnson)

Peter Herbert Collection, pages 125, 130

© Jonathan Hession, page 227

Hestercombe Gardens Trust, page 134, 244 (Jason Ingram), 256 bottom (Jason Ingram)

Ladew Topiary Gardens, page 201

Langdale Chase Hotel, page 108 bottom

Library of Congress, Prints & Photographs Division (Frances Benjamin Johnston), page 208

© Patrick Mahoney, page 184

© Marianne Majerus, page 132

© Marion Mako, pages 52, 54, 60, 65 top left and top right, 172, 212

© Arthur H. Miller, page 186

© Tim Mowl, page 84

© Jonathan Myles-Lea, page 29 bottom

© Bill Noble, pages 240, 242, 261, 269 top left, 272 left

Private Collection, pages 15, 44, 48, 138, 151 bottom (© Jason Ingram), 152 (© Jason Ingram), 155 (© Jason Ingram), 198 bottom, 199 right, 210

RIBA Library Drawings Collection, pages 80, 94, 96

© Christina Salwitz/The Personal Garden Coach, pages 249, 252 bottom

© George Schoellkopf, pages 243, 247, 248, bottom right, 267 bottom right

Society of Antiquaries of London, pages 49, 51 left

The Stickley Museum at Craftsman Farms, Parsippany, New Jersey, pages 180 (Kristen H. Sensenig), 181

Nancy Angell Streeter Family, page 206

© John R. Tankard, pages 13, 98, 108 top, 246, 259 left, 266

© Judith B. Tankard, pages 14, 22, 26, 27 bottom, 32 bottom, 45, 56, 57, 59, 61, 62, 65 bottom left and bottom right, 67, 68, 70, 71, 76, 93, 99, 104, 105, 106, 114, 116, 117, 133, 139 top right, 146, 156, 157, 158, 160, 163, 170, 173, 175, 188, 193, 197, 200 bottom, 202, 204 right, 209, 213, 214, 216, 219 bottom right, 220, 223 middle and bottom, 225, 226, 228, 230, 231, 234, 235, 236, 238, 239, 241, 248 left, 250, 254, 255 top, 256 top, 257 bottom, 258, 259 top right and bottom right, 262, 263 top left and bottom left, 264, 265, 267 top right and middle right, 268, 269 bottom left and bottom right, 271

© Philip Tankard, page 248 top right

Trustworth Studios, pages 6, 38, 41, 42, 47, 74, 88, 92

© Martin Wood, page 139 bottom right

INDEX

294

295

297

298

JUDITH B. TANKARD is an art historian specializing in landscape history. She received an M.A. in art history from the Institute of Fine Arts, New York University, and taught at the Landscape Institute of Harvard University for more than twenty years. She is the author or coauthor of ten illustrated books on landscape history, including her most recent publications, *Ellen Shipman and the American Garden* and *Gertrude Jekyll at Munstead Wood*. Her book *Beatrix Farrand: Private Gardens, Public Landscapes* was named an Honor Book for the 2010 Historic New England Book Prize. *A Place of Beauty: The Artists and Gardens of the Cornish Colony* won a Quill and Trowel Award from the Garden Writers Association in 2001. *The Gardens of Ellen Biddle Shipman* was a recipient of a 1998 book award from the American Horticultural Society. She is a frequent contributor to *Hortus: A Gardening Journal*, and her reviews and articles have been published in *Apollo, Country Life, Horticulture, Landscape Architecture Magazine, Pacific Horticulture*, and other publications. For ten years she was the editor of the *Journal of the New England Garden History Society* and presently serves on the editorial board of *Garden History* (UK). She is a Garden Conservancy Fellow and a stewardship council member of The Cultural Landscape Foundation. She is an advisor for the Beatrix Farrand Garden Association, Dumbarton Oaks Park Conservancy, Tregaron Conservancy, and other preservation organizations. She was vice president of the Beatrix Farrand Society and a board member for ten years. She lives in Boston and has a small garden on Martha's Vineyard.